A Modern Reader in Institutional and Evolutionary Economics

EUROPEAN ASSOCIATION FOR EVOLUTIONARY POLITICAL ECONOMY

Series Editor: Geoffrey M. Hodgson, *University of Hertfordshire Business School, UK*

Mixed Economies in Europe: An Evolutionary Perspective on their Emergence, Transition and Regulation
Edited by Wolfgang Blaas and John Foster

The Political Economy of Diversity: Evolutionary Perspectives on Economic Order and Disorder
Edited by Robert Delorme and Kurt Dopfer

On Economic Institutions: Theory and Applications
Edited by John Groenewegen, Christos Pitelis and Sven-Erik Sjöstrand

Rethinking Economics: Markets, Technology and Economic Evolution
Edited by Geoffrey M. Hodgson and Ernesto Screpanti

Environment, Technology and Economic Growth: The Challenge to Sustainable Development
Edited by Andrew Tylecote and Jan van der Straaten

Institutions and Economic Change: New Perspectives on Markets, Firms and Technology
Edited by Klaus Nielsen and Björn Johnson

Pluralism in Economics: New Perspectives in History and Methodology
Edited by Andrea Salanti and Ernesto Screpanti

Beyond Market and Hierarchy: Interactive Governance and Social Complexity
Edited by Ash Amin and Jerzy Hausner

Employment, Technology and Economic Needs: Theory, Evidence and Public Policy
Edited by Jonathan Michie and Angelo Reati

Institutions and the Evolution of Capitalism: Implications of Evolutionary Economics
Edited by John Groenewegen and Jack Vromen

Is Economics an Evolutionary Science? The Legacy of Thorstein Veblen
Edited by Francisco Louçã and Mark Perlman

Technology and Knowledge: From the Firm to Innovation Systems
Edited by Pier Paolo Saviotti and Bart Nooteboom

Evolution and Path Dependence in Economic Ideas: Past and Present
Edited by Pierre Garrouste and Stavros Ioannides

A Modern Reader in Institutional and Evolutionary Economics: Key Concepts
Edited by Geoffrey M. Hodgson

A Modern Reader in Institutional and Evolutionary Economics

Key Concepts

Edited by

Geoffrey M. Hodgson

Research Professor, University of Hertfordshire Business School, UK

EUROPEAN ASSOCIATION OF EVOLUTIONARY POLITICAL ECONOMY

Edward Elgar
Cheltenham, UK • Northampton, MA, USA

Published by
Edward Elgar Publishing Limited
Glensanda House
Montpellier Parade
Cheltenham
Glos GL50 1UA
UK

Edward Elgar Publishing, Inc.
136 West Street
Suite 202
Northampton
Massachusetts 01060
USA

A catalogue record for this book
is available from the British Library

Library of Congress Cataloguing in Publication Data
A modern reader in institutional and evolutionary economics : key concepts / edited by Geoffrey M. Hodgson.
    p. cm.
    "European Association of Evolutionary Political Economy."
    Includes bibliographical references and index.
    1. Institutional economics. 2. Evolutionary economics. I. Hodgson, Geoffrey
Martin, 1946– II. European Association for Evolutionary Political Economy.

HB99.5 .M63 2002
330—dc21

                                                                    2002016665

ISBN 1 84064 474 5 (cased)
      1 84064 495 8 (paperback)

Typeset by Manton Typesetters, Louth, Lincolnshire, UK.
Printed and bound in Great Britain by Biddles Ltd, *www.biddles.co.uk*

Contents

II PLURALISM AND COMPARATIVE PARADIGMS

III VARIETIES OF CAPITALISM

Figures

Tables

Contributors

Eileen Appelbaum is Research Director at the Economic Policy Institute, USA. She was formerly Professor of Economics at Temple University, USA, and Guest Research Fellow at the Wissenschaftszentrum Berlin, Germany. She has published numerous articles on employment and labour markets. She is co-editor of *Labor Market Adjustments to Structural Change and Technological Progress* (1990) and author or co-author of *Back to Work: Determinants of Women's Successful Reentry* (1981), *Job Saving Strategies: Worker Buyouts and QWL* (1988), *The New American Workplace* (1994) and *Manufacturing Advantage: Why High Performance Work Systems Pay Off* (2000).

Hans Berger is Assistant Professor of Marketing at the Faculty of Management and Organization, University of Groningen, the Netherlands. His research interests include subcontracting, transaction cost theory, relational contracting and strategic positioning.

Bernard Chavance is Professor of Economics at the University Paris VII – Denis Diderot, France. He has published *Le Capital Socialiste: Histoire Critique de l'Economie Politique du Socialisme (1917–1954)* (1980), *Le Système Economique Soviétique: De Brejnev à Gorbatchev* (1989), *The Transformation of Communist Systems: Economic Reforms since the 1950s* (1994), *La Fin des Systèmes Socialistes: Crise, Réforme et Transformation* (1994), *Capitalisme et Socialisme en Perspective: Evolution et Transformation des Systèmes Economiques* (1999). He is an editor of *Marx et le Capitalisme: La Dialectique d'un Système* (1996).

Benjamin Coriat is a Professor at the University of Paris XIII, UFR Sciences Economiques et de Gestion, Centre de Recherche en Economie Industrielle (CREI), France. He is the author of several articles on industrial and labour economics in the academic literature.

Giovanni Dosi is Professor of Economics at Sant'Anna School of Advanced Studies of Pisa, Italy. He is the author of *Innovation, Organization and Economic Dynamics: Selected Essays* (2000), *The Nature and Dynamics of Organizational Capabilities* (2000, with S. Winter and R. Nelson), *Technology, Organization and Competitiveness* (1998, with D. Teece and J. Chytry), *The Economics of Technical Change and International Trade* (1990, with K.

Pavitt and L. Soete) and several dozen articles in major international journals. He is listed in *Who's Who in Economics* (1999).

Sheila C. Dow is a Professor of Economics at the University of Stirling, UK. She is author of several books, including *The Methodology of Macroeconomic Thought: A Conceptual Analysis of Schools of Thought in Economics* (1996) and *Money and the Economic Process* (1993), co-editor of several volumes, and author of articles in academic journals on methodology, history of economic thought, Post Keynesian economics, monetary theory and regional finance. She is listed in *Who's Who in Economics* (1999).

Sandye Gloria-Palermo is a Researcher at the University of Saint-Etienne, France. She is author of *The Evolution of Austrian Economics: From Menger to Lachmann* (1999) and several scholarly articles.

Geoffrey M. Hodgson is Research Professor in Business Studies at the University of Hertfordshire, UK. He was formerly Reader in Economics at the University of Cambridge. He is the author of *How Economics Forgot History* (2001), *Economics and Utopia* (1999), *Evolution and Institutions* (1999), *Economics and Evolution* (1993), *After Marx and Sraffa* (1991), *Economics and Institutions* (1988), *The Democratic Economy* (1994) and over 60 articles in academic journals. He is listed in *Who's Who in Economics* (1999) and his website is www.herts.ac.uk/business/esst/Staff/g-hodgson/hodgson.html.

Bengt-Åke Lundvall is Professor in Economics at the Department for Business Studies, Aalborg University, Denmark. In 1992–5 he was Deputy Director at the Directorate for Science, Technology and Industry in the OECD. He introduced the concept of 'innovation system' in 1985 and, together with Björn Johnson, the concept of the 'learning economy' in 1994. His current research is focused on innovation and competence building in the globalizing learning economy. He edited, with Daniele Archibugi, *Europe in the Globalising Learning Economy* (2001).

Eric Magnin is Associate Professor in Economics at the University of Paris VII – Denis Diderot, France. He has published *Les Transformations Economiques dans les Pays de l'Est depuis 1989* (1999), *Capitalisme et Socialisme en Perspective* (co-edited with Bernard Chavance, Ramine Motamed-Nejad and Jacques Sapir, 1999), *Les Economies Post-socialistes: Une Décennie de Transformations* (co-edited with Ramine Motamed-Nejad, 1999), *Les Trajectoires de Transformation en Europe Centrale Post-socialiste (Hongrie, Pologne, République Tchèque)* and *Institutions, Evolution, Complexité* (forthcoming 2002).

Uskali Mäki is Professor of Philosophy at Erasmus University, Rotterdam, the Netherlands. His research focuses on issues in economic methodology, such as realism, explanation, rhetoric, the sociology and economics of economics, and foundations of new institutional and Austrian economics. He is co-editor of the *Journal of Economic Methodology*, *The Handbook of Economic Methodology* (1998), *Economics and Methodology, Crossing Boundaries* (1998) and *Rationality, Institutions and Economic Methodology* (1993), and editor of *The Economic World View: Studies in Economic Ontology* (2001) and *Fact and Fiction in Economics: Realism, Models and Social Construction* (2001).

Niels G. Noorderhaven is Professor of International Management at Tilburg University, the Netherlands (since 1997) and Associate Dean Educational Programmes (since 1999). He was Director of the Institute for Research on Intercultural Cooperation (IRIC) until March 2000 and is now associated with the IRIC as a senior researcher. His research focuses on (international) cooperation in business, with a special interest in issues of culture and trust. His website is http://cwis.kub.nl/~few5/center/staff/noorderh/index.htm.

Bart Nooteboom is Professor of Organizational Dynamics at Erasmus University, Rotterdam, the Netherlands. He was formerly Professor of Industrial Organization at Groningen University and a researcher at Shell International. He is author of *Trust: Forms, Foundations, Functions, Failures and Figures* (2002), *Learning and Innovation in Organizations and Economies* (2000), *Inter-firm Alliances: Analysis and Design* (1999) and 160 articles on small business, entrepreneurship, innovation and diffusion, technology policy, transaction costs, inter-firm relations, organizational learning and philosophy of economics and management. He is listed in *Who's Who in Economics* (1999) and his website is www.fbk.eur.nl/DPT/VG2/index.html.

Ronald Schettkat is Professor of Economics at Utrecht University, the Netherlands. His areas of research include labour economics, macroeconomics and economic policy. He was formerly a fellow of the Netherlands Institute for Advanced Study and the Wissenschaftszentrum Berlin, Germany and guest professor at several European and American universities. He wrote *The Labor Market Dynamics of Economic Restructuring: The United States and Germany in Transition* (1992) and edited *Flow Analysis of Labor Markets* (1996), and *The Growth of Service Industries* (with Thijs ten Raa, 2001). He joined the Institute for Labour Studies (IZA) as a Research Fellow in January 2001.

Marc R. Tool is Professor Emeritus of Economics at California State University, Sacramento, USA. He is author of *The Discretionary Economy* (1979), *Essays in Social Value Theory* (1986), *Pricing, Valuation and Systems* (1995),

Value Theory and Economic Progress (2000) and over 25 articles. He is editor of four volumes and co-editor of seven volumes. He was editor of *Journal of Economic Issues*, 1981–91. He was recipient of the Veblen–Commons Award in 1988. He is listed in *Who's Who in Economics* (1999) and the *Dictionary of Dissenting Economists* (2000).

David Young is a Senior Lecturer in Economics at the University of Manchester, UK. He was previously a lecturer in Economic Studies at the University of East Anglia. Originally an industrial economist, his principal interests are now in political economy and the philosophy of the social sciences. He has published widely on alternative theories of competition, the methodology of economics and public policy.

Introduction

Geoffrey M. Hodgson*

The book is the first of what is hoped to be a series of readers produced by the European Association for Evolutionary Political Economy (EAEPE) through Edward Elgar Publishing. The aim of these volumes is to present an exciting and diverse body of work in economics and related disciplines, to undergraduate students, graduate students and lecturers. Much of this work is not discussed in standard textbooks. Yet it is of enormous importance in understanding the manifest turbulence and transformations in the modern world.

With the exception of the present introduction, the essays reprinted here have all been published before. They all appeared in collections of papers presented at successive EAEPE conferences and workshops since 1990. In compiling this reader, key papers have been selected from conference volumes between 1990 and 1996 inclusive.[1] The papers have been selected not simply on their merit and importance but also to provide a coherent structure for the reader as a whole. Furthermore, the specific focus of this reader is on 'key concepts' and that too is reflected in the choice of papers.

The first aim of this introductory essay is to place these essays in the historical and theoretical background of recent developments in economics and other social sciences. In recent years there have been enormous changes, especially within and on the fringes of economics itself. Some of these developments are sketched in section 1. Section 2 outlines the conceptual and theoretical foundations of institutional and evolutionary economics. Section 3 briefly summarizes the contents of the essays reprinted here.

1. ECONOMICS FROM THE 1970s TO THE 1990s

If we could travel back in time just a few years to 1970, we would be struck by the remarkable difference between economics as taught then and as taught today. First, although the formalization of mainstream economics was then proceeding apace, it had not reached the levels that we find now. In the 1970s, even prestigious journals such as the *American Economic Review* and the

Economic Journal carried a significantly lower proportion of mathematical articles.

Second, non-mainstream viewpoints within economics had a stronger following and could be found in many university departments of economics. 'Post Keynesian' economics was launched in the early 1970s by Joan Robinson, Alfred Eichner, Sidney Weintraub and Paul Davidson (Lee, 2001). Within this grouping, a minority were engaged in the famous 'Cambridge' debates over capital theory (Harcourt, 1972). It seemed to many at the time that a major theoretical flaw in mainstream economics had been identified. However, the main preoccupation of Post Keynesianism was macroeconomics. In addition, Marxian economics experienced a major global revival, partly as a consequence of the political radicalization of the student movement. Accordingly, during the 1970s, economics included sizeable non-mainstream tendencies, such as Marxism and Post Keynesianism.

Herbert Simon was awarded the Nobel Prize for economics in 1978, and his criticisms of mainstream economics became more influential. In addition, Nicholas Georgescu-Roegen (1971) published an important theoretical work with major implications for both economic theory and policy. Friedrich Hayek received the Nobel Prize in 1974 and this heralded a revival of 'Austrian' economics, particularly in the United States. Economists of the Austrian school were highly critical of the informational assumptions and equilibrium analyses of mainstream economics. However, unlike most other critics of mainstream economics, they promoted a highly pro-market policy agenda. This helped them to survive in the 1980s, in the ideological environment of Ronald Reagan and Margaret Thatcher.

Several important developments occurred within mainstream economics in the 1970s, of which a few can be mentioned. In microeconomics, neoclassical approaches remained dominant, with their common emphasis on rationality, maximization and equilibrium. In some respects there was a growing self-confidence in this approach, with theorists such as Gary Becker applying it to new areas of enquiry such as the family. The perceived cutting edge of neoclassical theory was general equilibrium analysis. However, in the 1970s, general equilibrium theorists such as Gerard Debreu, Rolf Mantel and Hugo Sonnenschein discovered severe problems within this approach. These problems would eventually prove fatal for this research programme (Kirman, 1989; Rizvi, 1994a).

Another striking event in the 1970s was the inauguration of the 'new institutional economics'. The term was coined by Oliver Williamson (1975) and was also broadly associated with work from a variety of viewpoints by Ronald Coase, Douglass North, Mancur Olson, Richard Posner and others. These were important developments, not least because they opened for analysis the 'black box' of the firm and other institutions.

In macroeconomics, perhaps the most significant mainstream development in the 1970s was the renewed assault on all varieties of Keynesianism. It was argued that Keynesian theory involved '*ad hoc*' assumptions, and instead macroeconomics should be placed on the 'sound microfoundations' of general equilibrium theory (Weintraub, 1979). Milton Friedman promoted his own version of monetarism as an alternative to Keynesianism. The 'new classical economics' of Robert Lucas and others also became prominent.

The ideological climate changed markedly in the late 1970s. On the whole, Marxian economics failed to extricate itself from its arcane doctrinal debates and lost its theoretical momentum by the early 1980s. The only significant grouping of Marxian economists to survive the 1980s were those – such as John Roemer and John Elster – who had openly embraced mainstream theoretical and mathematical tools, such as neoclassical equilibrium analysis and game theory.

As a result, the 1980s opened with the main non-mainstream approaches to economics in difficulties. Post Keynesianism was under severe attack from the monetarists and Marxism was in severe decline. The Cambridge critique of the neoclassical aggregate production had been largely ignored. Frank Hahn (1982) rightly pointed out that the Cambridge critique of capital theory does not apply to disaggregated approaches such as general equilibrium theory. In these new circumstances, no school of non-mainstream economics made much headway.

Furthermore, mainstream economics itself, dramatically but quietly, shifted its cutting edge from general equilibrium theory to game theory. This became the main theatre of theoretical controversy within mainstream economics (Rizvi, 1994b).

At the same time, new critiques and alternatives began to develop. On the fringes, there was a steady increase in both 'evolutionary' and 'institutional' themes in the 1980s. Kenneth Boulding's (1981) book *Evolutionary Economics* appeared as one of the first of many in this new evolutionary wave. It was followed quickly by the classic work of Richard Nelson and Sidney Winter (1982) *An Evolutionary Theory of Economic Change*. These and other works brought into the limelight a very different type of approach to economic theory and analysis.

At roughly the same time, and especially in France, the *régulation* school had come into being through a work published originally in French in 1976 by Michel Aglietta (1979). In the 1980s, the *régulation* approach provided a bridge between Marxism and some newer evolutionary and institutionalist themes.

Also during the 1980s, there were significant developments in both the 'new' and the 'old' institutionalism. While the new institutionalism proved increasingly influential, some of its followers made links with the Austrian school, establishing links with the work of Carl Menger and subsequent Austrians (Schotter, 1981; Langlois, 1986).

In North America, a small group of 'old' institutionalists had formed the Association for Evolutionary Economics and the *Journal of Economic Issues* in the 1960s. While the old institutionalists had been overshadowed by Marxism and Post Keynesianism in the 1970s, the new situation in the 1980s provided the old institutionalists with an opportunity. After all, developments within or close to mainstream economics had put institutions back on the agenda. In addition, through the efforts of Americans such as Warren Samuels (1979), Marc Tool (1979) and others, the 'old' institutional economics began once again to be noticed. In addition, the Association for Institutionalist Thought was founded in the early 1980s. It continues to meet alongside the gatherings of the Western Economic Association in the USA.

These initiatives helped to revive interest in the works of such institutionalists as Thorstein Veblen, Wesley Mitchell, John Commons and Clarence Ayres. Significantly, several of their books were reprinted in the 1980s and 1990s. The most important living representative of the American institutionalist tradition – John Kenneth Galbraith – had already achieved prominence through his popular and challenging works.

The Santa Fe Institute was founded in 1984. It had an impact on the development of complexity theory and promoted non-reductionist discourses in both the social and the natural sciences (Waldrop, 1992). Another important and fertile development in the 1980s was the growth in interest in the methodology of economics, stimulated by publications such as those by Mark Blaug (1980) and Bruce Caldwell (1982).

The year 1988 was marked by a remarkable number of influential publications and developments. An influential work by Amitai Etzioni (1988) led to the foundation of the Society for the Advancement of Socio-economics (SASE). Horst Hanusch (1988) produced an edited volume on *Evolutionary Economics* that signalled a strong revival of interest in the ideas of Joseph Schumpeter and the formation of the International Joseph Schumpeter Association. A larger, seminal collection of essays – edited by Giovanni Dosi, et al. (1988) – focused on technical change and also proclaimed some strong 'evolutionary' themes. Finally, a work of mine may have helped the revival of the old institutional economics in Europe and America (Hodgson, 1988). The European Association for Evolutionary Political Economy was conceived at a meeting near London in 1988. It emerged as a broadly based and pluralist forum for the development of institutional and evolutionary economics.

Between 1980 to 1990, the profile of non-mainstream economics had changed globally and dramatically. In 1980, dissident economics was dominated by macroeconomics of Marxist and Post Keynesian hues. By contrast, in 1990, the picture was much more diverse. It involved unorthodox developments in microeconomics as well as in macroeconomics, and it included novel and prominent evolutionary and institutionalist themes.

However, in the meantime, mainstream economics had become more formal and narrow. Several departments of economics that had formerly accommodated non-mainstream economists, were by 1990 entirely under mainstream control. This was particularly noticeable at the University of Cambridge. Its leading non-mainstream theorists, Nicholas Kaldor, Joan Robinson and Piero Sraffa, all died in the 1980s. By 1990 the department was under neoclassical control. Similar changes occurred at many other institutions, including Rutgers University in New Jersey, which had previously been a Post Keynesian citadel.

After the fall of the Berlin Wall in 1989 and the end of the Cold War, the ideological environment changed. An important effect of this was to create more space within mainstream economics for analyses of the limitations of the market mechanism and justifications for some forms of state intervention. In addition to the extreme pro-market views that were still propounded in Chicago and elsewhere, rising mainstream theorists such as Joseph Stiglitz and Paul Krugman defended some role for state intervention and the regulation of markets. A wider variety of ideological viewpoints could be found among leading mainstream economists. The mistaken view that the debate between mainstream and dissident economics was primarily over ideology or policy was undermined.

However, what was noticeable about this ideological shift within the mainstream was that all positions had to be articulated within the increasingly formal language of mathematical economics, with less attention than in the 1970s to real world institutions and history. Although mainstream economics itself had changed enormously in the period, it increasingly defined itself in narrow, formalistic terms.

As a result, many non-mainstream economists were excluded from mainstream departments and journals. Institutional and evolutionary economists did not entirely reject mathematics as a tool, but they were critical of the tendency of the mainstream to become immersed in mathematical technique for its own sake. Consequently, many non-mainstream economists working in this area found employment in business schools, science policy units, departments of public policy and so on. Important work on the nature of social institutions was also carried out in social theory and philosophy (Searle, 1995). These matters of disciplinary demarcation affected the development of both mainstream and non-mainstream economics in the 1990s.

Institutional and evolutionary economics developed a broad global network, with a particular concentration in Europe. As well as important theoretical developments, it had an impact on economic policies, particularly in the areas of technology policy, innovation policy, competition policy and corporate strategy. Several governments in Europe had advisors who were particularly inspired by these approaches. As the millennium drew to a close, it was clear that institutional and evolutionary economics had had a major impact, and it faced exciting new challenges for the next century.

In addition, important developments within mainstream economics pointed to issues raised already by the dissident economists. For example, Douglass North (1990) and Masahiko Aoki (2001) moved towards more open-ended and evolutionary theoretical analysis. The idea that all theory has to start simply from given individuals was abandoned by some. Instead, individuals were placed in a historical and institutional context. This work led to a degree of convergence with the evolutionary ideas of the 'old' institutionalists.

2.   THE HISTORICAL AND THEORETICAL FOUNDATIONS OF INSTITUTIONAL AND EVOLUTIONARY ECONOMICS

Indeed, the developments in the last three decades of the twentieth century generally helped to rehabilitate the approaches of the historical school and the 'old' institutionalists. The historical school prevailed in Germany from the 1840s to the 1940s. The 'old' institutionalists were dominant in America between the First and Second World Wars. Within these schools of thought, evolutionary and institutional themes were common. These former schools still provide quarries of ideas. Their systems of thinking were not centred on, nor overly encumbered by, the neoclassical concepts of rationality, maximization and equilibrium.

Both American institutionalism and German historicism were immense and diverse movements and it is impossible to summarize their ideas in detail here. What should be emphasized, however, is that they held to a conception of economics that was much broader than the idea of the subject promoted by mainstream economists today. Within their capacious conception of the subject a number of important theoretical themes can be found. Some of these themes have been revived in modern institutional and evolutionary economics today.

Historical Specificity

Modern institutional and evolutionary economists endorse a theme that has been prominent in the writings of American institutionalists, German historicists and Marxists. From their viewpoints, it is recognized that socio-economic systems have changed substantially and enormously through history and that there are also important variations between different socio-economic systems at any point in time. From a realist point of view, changes and differences in reality have implications for the type of theory to be developed (Mäki, 1989; Lawson, 1997). Consequently, attempts to create general or universal theories in social science face the problem of dealing with this real variation and diversity. General theorizing faces an ontological constraint. Attempts to erect general theories in social science have either failed in their own terms to be truly general, or have acquired highly limited explanatory powers (Hodgson, 2001).

As a result, economic and social theorists are obliged to build theories that in part involve historically or geographically specific assumptions. Although all theorizing involves some general categories and elements, effective theories also involve specific and particular assumptions. Marx recognized this in his analysis of capitalism. The German historical school developed methods and taxonomies to deal with particular historical developments. The American institutionalists focused on the nature of specific economic institutions. These schools recognized that the value of any general theory in social science is, at best, highly limited. Instead their focus was on particular systems, institutions and mechanisms.

Similarly, the essays in the present volume do not pursue the chimera of a purely universal theory. Of course, some general concepts – such as knowledge, power, evolution and open systems – are thematic for institutional and evolutionary economics. But an attempt is made to link their exposition to real economic processes and relations. For example, it is important to understand and explain key phenomena such as prices, but the exposition of price theory in large part depends on the analysis of historically and institutionally specific market relations and pricing mechanisms. In addition, markets are not the universal ether of all human interaction but a highly specific type of social formation. In short, markets themselves are historically specific institutions.

Evolutionary Orientation

In contrast to the traditional equilibrium and steady-state orientation of much economic theory, institutional and evolutionary economists place much greater emphasis on processes, changes and structural transformations. The recognition of the historical specificity of socio-economic systems itself points to the processes of evolution and system change through time. While much of economic theory attempts to focus principally on that which is common to all socio-economic systems, institutional and evolutionary economics also emphasizes the differences and the changes in socio-economic systems.

Of course, all theorizing must take some items as given. But from an evolutionary perspective a theorist is obliged to give some justification and explanation of the assumptions that are made. If assumptions are made about human individuals or social institutions, then the theorist is obliged to point to a plausible evolutionary or historical explanation of the origin of the assumed circumstances. If no such explanation is yet available, then as scientists we are obliged to place this omission on the agenda for future enquiry.

For example, if humans are assumed to be capable of rational deliberation then we have to provide, at least in outline, an evolutionary explanation of such capacities. Rationality cannot be assumed to have dropped from heaven during some stage of human evolution. Consequently, we required some evolutionary picture, similar to the one developed by William James (1890) and others, in which reason is built upon habit, and in turn habit is built upon instinct. In practice, as the institutional economist John Maurice Clark (1918, p. 26) put it: 'it is only by the aid of habit that the marginal utility principle is approximated in real life'. Even if agents are rational according to the assumptions of neoclassical economics, then their capacity to be rational itself depends upon prior habituation. In humans, reason evolved after habits, and all human reason is dependent upon prior habits.

Essentially, a commitment to evolutionary explanation involves an ongoing quest for causal explanations. Of course, the process of enquiry can never be complete and explanations are always limited. All explanation involves theoretical isolation or abstraction (Mäki, 1992). It is impossible to bring every real causal link into the theoretical picture. Nevertheless, the evolutionary commitment remains. The obligation is to push back the boundaries of explanation, and not to be satisfied with abstractions simply on the basis of their apparent elegance or mathematical appeal.

The recognition that scientific enquiry can never reach finality or closure encourages a tolerant attitude to the conduct of science. The fact that all theory is necessarily incomplete and provisional obliges the scientist to accept, in principle, the viability of some alternative explanation. Like evolution in the real world, science itself thrives on diversity and plurality (Salanti and Screpanti, 1997).

A reason why the boundaries of explanation are never all-embracing is that open, complex systems exhibit novelty (Witt, 1992). Complex interactions and exchanges within and across the boundaries of the system bring about novel, emergent and unpredictable forms and events. Variation and diversity are part of both the natural and the economic order (Saviotti, 1996; Metcalfe, 1998). As the institutionalist and historicist John Atkinson Hobson (1936, p. 216) put it: 'Emergent evolution brings unpredictable novelties into the processes of history, and disorder, hazard, chance, are brought into the play of energetic action'.

The ongoing quest for causal explanations has another important implication. Given that there is no finality in each chain of cause and effect, and in principle there are no limits to the probing extent of scientific enquiry, then economists must also be concerned with the interactions between the social and the natural domain. There are no hermetic analytical boundaries between the social and the natural world. All socio-economic systems are embedded in, and dependent upon, a natural environment. Accordingly, the interactions between socio-economic and ecological systems, including effects such as pollution and ecological degradation, have to be taken into account (Georgescu-Roegen, 1971).

The extent to which evolutionary principles or laws from the natural world also apply to society and the economy has long been a matter of controversy among evolutionary and institutional economists (Penrose, 1952; Campbell, 1965). However, the adoption of a view that some laws or principles may apply across both the social and the natural domain does not itself imply that explanations of social and economic phenomena have themselves to be reduced to biological terms (Hodgson, 1993). The prevailing view among institutional and evolutionary economists is that socio-economic systems are governed by principles that are not entirely reducible to those pertaining to the natural world.

As the institutional and evolutionary economist Thorstein Veblen (1909, p. 300) put it, if conventions and institutions were mere outcomes – not the principal basis of social action – and instead people acted 'solely and directly on the grounds and values afforded by the unconventionalised propensities and aptitudes of hereditary human nature, then there would be no institutions and no culture'. The socio-economic domain has emergent properties and causal powers that are not reducible to biology, just as biology itself is not completely reducible to physics or chemistry.

Encultured Individuals

The general implication of the ongoing quest for causal explanations is that no entity is ultimately taken as given. This importantly applies to the human individual. In contrast, mainstream economists have typically taken the individual as given. In particular, Menger and the new institutionalists have been committed to the theoretical project of explaining the emergence of institutions in terms of the interactions of given individuals alone, starting from an institution-free 'state of nature'. It has been suggested above that this project has insurmountable internal theoretical problems (Hodgson, 1998a).

Among these difficulties is the problem of incorporating some notion of learning into the notion of fixed preferences. Although some attempts have been made to reconcile learning with Bayesian or other conceptions of rationality, the fundamental problem is that learning, if real and substantial, must in part *reconstitute* the preferences or purposes of the individual (Nonaka and Takeuchi, 1995; Nooteboom, 2000).

The tradition of institutional and evolutionary economics that is promoted here does not confine itself to the 'upward causation' from individuals to institutions. Although institutions clearly depend upon the actions of individuals, in addition individuals are affected by their institutional environment. There is 'downward causation' as well. Just as institutions are constituted by individuals, individuals are constituted by institutions (Giddens, 1984; Archer, 1995). Accordingly, Veblen (1898, p. 389) criticized Menger and others for assuming 'a passive and substantially inert and immutably given human nature'.

The idea that individuals are moulded by circumstances is thematic to the old institutionalism and follows from a commitment to an evolutionary approach (Hodgson, 2000). Individual preferences and purposes can be affected by behaviours, experiences, cultures and institutions. Instead of the atomistic individual, institutional and evolutionary economists focus on the social and encultured individual.

Consider a relevant example. Trust is an interpersonal relationship of some economic significance. Trust is an emergent property of an enduring and reciprocal relationship between multiple individuals in an institutional context. It is a relational property; not something that is a property of isolated individuals. Accordingly, the environment of trust, or lack of it, affects individual aims and preferences. The study of the role of trust in corporate organizations is an important area of research today (Lazaric and Lorenz, 1998; Nooteboom *et al.*, 1997).

Of course, once we adopt the view that there can be 'downward causation' from institutions and other entities at a 'higher' level to individuals then one is obliged to explain the causal mechanisms involved. Mere mention of cultural or social 'forces' is not enough. The danger is that the greater emphasis will be put on 'downward causation', to the neglect of the individual and causality in the opposite direction. The causal relationship between actor and structure remains an enduring problem in all the social sciences.

The argument of Veblen (1899, p. 192) and those inspired by him was that institutions acted upon individuals by changing their habits. Furthermore: 'Social structure changes, develops, adapts itself to an altered situation, only through a change in the habits of thought of the several classes of the community; or in the last analysis, through a change in the habits of thought of the individuals which make up the community'. Once again the concepts of habit and routine are central to evolutionary and institutional economics.

Multiple Levels of Analysis

Once we abandon the false dichotomy of methodological individualism (in which explanations of social phenomena are reduced to the preferences and purposes of individuals alone) and methodological collectivism (in which explanations of social phenomena are reduced to the collectives, structures, cultures or institutions alone) then the way is open to explore a third perspective, involving the interaction of individual and structure.

The old institutionalists took institutions as well as individuals as units of analysis. According to the argument pursued here, taking institutions as well as individuals as units of analysis should exclude a reductionist approach in which explanations of one are reduced entirely to the terms of the other. Both types of unit of analysis should come into the picture.

It has already been noted that Veblen saw the institutional and cultural, the individual, and the biological, all as legitimate levels of analyses. But in his view no level was entirely reducible to another. This multi-levelled approach has since been thematic in institutional and evolutionary economics.

For example, in his 1924 Presidential Address to the American Economic Association, Mitchell – a former student of Veblen – argued that economists need not begin with a theory of individual behaviour but with the statistical observation of 'mass phenomena'. Mitchell (1937, p. 30) went on: 'The quantitative workers will have a special predilection for institutional problems, because institutions standardize behavior, and thereby facilitate statistical procedure'. Subsequently, Rutledge Vining (1949, p. 85) noted how 'much orderliness and regularity apparently only becomes evident when large aggregates are observed' and noted the limitations of a reductionist method in economics. Modern computer simulations and other studies of complex systems seem to underline similar points (Cohen and Stewart, 1994; Chiaromonte and Dosi, 1993).

Mitchell and his colleagues in the US National Bureau for Economic Research in the 1920s and 1930s played a vital role in the development of national income accounting and suggested that aggregate, macroeconomic phenomena have an ontological and empirical legitimacy. Arguably, this important incursion against reductionism created space for the Keynesian revolution in economics. Through the development of national income accounting, the work of Mitchell and his colleagues helped to establish modern macroeconomics and inspired the macroeconomics of Keynes (Mirowski, 1989, p. 307; Colander and Landreth, 1996, p. 141). Accordingly, a consequence of the Veblenian emphasis on multiple levels of analysis was the legitimation of a macroeconomics that could not be reduced entirely to microeconomic elements.

Similarly, the German historical school had previously established a level of analysis of the 'national economy'. As Christopher Freeman (1995) and others have noted, this historicist work is a root of the modern study of 'national systems of innovation' (Lundvall, 1992; Nelson, 1993). Clearly, once we adopt the idea of multiple levels of analysis, additional levels are possible, such as the firm, the industry, the region and the global economy.

The 'old' institutional economics did not attempt to build up a picture of the whole system by moving unidirectionally from given individuals. Instead there is the idea of interactive agents, mutually entwined in durable and self-reinforcing institutions. This provides a quite different way of approaching the problem of theorizing the relationship between actor and structure.

3.   THE CONTENTS OF THIS READER

This volume is intended to provide introductions to, and illustrations of, some of the key themes touched upon in this introductory essay.

Part I focuses on key concepts such as learning, power, trust, prices and markets. In Chapter 1, Marc R. Tool provides a survey of institutionalist works on pricing theory. Not only does this essay refute the allegation that the 'old' institutional economics was 'atheoretical' or 'against theory', but also it shows that institutionalist theories of pricing are rooted in an analysis of the institutional routines and market conditions associated with the pricing process.

In Chapter 2 Bengt-Åke Lundvall examines the challenge that the concept of learning provides to mainstream economics. He dramatizes this argument in the context of the modern, knowledge-intensive, learning economy.

In Chapter 3 David Young examines different conceptions of power in economic analysis. Building on earlier work by Steven Lukes (1974) and others, Young shows that much economic and social theory relies on an overly limited conception of power. In contrast, an enhanced concept of power involves a reconstitution of the aims and purposes of those individuals over whom power is exercised.

In chapter 4, Sandye Gloria-Palermo examines the Austrian view of the market process and finds it deficient in its treatment of creativity and novelty. This argument has important implications for the institutionalist understanding of markets (Gloria-Palermo, 1999).

In Chapter 5, Hans Berger, Niels G. Noorderhaven and Bart Nooteboom report an important and pioneering empirical study of the role of trust in economic relationships.

Part II is devoted to varieties of economic theory. It has a more specific focus, involving comparisons between schools of thought and the general role of theoretical pluralism in economic science. In Chapter 6 Benjamin Coriat and Giovanni Dosi offer a forensic examination and comparison of the 'regulationist' (or *régulationniste*) and 'evolutionary' research programmes, focusing especially on their strengths and complementarities.

In Chapter 7 Uskali Mäki discusses the relationship between the realist commitment to the existence of a real world outside ourselves and the existence of multiple theories describing that single world. He shows that the possible relationships between different theories include complementarity and incompatibility.

Sheila C. Dow further explores this methodological theme in Chapter 8. She argues that the methodological pluralism of Bruce Caldwell (1982) and others, at least in a pure form, is untenable as a basis for knowledge. Further, the justification of methodological pluralism becomes opaque when it is combined with a unitary, closed-system epistemology or ontology.

Part III of this book is devoted to varieties of capitalism. In Chapter 9 Eileen Appelbaum and Ronald Schettkat analyse and compare different growth regimes, both through time and in different capitalist countries. They focus in particular on the impact of different wage-bargaining institutions on economic performance.

In Chapter 10, Bernard Chavance and Eric Magnin examine the evolution of some of the transitional economies in Central Europe in the 1990s. They show that the outcomes were highly dependent both on the particular national historical legacies and the types of privatization arrangement, financial institutions and industrial structures that were promoted by the early transition governments. Hence, despite the pressures of market globalization, highly diverse capitalist economies have emerged in Central and Eastern Europe.

Finally, in Chapter 11, Geoffrey M. Hodgson places the manifest variety of capitalist forms alongside a number of theoretical approaches. He argues that neoclassical, Austrian and Marxist approaches all have theoretical problems in fully recognizing and dealing with this institutional and cultural variety. He sketches an institutional approach to this problem that is directed at overcoming some of these limitations and defects.

NOTES

* The author is very grateful to Eileen Appelbaum, Albert Jolink, Uskali Mäki, Bart Nooteboom and Marc Tool for helpful comments on an earlier draft of this essay.
1. The complete list of volumes for the 1990–96 EAEPE conferences are: from the 1990 conference in Florence – Amin and Dietrich (1991) and Hodgson and Screpanti (1991); from the 1991 conference in Vienna – Blaas and Foster (1992); from the 1992 conference in Paris – Delorme and Dopfer (1994); from the 1993 conference in Barcelona – Groenewegen et al. (1995) and Tylecote and van der Straaten (1997); from the 1994 conference in Copenhagen – Nielsen and Johnson (1998); from the 1994 workshop in Bergamo – Salanti and Screpanti (1997); from the 1995 conference in Krakow – Amin and Hausner (1997); from the 1996 conference in Antwerp – Michie and Reati (1998) and Groenewegen and Vromen (1999). The essays reprinted here have been slightly revised and updated.

REFERENCES

Aglietta, Michel (1979), *A Theory of Capitalist Regulation: The US Experience*, translated by David Fernbach from the French edition of 1976, London: NLB.

Amin, Ash and Michael Dietrich (1991), *Towards a New Europe? Structural Change in the European Community*, Aldershot: Edward Elgar.

Amin, Ash and Jerzy Hausner (eds) (1997), *Beyond Market and Hierarchy: Interactive Governance and Social Complexity*, Cheltenham: Edward Elgar.

Aoki, Masahiko (2001), *Toward a Comparative Institutional Analysis*, Cambridge, MA: MIT Press.

Archer, Margaret S. (1995), *Realist Social Theory: The Morphogenetic Approach*, Cambridge: Cambridge University Press.

Blaas, Wolfgang and John Foster (eds) (1992), *Mixed Economies in Europe: An Evolutionary Perspective on Their Emergence, Transition and Regulation*, Aldershot: Edward Elgar.

Blaug, Mark (1980), *The Methodology of Economics: Or How Economists Explain*, 1st edition, Cambridge: Cambridge University Press.

Boulding, Kenneth E. (1981), *Evolutionary Economics*, Beverly Hills, CA: Sage Publications.

Caldwell, Bruce J. (1982), *Beyond Positivism: Economic Methodology in the Twentieth Century*, London: Allen & Unwin.

Campbell, Donald T. (1965), 'Variation, selection and retention in sociocultural evolution', in Barringer, H.R., Blanksten, G.I. and Mack, R.W. (eds), *Social Change in Developing Areas: A Reinterpretation of Evolutionary Theory*, Cambridge, MA: Schenkman), pp. 19–49. Reprinted in *General Systems*, 14, 1969, pp. 69–85 and in Hodgson (1998b).

Chiaromonte, Francesca and Giovanni Dosi (1993), 'Heterogeneity, competition, and macroeconomic dynamics', *Structural Change and Economic Dynamics*, 4(1), June, pp. 39–63.

Clark, John Maurice (1918), 'Economics and modern psychology' Parts I and II, *Journal of Political Economy*, 26(1–2), January–April, pp. 1–30, 136–66. Reprinted in John Maurice Clark (1967), *Preface to Social Economics*, New York: Augustus Kelley, and in Hodgson (1998b).

Cohen, Jack and Ian Stewart (1994), *The Collapse of Chaos: Discovering Simplicity in a Complex World*, London and New York: Viking.

Colander, David C. and Harry Landreth (eds) (1996), *The Coming of Keynesianism to America: Conversations with the Founders of Keynesian Economics*, Aldershot: Edward Elgar.

Delorme, Robert and Kurt Dopfer (eds) (1994), *The Political Economy of Diversity: Evolutionary Perspectives on Economic Order and Disorder*, Aldershot: Edward Elgar.

Dosi, Giovanni, Christopher Freeman, Richard Nelson, Gerald Silverberg and Luc L.G. Soete (eds) (1988), *Technical Change and Economic Theory*, London: Pinter.

Etzioni, Amitai (1988), *The Moral Dimension: Toward a New Economics*, New York: Free Press.

Freeman, Christopher (1995), 'The "national system of innovation" in historical perspective', *Cambridge Journal of Economics*, 19(1), February, pp. 5–24.

Georgescu-Roegen, Nicholas (1971), *The Entropy Law and the Economic Process*, Cambridge, MA: Harvard University Press.

Giddens, Anthony (1984), *The Constitution of Society: Outline of the Theory of Structuration*, Cambridge: Polity Press.

Gloria-Palermo, Sandye (1999), *The Evolution of Austrian Economics: From Menger to Lachmann*, London: Routledge.

Groenewegen, John and Jack Vromen (eds) (1999), *Institutions and the Evolution of Capitalism: Implications of Evolutionary Economics*, Cheltenham: Edward Elgar.

Groenewegen, John, Christos Pitelis and Sven-Erik Sjöstrand (eds) (1995), *On Economic Institutions: Theory and Applications*, Aldershot: Edward Elgar.

Hahn, Frank H. (1982), 'The neo-Ricardians', *Cambridge Journal of Economics*, 6(4), December, pp. 353–74.

Hanusch, Horst (ed.) (1988), *Evolutionary Economics: Applications of Schumpeter's Ideas*, Cambridge: Cambridge University Press.

Harcourt, Geoffrey C. (1972), *Some Cambridge Controversies in the Theory of Capital*, Cambridge: Cambridge University Press.

Hobson, John A. (1936), *Veblen*, London: Chapman and Hall.

Hodgson, Geoffrey M. (1988), *Economics and Institutions: A Manifesto for a Modern Institutional Economics*, Cambridge and Philadelphia: Polity Press and University of Pennsylvania Press.

Hodgson, Geoffrey M. (1993), *Economics and Evolution: Bringing Life back into Economics*, Cambridge, UK and Ann Arbor, MI: Polity Press and University of Michigan Press.

Hodgson, Geoffrey M. (1998a), 'The approach of institutional economics', *Journal of Economic Literature*, 36(1), March, pp. 166–92.

Hodgson, Geoffrey M. (ed.) (1998b), *The Foundations of Evolutionary Economics: 1890–1973*, 2 vols, International Library of Critical Writings in Economics, Cheltenham: Edward Elgar.

Hodgson, Geoffrey M. (2000), 'What is the essence of institutional economics?', *Journal of Economic Issues*, 34(2), June, pp. 317–29.

Hodgson, Geoffrey M. (2001), *How Economics Forgot History: The Problem of Historical Specificity in Social Science*, London and New York: Routledge.

Hodgson, Geoffrey M., Warren J. Samuels and Marc R. Tool (eds) (1994), *The Elgar Companion to Institutional and Evolutionary Economics*, Aldershot: Edward Elgar.

Hodgson, Geoffrey M. and Ernesto Screpanti (eds) (1991), *Rethinking Economics: Markets, Technology and Economic Evolution*, Aldershot: Edward Elgar.

James, William (1890), *The Principles of Psychology*, 1st edition, New York: Holt.

Kirman, Alan P. (1989), 'The intrinsic limits of modern economic theory: the emperor has no clothes', *Economic Journal (Conference Papers)*, 99, pp. 126–39.

Langlois, Richard N. (ed.) (1986), *Economics as a Process: Essays in the New Institutional Economics*, Cambridge: Cambridge University Press.

Lawson, Tony (1997), *Economics and Reality*, London: Routledge.

Lazaric, Nathalie and Edward Lorenz (eds) (1998), *Trust and Economic Learning*, Cheltenham: Edward Elgar.

Lee, Frederick S. (2002), *Alfred S. Eichner, Joan Robinson and the Founding of Post Keynesian Economics*, Armonk, NY: M.E. Sharpe, forthcoming.

Lukes, Steven (1974), *Power: A Radical View*, London: Macmillan.

Lundvall, Bengt-Åke (ed.) (1992), *National Systems of Innovation: Towards a Theory of Innovation and Interactive Learning*, London: Pinter.

Mäki, Uskali (1989), 'On the problem of realism in economics', *Ricerche Economiche*, 43(1–2), Gennaio–Giugno, pp. 176–98.

Mäki, Uskali (1992), 'On the method of isolation in economics', in Craig Dilworth (ed.), *Idealization IV: Intelligibility in Science*, Amsterdam: Rodopi, pp. 317–51.

Metcalfe, J. Stanley (1998), *Evolutionary Economics and Creative Destruction*, London: Routledge.

Michie, Jonathan and Angelo Reati (eds) (1998), *Employment, Technology and Economic Needs: Theory, Evidence, and Public Policy*, Cheltenham: Edward Elgar.

Mirowski, Philip (1989), *More Heat than Light: Economics as Social Physics, Physics as Nature's Economics*, Cambridge: Cambridge University Press.

Mitchell, Wesley C. (1937), *The Backward Art of Spending Money and Other Essays*, New York: McGraw-Hill.

Neilsen, Klaus and Johnson, Björn (eds) (1998), *Institutions and Economic Change: New Perspectives on Markets, Firms and Technology*, Cheltenham: Edward Elgar.

Nelson, Richard R. (ed.) (1993), *National Innovation Systems: A Comparative Analysis*, Oxford: Oxford University Press.

Nelson, Richard R. and Sidney G. Winter (1982), *An Evolutionary Theory of Economic Change*, Cambridge, MA: Harvard University Press.

Nonaka, Ikujiro and Hirotaka Takeuchi (1995), *The Knowledge-creating Company: How Japanese Companies Create the Dynamics of Innovation*, Oxford and New York: Oxford University Press.

Nooteboom, Bart (2000), *Learning and Innovation in Organizations and Industries*, Oxford and New York: Oxford University Press.

Nooteboom, Bart, Hans Berger and Niels G. Noorderhaven (1997), 'Effects of trust and governance on relational risk', *Academy of Management Journal*, 40(2), pp. 308–38.

North, Douglass C. (1990), *Institutions, Institutional Change and Economic Performance*, Cambridge: Cambridge University Press.

Penrose, Edith T. (1952), 'Biological analogies in the theory of the firm', *American Economic Review*, 42(4), December, pp. 804–19. Reprinted in Geoffrey M. Hodgson (ed.) (1995), *Economics and Biology*, Aldershot: Edward Elgar, and in Hodgson (1998b).

Rizvi, S. Abu Turab (1994a), 'The microfoundations project in general equilibrium theory', *Cambridge Journal of Economics*, 18(4), August, pp. 357–77.

Rizvi, S. Abu Turab (1994b), 'Game theory to the rescue?', *Contributions to Political Economy*, 13, pp. 1–28.

Salanti, Andrea and Ernesto Screpanti (eds) (1997), *Pluralism in Economics: New Perspectives in History and Methodology*, Aldershot: Edward Elgar.

Samuels, Warren J. (ed.) (1979), *The Economy as a System of Power*, 2 vols, New Brunswick, NJ: Transaction.

Saviotti, Pier Paolo (1996), *Technological Evolution, Variety and the Economy*, Aldershot: Edward Elgar.

Schotter, Andrew R. (1981), *The Economic Theory of Social Institutions*, Cambridge: Cambridge University Press.

Searle, John R. (1995), *The Construction of Social Reality*, London: Allen Lane.

Tool, Marc R. (1979), *The Discretionary Economy: A Normative Theory of Political Economy*, Santa Monica, CA: Goodyear.

Tylecote, Andrew and Jan van der Straaten (eds) (1997), *Environment, Technology and Economic Growth*, Cheltenham: Edward Elgar.

Veblen, Thorstein B. (1898), 'Why is economics not an evolutionary science?', *Quarterly Journal of Economics*, 12(3), July, pp. 373–97. Reprinted in Thorstein

B. Veblen (1919), *The Place of Science in Modern Civilisation and Other Essays*, New York: Huebsch.

Veblen, Thorstein B. (1899), *The Theory of the Leisure Class: An Economic Study in the Evolution of Institutions*, New York: Macmillan. Republished 1961, New York: Random House.

Veblen, Thorstein B. (1909), 'Fisher's rate of interest', *Political Science Quarterly*, 24, June, pp. 296–303. Reprinted in Thorstein B. Veblen (1934), *Essays on Our Changing Order*, ed. Leon Ardzrooni, New York: Viking Press.

Vining, Rutledge (1949), 'Methodological issues in quantitative economics', *Review of Economics and Statistics*, 31(2), May, pp. 77–86.

Waldrop, M. Mitchell (1992), *Complexity: The Emerging Science at the Edge of Order and Chaos*, New York: Simon and Schuster.

Weintraub, E. Roy (1979), *Microfoundations*, Cambridge: Cambridge University Press.

Williamson, Oliver E. (1975), *Markets and Hierarchies: Analysis and Anti-trust Implications: A Study in the Economics of Internal Organization*, New York: Free Press.

Witt, Ulrich (ed.) (1992), *Explaining Process and Change: Approaches to Evolutionary Economics*, Ann Arbor, MI: University of Michigan Press.

PART I

Learning, Trust, Power and Markets

1. Contributions to an institutionalist theory of price determination

Marc R. Tool*

Since all modern economies are, and will remain, monetary exchange economies, theoretical explanations of ratios of exchange – prices – and their determination must constitute a major area of inquiry in any encompassing examination of the economic process. This chapter is a part of a more extensive inquiry into the character and explanatory capabilities of an institutionalist theory of price determination. My general concern is to help formulate a logically coherent and empirically grounded theory of discretionary pricing. 'Discretionary pricing' here refers to the use by individuals of achieved economic power significantly to specify or to influence monetary terms of exchange.

Following Eichner (1987, p. 1558), I distinguish at the outset between *prices*, which as ratios of exchange refer to numerical values indicating the amount of funds that must be given up for a good or service, and *pricing*, which refers to the behaviour and judgements that determine prices. This chapter is addressed primarily to *pricing*, that is, to matters relating to the *formulation* of prices.

In this chapter, I examine (a) the theoretical context of price determination; (b) the institutional context of price determination, and (c) contributions of institutional economists to a theory of discretionary pricing, especially with regard to the corporate oligopolistic sector. I give particular attention to the views of Thorstein Veblen, Walton Hamilton, Gardiner Means, John Kenneth Galbraith, and to contributions of Alfred Eichner and Arthur Okun that are correlative with institutional economics.[1]

1. THE THEORETICAL CONTEXT

Neoclassical economists have long understood the significance of price determination as a part of the exchange process. Indeed, their primary interest has been to offer analyses of market pricing in differing settings on the assumption that to explain market price determination is tantamount to explaining virtually all that is of importance in the economic process. Their universe of inquiry has typically been confined to an analysis of pricing phenomena tending to market equilibria that define economic efficiency. The model of a free competitive market system is advocated as the most efficient allocative mechanism. Unfettered price determination within such markets, as explained through marginal analysis, accomplishes the efficient allocation. This perspective reflects the 'intuitive belief', as Nicholas Kaldor (1985, pp. 13–14) characterizes it,

> that the price mechanism is the key to everything, the key instrument in guiding the operation of an undirected, unplanned, free market economy. The Walrasian model and its most up-to-date successor may both be highly artificial abstractions from the real World but the truth that the theory conveys – that prices provide the guide to all economic action – must be fundamentally true, and its main implication that free markets secure the best results must also be true.

Here 'truth' is a matter of logical and rhetorical affirmation, not of comprehensive evidential demonstration, and 'best', in a typical case, is an approximation of Paretian optimality. The better-off–worse-off calculations in such Paretian judgements are undergirded by a tacit acceptance of utility as the meaning of social value and utility maximization as the preferred social goal (Hodgson, 1988, pp. 73–4; Tool, 1986, p. 84). Prices paid in unfettered markets are the valuation measures.

This *a priori* focus of neoclassical inquiry has defined the discipline of economics for mainstream scholars for most of this century. Its advocates have generated 'market mentalities' (Polyani, Kindleberger) as the products of their instruction and dominion. Neoclassical orthodoxy constitutes the 'conventional wisdom' (Galbraith) on all manner of policy options. Vigorous advocacy of shrinking governments, deregulation and enterprise zones are among recent policy reflections of this view. Moreover, positivist claims notwithstanding, such price determination is presumed by such market mentalities to have both practical and *moral* significance (Ayres, 1944, pp. 3–38). The neoclassical 'price system' is alleged to be *concurrently* a pervasive characterization of how prices *tend to be* determined in most markets and a stipulation of how prices *ought to be* determined in virtually *all* markets. Departures from price-competitive market determinations are examined as pathology. The abstract ideal defines the *proper* price system. The normative use of this competitive model remains endemic in orthodox neoclassical theory generally (Tool, 1986, pp. 87–103).

But within the sometimes contentious house of orthodoxy there is widespread recognition that the postulated theory of automatic, mechanistic price determination in free competitive markets is not necessarily descriptively adequate. Orthodox economists do not contend that free-market pricing under conditions of pure or perfect competition actually and comprehensively prevails in any economy. The earlier literature on monopolistic competition (Chamberlin, 1933) and imperfect competition (Robinson, 1933) and the more recent literature on externalities and market failures (Spulber, 1989) are troublesome contributions, among others, that confirm extensive behaviour at variance with the general model (Tool, 1986, pp. 104–25). They suggest that neoclassical theory does not provide the *general* theory of price determination after all (Joskow, 1975, pp. 270–79). One can hardly claim generality when confronted with substantial non-conforming conduct and events.

As I explore below, managers, at least of large-scale enterprises, are increasingly perceived as *price makers* rather than *price takers*. *Fix-price* models usually come closer to reality than *flex-price* models. As Arthur Okun (1981, p. 23) observed, 'models that focus on price takers and auctioneers and that assume continuous clearing of the market generate inaccurate microeconomics as well as misleading macroeconomics'. Even so, it appears that neoclassical theorists assume that the *general* theory is one of free-market price determination, regarding which there are occasional departures. Institutionalists, in contrast, argue that the more inclusive and descriptively accurate theory must be one of discretionary pricing and that instances of free-market determination are exceptionally rare.

2.   THE INSTITUTIONAL CONTEXT

All social orders, of necessity, provide for the *function* of exchange to occur. Institutional arrangements are everywhere used to facilitate the reciprocal activity of trading money in some form for goods or services. Monetary exchange typically involves the transfer of discretion over the objects of exchange.

'Institutions' are often defined by institutionalists as 'socially prescribed patterns of correlated behavior' (Bush, 1987, p. 1076). Institutional arrangements comprising markets condition and correlate behaviour in the exchange process. Such patterns of correlation do include the establishment and publication of prices. Markets are defined by Hodgson (1988, p. 174) as 'a set of social institutions in which a large number of commodity exchanges of a specific type regularly take place, and to some extent are facilitated and structured by those institutions'.

In the neoclassical market model, the primary institutions facilitating exchange are private ownership and legally enforceable contracts. Ownership consists of a legally sanctioned area of discretion over the possession, use and disposition of an item. Ownership is transferred with agreed-upon exchange; contracts stipulate the terms of the exchange; governments ensure compliance with contracts. But in the neoclassical formulation, markets themselves remain largely unspecified; they are accorded no other structural character (Hodgson, 1988, pp. 182–3). The neoclassical analyses do not reflect the breadth and complexity of behaviour actually correlated in markets, nor the roles of customs and habits in conditioning market conduct, nor the patterns and varying criteria of choice-making exhibited. Market motivations are simplistically affirmed as profit and/or utility maximization; market participation reflects 'constrained maximization'.

Institutionalists recognize that modern markets are comprised of a large number of usually complex, correlated patterns of behaviour, all of which, though typically habitual, are initially creations of people as discretionary agents. Such correlated patterns organize and structure exchange activity. They specify behaviour not only with reference, at times, to property and contract, but also, for example, to acquisition of information, communication among participants, and transportation of items exchanged (Hodgson, 1988, p. 174). Customary, legal, political and economic patterns of behaviour are all present to regularize exchange practices and to provide some measure of predictability or security of expectations for participants. *Customary*: tradition may stipulate who in a family or a corporate firm is (are) the power-wielding, and status-bearing, market participant(s). *Legal*: laws specify the place, time, character, media and terms of exchange. *Political*: stipulations of governing bodies define where, and to what extent, discretion over market exchange shall reside, and whose economic interests are to be served. *Economic*: organizations of market participants – unions, megacorps, cartels, marketing co-ops, trade associations, business 'clubs' – impinge on and help shape market conduct. In brief, 'markets are organized and institutionalized exchange' (Hodgson, 1988, p. 174). But the customary and conventional character of market institutional structures, including prices, requires emphasis. Established exchange arrangements, once created, tend to persist. Habitual patterns of behaviour as conventions in price-setting are commonplace (Hodgson, 1988, pp. 125–34, 182–7). G.L.S. Shackle (1972, p. 227) suggests a reason:

> Prices which have stood at particular levels for some time acquire thereby some sanction and authority. They are the 'right' and even the 'just' prices. But also they are the prices to which the society has adapted its ways and habits, they are prices which mutually cohere in an established frame of social life.

We shall see this recognition also in the contributions of Galbraith and Okun below.

As with other facets of the economic order, both the *structures of prices*, the lists, schedules and patterns of relative prices, and the *price-setting practices* vary widely among economies and among sectors within economies. The customs and conventions of pricing in the National Health Service in Great Britain, for example, reflected indigenous judgements somewhat unique to that culture; they diverged from the pricing of socialized medicine on the Continent, and from fee-for-service medicine and private health insurance in the United States. Similarly, pricing patterns and practices in agriculture, accomplished by subsidies and management of aggregate supplies, or in the learned professions through fee schedules, will differ dramatically from price leadership and mark-up pricing in industry, and control of prices by regulatory commission in public utilities. There is extensive variation among political economies and among economic sectors within a political economy both in the structure of prices and the correlating patterns through which the determination of prices is accomplished. But the generalization that virtually all significant prices are set as discretionary acts of identifiable persons – that existential markets are, in large part, shaped and staffed by *price makers* rather than *price takers* – is an argument I make here and through the rest of the chapter. As Galbraith (1967, p. 190) observed:

> We are profoundly conditioned by the theology of the market. ... A price that is fixed by the seller, to a singular degree does not seem good. Accordingly, it requires a major act of will to think of price-fixing as both normal and having economic function. In fact, it is normal in all advanced industrial societies.

Why, from an institutional perspective, is price-*fixing* 'normal' in all major economies? Why has *discretionary price-setting* become endemic? *Market participants seek and acquire control over price-setting in order to reduce uncertainty of judgement.* The reason one looks virtually in vain for examples of an actual pure or perfect market in the real world is that no market seller, in such a setting, can get sufficient relevant information to make informed economic judgements. The continuing uncertainties are destabilizing. Continuous actual unfettered competition, where markets actually determine prices, would be traumatic and intolerable. The inability reasonably to predict and control the character and direction of exchange phenomena, most particularly price changes, and the difficulties of influencing price elasticities of demand, makes reflective, means–consequence judgements concerning the level and character of production, the nature and extent of investment, the creation and/ or employment of new technology, hiring policies and practices, and the like, exceedingly difficult, if not impossible. The most critically significant variables are unpredictable. Having to adjust to prices determined elsewhere narrows one's own choices; gaining the ability to adjust one's own prices widens choices. An observation made by Jan Kregel (1980, p. 40) with regard to investment decision-making in Keynesian theory, applies, in my view, more generally:

The information required for rational decision making does not exist; the market mechanism cannot provide it. But, just as nature abhors a vacuum, the economic system abhors uncertainty. The system reacts to the absence of the information the market cannot provide by creating uncertainty-reducing institutions: wage contracts, debt contracts, supply agreements, administered prices [and] trading agreements.

I would modify this view only by attributing the reaction to the absence of market information, not to the 'system', but to those in the polity and/or economy who have achieved discretionary control over institutional adjustments, and are willing and able to use it. The discretionary agent(s) responsible for any significant economic organization (public or private) must gain and retain some appreciable control over prices charged and, if possible, over prices paid.

The quest for increasing security of expectation is unending. To seek and acquire as much control as possible over the forces and factions which ultimately determine the extent of discretion, the character of discretion and the duration of the organization constitute the *real* 'bottom line'. Among such 'forces and factions' price-setting powers figure prominently. Price-fixing is and must continue to be 'normal', meaning typical, habitual and, in some considerable measure, predictable.

Having now considered the institutional character of markets and pricing, and why discretionary control over price determination is sought, I conclude this section with a brief illustrative exploration of institutional configurations in and through which pricing judgements are made.

In most advanced economics, the modern large corporation is the major institutional complex through which industrial goods and major services are produced and distributed. Although its specific form varies, it is usually created only with governmental permission. As a legal *person* in the eyes of the law, it has legal-entity status and standing; it can sue and be sued. Ownership is nominally 'private' but private owners' discretion may or may not be a viable instrument of attaining and retaining control. In most megacorps, through fragmentation and wide dispersion of shares, discretion for ordinary stockholders may well be limited to a passive claim to dividends. Ownership is dispersed; control is concentrated, as Veblen observed (1904) and Adolf Berle and Gardiner Means demonstrated (1932).

The modern large corporation is, in effect, a legally sanctioned private government usually run by a self-perpetuating dynastic management. Its government-like powers include the abilities to impose, deny and manipulate behaviour of persons subject to its hegemonic power. It is subject to constraints of competitive rivalry but normally not price competition. It defines cultural tastes; it creates demand for its own products; it influentially participates in the determination of what higher education consists; it significantly shapes the social life of its employees (Dugger, 1989). It exhibits a continuing participatory role in bringing pressure and influence to bear on political processes at all levels.

The modern oligopolistic corporation is subject, in varying degrees, to public constraints of environmental compliance, labour laws and anti-discrimination and fair employment rules, among others. Firms may confront governmental price constraints (general or industry-specific), negative political responses to pricing judgements made, and government macromanagement policies, fiscal and monetary, that help importantly to define the context for price administration. The megacorp may be a recipient of public largess through subsidies (including tax expenditures), trade protections, public education of its employees and, at times, mandated exemption status to regulations (pollution controls, safety standards) and the like.

In their unique concerns with price determination, in a typically oligopolistic organization, the corporation's price setters do not necessarily have an easy time of it (Hamilton, 1974, essay no. 3). They must, of course, set prices which cover their continuing costs of materials and labour, and a mark-up margin to generate the pecuniary options which residual balances provide. But also, they must function in a difficult, risk-filled, institutional environment that may well include intra-industry concerns over retaliatory pricing responses from industry rivals at home; accommodation to or adjustment of pricing judgements of material suppliers; negotiation of wage agreements under collective-bargaining rules and regulations; and market-sharing agreements, among others. In addition, they may face inter-industry pressures from aggressive, state-subsidized and supported rival contenders from abroad and negotiation of pricing accords (cartel or otherwise) with international firms.

Given the foregoing, and the significance and complexities of price-making in large corporations, it comes as no surprise that corporations have developed highly trained specialists as price setters who work in specific and sophisticated agencies (bureaux or divisions) within the corporate or conglomerate complex and concentrate solely on the price determination responsibility (Kaplan *et al.*, 1958, pp. 220–47).

When one asks, then, where discretionary prices are determined, the loci of discretionary determination of prices must be sought among the complexities and intricacies of the institutional fabric through which pricing power has been achieved, retained and exercised. In any problematic context, where access to such information is crucial, *only enquiry into the complexities of the structural fabric involved can disclose the particular pricing power centres, who the price-setting agents are, the criteria reflected in their decisions, and the consequences that flow therefrom.*

At this point, the focus of this chapter narrows, given space constraints, to consideration of price determination mainly in oligopolistic enterprises. It is in this realm that disarming apologias for price-setting power, rooted in neoclassical price theory, are most persistent; it is in this area that many of the major price-fixing decisions are initiated, with wide repercussions through the economy.

3.   INSTITUTIONALIST CONTRIBUTIONS TO A THEORY OF DISCRETIONARY PRICING

Institutionalists have been contributing to a theory of discretionary pricing for nearly a century. That contribution began with Thorstein Veblen, and involves two largely complementary and converging approaches: the older tradition encompasses a literature on *administered* pricing, to which Walton H. Hamilton, Gardiner C. Means, John Kenneth Galbraith, among others, contributed. The more recent and more technical tradition is reflected in writings on *mark-up* or *cost-plus* pricing of Alfred Eichner and other such heterodox-leaning and empirically oriented scholars as Arthur Okun. After touching base with Veblen, I canvass selected examples of the work of these contributors, seeking conceptual tools, analytical formulations and synthetic characterizations for an institutional theory of discretionary pricing.

Thorstein B. Veblen

Although Veblen certainly was among the first American scholars to observe and explain the nature and significance of the corporate revolution in the organization of the economy, he did not dwell at length on the pricing power of the then newly emerging giant corporations. He did, however, see a general trend towards the development of 'business coalitions' that had an important bearing on price-setting:

> 'Cutthroat' competition … can be done away by 'pooling the interests' of the competitors, so soon as all or an effective majority of the business concerns which are rivals in the market combine and place their business management under one directive head. When this is done, by whatever method, selling of goods or services at competitively varying prices is replaced by collective selling … at prices fixed on the basis of 'what the traffic will bear'. (Veblen, 1904, p. 258)

Moreover,

> [W]hen the coalition comes effectually to cover its special field of operations, it is able not only to fix the prices which it will accept … but also in a considerable measure to fix the prices or rates which it will pay for materials, labor, and other services (such as transportation) on a similar basis. (ibid., p. 261)

For Veblen, the drive to create monopolies, what he called 'business coalitions', is motivated by the quest for pecuniary gain, is prompted by the need to employ and control newly emerging technologies, and is required to provide 'the only refuge from chronic depression'. The incorporation of newer machine technology 'makes competitive business impracticable ... but it makes coalition practicable' (ibid., p. 263). At the time he wrote, the trend to concentration was already well advanced: 'it is doubtful if there are any successful business ventures within the range of the modem industries from which the monopoly element is wholly absent' (ibid., p. 54).

With Veblen, then, we get an early characterization of a corporate-dominated, administered-price, industrial economy.

Walton Hale Hamilton

In the published writings of the distinguished lawyer and economist, Walton Hamilton, which cover more than 40 years, are to be found some of the most penetrating and significant analyses of the emergent corporate economy. In analysis less sardonic and somewhat more empirically grounded than Veblen, Hamilton explores the evolutionary transformation of the locus and use of economic power by corporations in labour relations and wage-setting (Hamilton and May, 1923), in the use of patents and their protection (Hamilton, 1957, pp. 63–99) and in administered-pricing judgements and practices (Hamilton, 1938), among others. Attention here is necessarily confined to his concern with administered pricing.

Heading a small research staff for the Cabinet Committee on Price Policy, appointed by President Roosevelt in 1934, Hamilton guided an inquiry into the actual pricing practices of a number of basic American industries. At issue was consideration of industrial policy, which he defined as 'an aggregate of the measures contrived for the guidance of industry by all the agencies which operate upon it' (Hamilton, 1938, p. 528). Of the completed studies, those on the automobile, tyre, gasoline, cottonseed, dress, whiskey and milk industries were published in the collection edited by Hamilton, *Price and Price Policies* (1938). In the 'Preface' he observes that

> the literature of industry was inadequate to the demands of price policy. Accounts of how in general industry is organized and how in the abstract prices are made were available in abundance. Yet, with notable exceptions, little was at hand upon the structures of particular industries, their distinctive habits, their unique patterns of control, and the multiplex of arrangements – stretching away from technology to market practice – which give magnitude to their prices. (Hamilton, 1938, p. vii)

Hamilton and his fellow researchers sought to fill that gap in knowledge and therewith to contribute to policy deliberations.

In his concluding chapter, Hamilton (1938, pp. 525–56) does not presume to draw general principles from this sampling of industrial practice. He distils no synthetic summary of price determination. What he finds in these empirical studies, rather, is an extraordinary complexity of institutional structure bearing on pricing practices. Each industrial area studied revealed an idiosyncratic fabric of diverse interrelations and interdependencies. Each had a different history of emergence; each exhibited a somewhat unique pattern of customary behaviours; each had its own way of arriving at pricing decisions and of implementing pricing judgements. Although cost considerations were of some significance in virtually all pricing judgements, nowhere were they an exclusive concern. Loci of discretion over price varied widely among the industries studied, but nowhere could one presume or show that atomistic, automatic, freely competitive market forces were determining prices in auction markets. Hamilton recognized the cultural origins of demand: tastes are acquired; preferences are learned; industries must lead in creating markets for their goods. They must also adapt to changes induced by the growth of knowledge and new technology. Custom influenced the cost structure too: he was aware of the differing habits and practices which impinge on workers' wages and salaries; acknowledging the complexity of production programmes, he recognized the difficulties of assigning cost in joint-product firms.

In sum, 'a touch of the motley rests upon the ways of price-making. Price bears the marks of the process from which it emerges' (ibid., p. 530). 'The business unit is not content to leave its affairs ... and its survival to the arbitration of an impersonal market. It must bestir itself to hold its own' (ibid., p. 549). 'Price, quality, service, blarney, guile, and the creative touch are alike weapons of promotion and devices of accommodation' (ibid., p. 550). But the *manipulation* of price, in quest of market control or shares, may be 'too dangerous a mechanism to be employed'. (That is, discretion over prices *is held* but prevailing circumstances in the industry may discourage its use.) Industrial leaders will then seek a formal or informal understanding to shift to non-price forms of rivalry (see ibid., p. 542). 'Thus price and the costs which attend it – are a pecuniary reflection of the usages which impinge upon the making and marketing of a good. These usages run through the whole industrial process. ... They are embedded in the ways of an industry just as the folkways are embedded in the culture of a primitive or a civilized people' (ibid.).

Hamilton's contribution to an institutionalist theory of discretionary pricing, then, consists of: (a) his recognition and demonstration of overt and pervasive pricing power in industry; (b) his showing of the role of convention and custom in actual industrial pricing practice; (c) his demonstration of the remarkable variability and complexity in pricing practices; and (d) his recognition of the probable need for an industrial policy to impinge on industrial leaders' discretion over pricing, and his implication of the need to examine and appraise criteria of pricing judgements.

Gardiner C. Means

For much of Gardiner Means's professional life, his research ambition was to provide a 'new paradigm for macrotheory'; it was to be a 'new macrotheory based on the realities of our modem economy' (Means, 1975a, p. 154). It would differ fundamentally from the neoclassical and Keynesian approaches. He had, early in his career, 'laid down basic postulates for the new theory'. Two are of special significance here: one 'is that a large part of production is carried on by a few great corporations in which final ownership is widely dispersed, ownership and control are largely separated, and management is largely a self-perpetuating body'. A second 'is that most prices are administered privately (or by agencies of government) and behave in a fashion quite different from that indicated by traditional theory' (ibid., p. 152). While the 'new paradigm' evidently was never completed, Means's contribution to a theory of discretionary pricing is revealed principally in his empirical demonstration of these two postulates.

Means was not academically trained as an institutional economist; his early empirical research into corporate structure and agricultural pricing drove him, as a fledgling scientist, to seek a theory that would better explain the factual realities he perceived. His heterodoxy was fuelled by his experience as a scholar. His research (with Adolf Berle) that culminated in *The Modern Corporation and Private Property* (Berle and Means, 1932) generated the first postulate; a long series of statements, incorporating his empirical research, and prepared as testimony for congressional hearings, undergirded the second postulate (Means, 1963, pp. 213–39).

Means is the principal formulator of 'the theory of administered pricing'. Following is one of his more illuminating presentations of this idea:

> An administered price has been defined as a price which is set, usually by a seller, and held constant for a period of time and a series of transactions. Such a price does not imply the existence of monopoly or of collusion. However, it can occur only where a particular market is dominated by one or relatively few sellers (or buyers). It is the normal method of selling in most markets today. Its significance ... rests, first on the fact that it lies entirely outside traditional economic theory and, second, that where the area of discretion in price administration is large, administered prices produce economic results and problems of economic policy quite different from those dealt with by traditional theory. (Means, 1959, p. 4)

The theory of administered pricing was the basis for some partially successful federal policies (Means, 1975a, pp. 14–22). Also it has been the object of considerable professional controversy (Stigler, 1963; Adams and

Lanzillotti, 1963; Blair, 1972; Kahn, 1975; Samuels and Medema, 1990), yet its credibility has survived (Kefauver, 1965). Price administration is accomplished in large corporations through the technique of target pricing, among other techniques. As perceived by Means (1975a) and John Blair (1975, pp. 33–67), price determination is customarily accomplished by the calculation of a 'target rate of return on capital'. What is sought is the highest rate of return on capital 'consistent with a healthy growth of the business'. Calculations of such target rates require decisions on the level of operation, estimates of the costs of production at various operating levels, determination of prices which will yield the desired target rates and, given costs and operating rates, the setting of discretionary prices in view of actual market conditions (Means, 1963, pp. 220–21). Recourse to this pricing technique was earlier confirmed in the Brookings study on *Pricing in Big Business* (Kaplan *et al.*, 1958) and later by John Blair (1976).

Finally, it is interesting to note that, although Means did not make explicit use of social value theory, he does recognize that judgements of appropriateness or propriety must be made concerning prices administratively set. In this particular context, he argues that target rate prices which yield returns on capital no greater than 'the competitive cost of capital' may be considered as consistent with the public interest. A rough approximation of such a rate is that allowed public utilities by effective regulatory commissions (Means, 1963, p. 222). Any 'form of regulation should ... bring about the same type of economic behavior that would prevail if the industry were competitive' (Means, 1975a, p. 66). In this latter deference to the normative use of the competitive model, Means's break with orthodoxy is clearly incomplete.

Means, however, did not believe that market forces would provide a sufficient constraint on the power to administer prices. Although his specific policy recommendations shifted over the years as the problems to which he addressed himself changed, he consistently advocated public government supervision sufficient to ensure that the public interest was served. He argued, for example, that: 'inflation in the concentrated industries can be restrained only by the imposition of direct price and wage controls', and that 'restraints should be imposed on sudden and substantial increases in the target rate of return' (Means, 1975a, p. 66).

In sum, Means repeatedly demonstrated, to his own satisfaction if not that of his neoclassical critics, the continuing fact and practice of administered pricing in American industry. He posed, but did not adequately answer, the question of how to decide when judgements reflected in private price determination are in the public interest.

John Kenneth Galbraith

Perhaps no American economist in this century has been confronted with a more dramatic or significant test of applying institutional analysis to an area of critical public policy than was John Kenneth Galbraith upon his appointment, in 1941, as head of what later would be called the Office of Price Administration (OPA). This 'Price Czar Novitiate' (Galbraith, 1981, pp. 124–44) had the task of introducing and managing a comprehensive programme of price control and rationing for the wartime American economy. As preparation for that task, a long tradition of market-deferential, neoclassical analysis was, in his view, largely irrelevant. Orthodox economists thought it was unwise for him to undertake such a responsibility and impossible for him to achieve the goal sought (Galbraith, 1952, pp. 2–7). In an important, if small and unfortunately neglected, book reflecting on this experience, *The Theory of Price Control* (1952), Galbraith explains how his understanding of actual corporate pricing behaviour was comprehensively expanded and empirically reconfirmed by his experience as head of the OPA. In brief, he could generate his own tautology and assert that 'it is relatively easy to fix prices that are already fixed' (ibid., p. iv).

Here he distinguished between markets that were imperfectly or monopolistically competitive (oligopolies) and those that still resembled price-competitive markets. This becomes a distinction between the 'planning' sector and the 'market' sector in his later work (see Galbraith, 1973). Imperfect markets could be controlled directly and with greater ease than was anticipated. Price-competitive markets could be controlled but with more difficulty and only if rationing was also employed.

In imperfect markets, OPA-administered price control was easier because a comparatively smaller number of firms was involved, enforcement was facilitated, and prices were already relatively inflexible and had become institutionalized (Galbraith, 1952, pp. 10–19). Supply-price conditions were also relatively stable at the time. Given unused capacity, production, except for agriculture and extractive industries, generally was expanded for war purposes without increasing fixed costs, and thus without creating major pressures for increasing prices. In a few instances, subsidies were used to 'offset higher "marginal" costs in increasing-cost industries' (ibid., pp. 20–25).

But even in efforts to control prices at the retail level, Galbraith came to realize that customary and conventional pricing was the rule. The price charged for the product or service is strictly a conventional mark-up. Profit *maximization* is not an operational option. The small seller 'has neither the information nor the capacity to adjust his margins commodity by commodity, week by week, or season by season, in such manner as might maximize his returns'. He relies on rule-of-thumb. 'The effect of a well-designed system of price control in markets of this kind is merely to continue accepted rules' (ibid., p. 18). In sum, price control in imperfect markets is comparatively easy and can be quite successful; price control in price-competitive markets – markets where market shares are small and pricing power is more limited than in oligopolistic firms – can also succeed but is more difficult. What is confirmed for our purposes, however, is the pervasiveness of administered pricing in the so-called private sector, and the fact that comprehensive public control of privately administered prices, in this instance at least, was demonstrated to be both feasible and successful.[2]

For Galbraith, the 'technostructure becomes the commanding power' in the modern giant corporation. As organized management, it is the locus of discretion over pricing decisions and much else that affects the character and continuity of the large corporation. Its decisions are collegial, but authoritarian (Galbraith, 1973, pp. 83–6). The technostructure consists of the technical specialists who exercise *de facto* power and are placed hierarchically just below the *pro forma* executives and directors of the organization. These specialists generate and pool the specialized and technical knowledge that is required to fashion the productive process, and generate and update technological innovations and product improvements. 'For the exercise of this power – for product planning, to devise price and market strategies, for sales and advertising management, procurement planning, public relations and governmental relations – specialists are also needed' (ibid., p. 82). Governance of a megacorp is necessarily conjoint; members of the technostructure respectively contribute their expertise and insights in reaching judgements. 'Collective intelligence' guides managerial decision-making; the positions of hierarchical 'heads' – president, chairman, director – are often status-conferring, anachronistic relics of an older order from which power is eroding. But members of the board can, if they are aggressive, sometimes influence the power of the technostructure and the direction in which it moves by eliciting sufficient support to change leadership officers (for example, the chief executive officer), 'directing the decision-making process into new areas', and/or by calling in outside experts to appraise the performance of the directive cadre (ibid., p. 89).

The purposive goals which drive the technostructure – the uses to which its *de facto* power are put – are twofold: to protect 'the autonomy of its decision-making primarily by seeking to secure a minimum level of earnings' and to reward 'itself affirmatively with growth' of the firm. Incident to these quests, technological innovation and *increasing* earnings may also be pursued. Profits will be sought; they are not typically maximized, orthodoxy notwithstanding (ibid., p. 107).

If these 'protective and affirmative purposes of the technostructure' are to be realized, prices must be set and must remain under the tightest possible control.[3] Productive technology is specialized, complex, time-consuming to create and expensive. Corporate planning of price-setting must be such as to ensure that the necessary materials and equipment can be acquired. Prices must be firmly under discretionary control so that they can be revised, as necessary, to cover costs not wholly under control of the technostructure – as with the wage bill. Increased wages can be (and are) readily covered with increased prices. Prices must be firmly controlled to permit management and manipulation of demand.

Discretionary agents in megacorps must control prices to maintain their position *vis-à-vis* other firms. They must participate in a communal effort to preclude unplanned or pre-emptive price-cutting. 'Oligopolistic cooperation'[4] with others is required to *avoid* losing control over their own enterprise. They must maintain a necessary level of earnings through adequate sales promotion. Prices must be set low enough to ensure adequate expanding sales. They must accommodate to existing price elasticities. Otherwise growth and its benefits for the technostructure cannot be realized. Roughly uniform prices will be commonplace in an industry. If there is a dominant firm, the technostructure of that firm will serve as price leader and its affirmative purposes and protective patterns will serve as the model for the industry. Given the complexity and interdependencies of the pricing patterns set, the intent is to leave most prices unchanged for an extended period of time. Each participant gains predictability and is able to sustain control more adequately.

In sum, Galbraith reconfirms the pervasiveness of discretionary pricing in the industrial sector, identifies the dominant price-setting group or cadre, and explains the protective and affirmative criteria that guide their pricing choices.

Alfred S. Eichner

Although Alfred Eichner generally described himself as a Post Keynesian, there is a great deal of commonality between his critique of neoclassical orthodoxy and his recommended alternative approach, and that of institutionalists. Indeed, he sought to bring the two approaches into closer analytical congruity with his edited volume on *Why Economics Is Not Yet a Science* (1983). He considers the neoclassical tradition, and especially its price theory, 'intellectually bankrupt'; its claims to generality and scientific status are without foundation. Because of its vacuousness, it is an unreliable guide to policy-making (Eichner, 1983, pp. 205–6). In these judgements, institutionalists concur.

Eichner sets the familiar institutional context: 'commodity markets have been largely superseded by industrial markets and the family business by the megacorp as the representative firm within those markets' (Eichner, 1987, p. 1555). Megacorps, by 'virtue of their size and dominant market position, have considerable discretion in setting prices'. These firms, 'with their administered pricing policies for financing growth and expansion, have become the locus of decision-making within the decentralized system of private planning that operates within the U.S. economy'.[5]

It is Eichner's central purpose to explain 'how prices are determined in the oligopolistic sector of the American economy, and how those prices, so determined, affect the growth and stability of the economy as a whole' (Eichner, 1976, p. 1). He seeks to provide a new micro foundation for Keynesian macroeconomic theory. The explanation offered may be characterized as a dynamic, extended cost-plus model in which the 'plus', as it varies over time and among industries, is also explained (ibid., pp. 4–5).

Two attributes in particular distinguish this pricing model from orthodox approaches. First, 'it is predicated upon realistic assumptions'. Second, it yields determinate solutions; empirically demonstrable accounts of pricing can be derived.

The realistic assumptions are rooted in institutionalist contributions: megacorps are characterized by a separation of ownership and managerial control. 'Production occurs within multiple plants or plant segments' in which the factor coefficients are fixed by both 'technological and institutional constraints'. 'The firm's output is sold under conditions of recognized interdependence'; oligopolistic cooperation prevails (ibid., p. 3). Indeed, Eichner's 'operational definition of an industry' is 'that group of firms which share a day-to-day interest in the same set of price quotations for a class of goods they are each capable of producing' (ibid., p. 10).

The deterministic solutions, as explanations, become evident 'only from the long-run perspective of the industry as a whole, with one megacorp, the price leader, acting as a surrogate for all members of that industry'. The long-run view does not explain the 'absolute price level but rather the change in that price level from one period to the next … the marginal adjustment'. The megacorp price leader 'will vary the industry price so as to cover (1) any change in per unit average variable and fixed costs, and (2) any increased need for internally generated funds' (ibid., p. 4). What is demonstrated is that the pricing decision for a price-leader megacorp 'is ultimately linked to the investment decision. … prices are likely to be set so as to assure the internally generated funds necessary to finance a firm's desired rate of capital expansion'. The substantial convergence of this view with the 'target return' arguments of Means and Blair above is now apparent.

Eichner (1987, p. 1582) summarizes his discretionary pricing theory as follows:

> Thus, once the institutional context in which firms find themselves has been correctly identified, it is possible to explain the price observed in any industry ... according to the change in cost ... or the change in markup ... from the preceding time period. The prices actually observed are therefore the outcome of a historical process, with the change in cost ... reflecting the changing input–output relationships that define the reigning technology, and the change in markup ... reflecting the need for investment funds relative to the pricing power of firms.

To pursue his more inclusive goals of inquiry, Eichner extends his analysis to a corollary microeconomic consideration of factor pricing, in the course of which he finds the neoclassical marginal productivity theory to be largely irrelevant. His own reformulation, in addressing the cost structure confronting megacorps, draws on the institutionalist literature on economic power, the sociologist focus on social norms, the Marxian interest in surplus value and the Keynesian stress on aggregate demand factors (Eichner, 1976, pp. 5–6). Beyond observing that factor prices are also largely administered, we need not, for present purposes, follow Eichner on this conceptual path.

In addition, Eichner explores the significance of his altered microeconomic theory for macroeconomic analysis. Here, given the megacorp's concern with price-setting and investment to assure growth, and consequent concern with aggregate demand, Eichner's analysis 'lends theoretical support to the accelerator model of investment', and to the recognition of the significance for the economy generally of the megacorp's investment spending from retained earnings. The megacorps play a central role in determining the secular growth rate for the economy (ibid., pp. 7–8). Economic power, reflected in discretionary pricing, matters.

Finally, in exploring policy implications, Eichner must address, as do other scholars, the character and consequences of price judgements made by megacorps. He concludes that 'effective social control over the individual megacorp can be achieved by no more and no less than regulating both the rate of growth, and the composition of aggregate investment'. The economic welfare of both individuals and the economy generally cannot otherwise be served. His major recommendation then is 'that a system of national indicative planning be established' (ibid., p. 9).

Arthur M. Okun

I have found nothing to suggest that Arthur Okun ever characterized himself as an institutionalist. Yet he, like institutionalists, was a theorist and a realist. I construe his analysis of pricing, with minor exceptions, to be both compatible with, and an extension of, earlier institutionalist contributions to a theory of discretionary pricing. More specifically, his work may be viewed as a plausible explanation of the conventional and customary mark-up pricing

Galbraith found in administering comprehensive price controls in non-oligopolistic markets during the days of OPA.

Okun appears to have been committed to the premise that theory ought actually to explain what it purports to explain. For him, mainstream orthodoxy has long since ceased to offer an adequate explanation of the pricing process; it does not provide the *general* theory of market behaviour.

As noted in section 1 above, Okun distinguishes between the realm of price *makers* and that of price *takers* in the modern economy. The portion of the economy exhibiting price takers in 'auction markets' is

> a small and shrinking sector of the U.S. economy. ... Most of our economy is dominated by cost-oriented prices and equity-oriented wages. Most prices are set by sellers whose principal concern is to maintain customers and market share over the long run. ... Prices are set to exceed costs by a percentage markup that displays only minor variations over the business cycle. (Okun, 1979, pp. 1–5)

The realm of price makers, then, is not confined to oligopolistic sellers only. It includes most of the economy except for 'active auction markets' reported on the financial pages of the daily newspaper: financial assets, agricultural commodities, some primary metals and the like (Okun, 1981, p. 134).

In a fairly elaborate analysis of the complexities price makers must face in determining the mark-ups to be reflected in selling prices, Okun demonstrates, as earlier institutionalists have shown, that actual markets are institutionally complex. Of particular importance for Okun are the conventions and expectations that develop between sellers and buyers. Sellers offer stable prices, continuing services, access to credit, refund prerogatives, advanced sales notices and the like to secure customer loyalty and repeat purchases (ibid., pp. 138–48). Such 'implicit contract' arrangements 'economize on a variety of information and transaction costs' (ibid., p. 154). Predictability, dependability and fulfilment of expectations through such correlated patterns give the firm some measure of control over its own demand, and insulation from the competitive rivalry of other firms. Decisions on the size and frequency of price changes, then, are of critical significance. Alienating or disruptive changes in the continuity of expectations regarding prices is to be avoided. Firms regularly engage in price-fixing as a routine effort to maintain their market shares. Their achieved market power is reflected in the degree to which their desires in that quest can be implemented.

Discretionary managers, in Okun's view, are more influenced in their pricing decisions by supply-side costs than by changes in demand:

> The setting of prices by marking up costs is a good first approximation to actually observed behavior in most areas of industry, trade, and transportation. Firms not

only behave that way, but also condition their customers to expect them to behave that way. ... Price increases that are based on cost increases are 'fair', while those based on demand increases often are viewed as unfair. (Okun, 1981, p. 153)

A significant hazard, however, in using 'cost-oriented pricing' as a standard in setting prices is that customers do not, and cannot, observe the price-setting deliberation process. They must take on faith any contention that price increases were caused or validated by cost increases.

The conceptual dilemma facing the price setters is itself quite complex. The definition and measurement of costs that are to become part of the bases for price determinations require price setters to take account of such standards or constructs as historical costs, replacement costs, valuation adjustments, standard volume unit costs, full or direct costs, and material costs (Okun, 1981, pp. 154–64). Even so, 'the empirical evidence for the United States suggests that cost-oriented pricing is the dominant mode of behavior' (ibid., p. 165). Okun has one main reservation concerning the Means–Blair theory of administered pricing: his own model

allows for various causal factors to determine the pricing behavior of an industry, while the administered-prices view focuses on the single explanation of industrial concentration. ... Markup rigidity seems to me simply too pervasive across the U.S. economy to be attributable to oligopoly. ... The aggregate evidence on pricing in private nonfarm business accords closely with the mark-up model. (Okun, 1981, pp. 175–6)

Okun's pricing theory, concerning customer–seller attachments, expectations and conventions, does appear to account for this limitation in the Means–Blair position. Recall, in addition, that Okun reconfirms Galbraith's earlier characterization that smaller, private, non-farm businesses employ mark-up pricing practices and reflect price rigidity. Discretionary price determination is not confined to oligopolies.

Finally, though only passing reference is made, Okun does regard his 'customer–market' view of inflexible prices as implying an approvable and acceptable market structure. It is 'an inherently desirable institutional arrangement' because it 'economizes on the expenses of shopping, trying out products, and otherwise engaging in transactions'. There arc significant 'benefits of customer attachments' (ibid., p. 178). Accordingly, these pricing conventions serve what are, for Okun, economically defensible purposes; they are normatively approvable.

4.   CONCLUSION

While no elaborate summary is provided, the following generalities summarizing institutionalist, and quasi-institutionalist, contributions to a theory of discretionary pricing may be noted:

- Exchange occurring in non-auction markets is not simplistic and reducible to maximizing tenets and singular behavioural constants. It is accomplished by a complex, and widely divergent, pattern of institutional arrangements that facilitate the making of pricing judgements. In all economies, these arrangements continue to evolve as new problems and their consequences are identified and new pricing judgements and structures are instituted to resolve them.

- To these institutionalists, the mainstream neoclassical theory of pricing does not explain the overwhelmingly dominant phenomenon of discretionary pricing in advanced industrial economies. In their view, the explanatory capabilities and policy relevance of that approach continue to erode as empirical inquiry and theoretical critiques undermine its claim to significance.

- At the level both of oligopolistic megacorps and of smaller, non-auction market sellers, prices are determined as deliberate decisions by price setters to serve a variety of individual and firm goals. The presumption that a Walrasian-like price mechanism – structure-free, atomistic auction-house – is the vehicle through which prices are determined becomes even more conjectural, in their view.

- Such discretionary pricing typically reflects the use of one or another variant of mark-up, cost-plus, target or similar pricing rule. Actual pricing rules as conventions are set; pricing judgements are made; markets are institutionally ordered; and market behaviour is correlated.

- Price-making decision bodies vary with industry structures, custom and conventions, and extant power bodies. The technostructure – an information, organization and/or technology-dominating managerial élite – appears to be a typical locus of price-making power in megacorps. But only extensive inquiry will disclose the particular loci of power, the pricing rules and structures employed and the character of pricing judgements made.

- All contributors acknowledge, but do not extensively address, the fact and need for external standards or criteria with which to judge the propriety of pricing decisions made. Such standards reflect conditioned views of what is a fair, proper, right or just price. Public appraisals of private pricing decisions, of course, have long been a common practice. But there is no agreement among these contributors on what standards or criteria should be used for such appraisals or what social-value theory to employ in quest of such standards. An agenda for further inquiry is suggested.

NOTES

*   The author wishes to thank Paul Dale Bush, Harry Trebing, John Henry, Ernesto Screpanti and Geoff Hodgson for instructive suggestions on earlier drafts of this paper.
1.   These contributions are presented as illustrative and indicative of what I characterize as institutionalist, or institutionalist-compatible, views, not as a definitive treatment of the subject field. The latter would require, in addition, consideration of contributions of Post Keynesian theories of the firm and of macro analysis, and other heterodox theories.
2.   The foregoing does not address Galbraith's views concerning the loci of price-setting power in imperfect markets as such, nor explain how, among oligopolies, prices are determined, nor consider criteria in terms of which pricing judgements are made.
3.   I draw heavily on Galbraith (1973, pp. 112–21) in this and the following paragraph.
4.   See also Munkirs and Sturgeon (1985).
5.   Eichner here cites Munkirs (1985), who presents a general theory of 'Centralized Private Sector Planning'.

REFERENCES

Adams, Walter and Robert F. Lanzillotti (1963), 'The reality of administered prices', in Subcommittee on Antitrust and Monopoly of the Committee on the Judiciary, United States Senate, Eighty-eighth Congress, First Session, *Administered Prices: A Compendium on Public Policy*, Washington, DC: US Government Printing Office.
Ayres, Clarence E. (1944), *The Theory of Economic Progress*, 1st edition, Chapel Hill, North Carolina: University of North Carolina Press.
Berle, Adolf A. and Gardiner C. Means (1932), *The Modern Corporation and Private Property*, New York: Commerce Clearing House.
Blair, John M. (1972), *Economic Concentration: Structure, Behavior, and Public Policy*, New York: Harcourt Brace Jovanovich.
Blair, John M. (1975), 'Inflation in the United States: a short-run target return model', in Means *et al.* (1975b), pp. 33–67.
Blair, John M. (1976), *The Control of Oil*, New York: Pantheon.
Bush, Paul Dale (1987), 'The theory of institutional change', *Journal of Economic Issues*, 21(3), September, pp. 1075–116. Reprinted in Geoffrey M. Hodgson (ed.) (1993), *The Economics of Institutions*, Aldershot: Edward Elgar.
Chamberlin, Edward H. (1933), *The Theory of Monopolistic Competition*, Cambridge, MA: Harvard University Press.
Dugger, William M. (ed.) (1989), *Corporate Hegemony*, Westport, CN: Greenwood Press.
Eichner, Alfred S. (1976), *The Megacorp and Oligopoly: Micro Foundations of Macro Dynamics*, Cambridge and New York: Cambridge University Press.
Eichner, Alfred S. (ed.) (1983), *Why Economics Is Not Yet a Science*, Armonk, NY: Sharpe.
Eichner, Alfred S. (1987), 'Prices and pricing', *Journal of Economic Issues*, 21(4),

December, pp. 1555–84. Reprinted in Marc R. Tool (ed.) (1988), *Evolutionary Economics, Vol. 2: Institutional Theory and Policy*, Armonk, NY: M.E. Sharpe.

Galbraith, John Kenneth (1952), *The Theory of Price Control: The Classic Account*, Cambridge, MA: Harvard University Press.

Galbraith, John Kenneth (1967), *The New Industrial State*, Boston, MA: Houghton Mifflin.

Galbraith, John Kenneth (1973), *Economics and the Public Purpose*, Boston, MA: Houghton Mifflin.

Galbraith, John Kenneth (1981), *A Life in Our Times*, Boston, MA: Houghton Mifflin.

Hamilton, Walton H. (ed.) (1938), *Price and Price Policies*, New York: McGraw-Hill.

Hamilton, Walton H. (1957), *The Politics of Industry*, New York: Alfred A. Knopf.

Hamilton, Walton H. (1974), *Industrial Policy and Institutionalism: Selected Essays*, with an introduction by Joseph Dorfman, New York: Augustus Kelley.

Hamilton, Walton H. and Stacy May (1923), *The Control of Wages*, New York: Macmillan.

Hodgson, Geoffrey M. (1988), *Economics and Institutions: A Manifesto for a Modern Institutional Economics*, Cambridge and Philadelphia: Polity Press and University of Pennsylvania Press.

Joskow, Paul L. (1975), 'Firm decision-making processes and oligopoly theory', *American Economic Review (Papers and Proceedings)*, 65(2), May, pp. 270–79.

Kahn, Alfred E. (1975), 'Market power and inflation: a conceptual overview', in Means *et al.* (1975b).

Kaldor, Nicholas (1985), *Economics without Equilibrium*, Cardiff: University College Cardiff Press.

Kaplan, A.D.H., Joel B. Dirlam and Robert F. Lanzillotti (1958), *Pricing in Big Business*, Washington, DC: Brookings Institution.

Kefauver, Estes (1965), *In Few Hands: Monopoly Power in America*, New York: Pantheon.

Kregel, Jan A. (1980), 'Markets and institutions as features of a capitalistic production system', *Journal of Post Keynesian Economics*, 3(1), Fall, pp. 32–48.

Means, Gardiner C. (1959), *Administered Inflation and Public Policy*, Washington, DC: Anderson Kramer Associates.

Means, Gardiner C. (1963), 'Pricing power and public interest', in Walter Adams and Robert F. Lanzillotti, 'The reality of administered prices', in Subcommittee on Antitrust and Monopoly of the Committee on the Judiciary, United States Senate, Eighty-eighth Congress, First Session, *Administered Prices: A Compendium on Public Policy*, Washington, DC: US Government Printing Office.

Means, Gardiner C. (1975a), 'Simultaneous inflation and unemployment', in Means *et al.* (1975b)

Means, Gardiner C. *et al.* (1975b), *The Roots of Inflation*, New York: Burt Franklin, pp. 152–4.

Munkirs, John R. (1985), *The Transformation of American Capitalism*, Armonk, NY: M.E. Sharpe.

Munkirs, John R. and James I. Sturgeon (1985), 'Oligopolistic cooperation: conceptual and empirical evidence of market structure evolution', *Journal of Economic Issues*, 19(4), December, pp. 899–921.

Okun, Arthur M. (1979), 'An efficient strategy to combat inflation', *Brookings Bulletin*, 15(1), Spring, pp. 1–5.

Okun, Arthur M. (1981), *Prices and Quantities*, Oxford: Basil Blackwell.

Robinson, Joan (1933), *The Economics of Imperfect Competition*, London: Macmillan.

Samuels, Warren J. and Steven C. Medema (1990), *Gardiner C. Means: Institutionalist and Post Keynesian*, Armonk, NY: M.E. Sharpe.

Shackle, George L.S. (1972), *Epistemics and Economics: A Critique of Economic Doctrines*, Cambridge: Cambridge University Press.

Spulber, Daniel F. (1989), *Regulation and Markets*, Cambridge, MA: MIT Press.

Stigler, George J. (1963), 'Administered Prices and Oligopolistic Inflation', in Walter Adams and Robert F. Lanzillotti (eds), *Administered Prices: A Compendium on Public Policy*, US Senate, Committee on the Judiciary, Subcommittee on Antitrust and Monopoly. 88th Congress, first session, Washington, DC: US Government Printing Office.

Tool, Marc R. (1986), *Essays in Social Value Theory: A Neoinstitutionalist Contribution*, Armonk, NY: Sharpe.

Veblen, Thorstein B. (1904), *The Theory of Business Enterprise*, New York: Charles Scribners.

2. The learning economy: challenges to economic theory and policy

Bengt-Åke Lundvall*

INTRODUCTION

In this chapter the focus is on new features in our societies that have to do with the changing roles of learning and knowledge in the economic process. Some of the new characteristics are reasonably well established in theoretical and empirical terms. Others are less so, and some of the propositions should be regarded as conjectures based upon a personal interpretation of empirically based trends, especially new trends in the demand for labour.

The starting point is the assumption that the current economy is one where knowledge is the most strategic resource and learning the most important process. This observation has important implications for economic theory. It challenges the fundamental focus on scarcity in economic theory and it implies that the economic process can only be understood as being socially embedded.[1] It becomes important to distinguish new trends in the knowledge base and their impact on the economy. In what follows we propose the following interpretations.

While the information technology revolution makes more kinds of knowledge codifiable, some elements of tacit knowledge become even more important for economic performance and success than before. The traditional dichotomy between collective and private knowledge is becoming less relevant. As indicated in a recent contribution by Kenneth Arrow (1994), hybrid forms of knowledge, which are neither completely private nor completely public, become increasingly important. More and more strategic know-how and competence is developed interactively and shared within subgroups and networks. Access to and membership of such subgroups is far from free. This change in the character of knowledge may be regarded as the other side of the more generally recognized organizational developments where the dichotomy between market and hierarchy is challenged by hybrid forms that have been called *industrial networks* (Freeman, 1991).

These changes are part of an even more far-reaching process of socio-economic change – we are moving towards a network society where the

26

opportunity and capability to get access to and join knowledge- and learning-intensive networks is determining the relative socio-economic position of individuals and firms. The economy is becoming a hierarchy of networks with some global networks at the top and an increasing proportion of social exclusion at the bottom of the pyramid. The acceleration in the rate of change and the rate of learning is at the roots both of the creation of new organizational forms such as industrial networks and the polarization in OECD labour markets.

This is why policies promoting information infrastructures and accelerating innovation risk reinforcing inequality and threatening the social cohesion of the economy, if the social and distributional dimensions are neglected. Computer literacy and access to network facilities tend to become even more important in determining the future of citizens than literacy in the traditional sense has been. Promoting broad access to skills and competencies, and especially the capability to learn, is the key element in any strategy aiming at limiting the degree of social exclusion. There is a growing risk that IT becomes an acronym for 'intellectual tribalism'. A 'New New Deal' focusing on the uneven distribution of knowledge and information is called for.

THE LEARNING ECONOMY – REMARKS ON TERMINOLOGY

The term 'the learning economy' signifies a society where the capability to learn is critical to economic success. It is akin to 'the information society', which indicates that a big and increasing proportion of the workforce is involved in the production, storing, handling and distribution of information. But the two concepts differ because the outcome of learning, namely knowledge, is a much wider concept than information. Information is the part of knowledge which can be transformed into 'bits' and easily transmitted through a computer network, while learning gives rise to know-how, skills and competencies, which are often tacit rather than explicit and which cannot easily be transmitted through telecommunication networks.

This distinction is important also in relation to economic analysis because it makes it clear that learning is something different from and more complex than a transfer of information and that learning cannot be reduced to acts of transaction. The economics of information is relevant to the analysis of the learning economy and so is transaction cost analysis but none of them covers more than a part of the analytical needs. The formation of individual skills and competencies in interactive processes, and the establishment of economic competence at the level of an organization and in networks of organizations, have characteristics akin to transactions. They may involve the exchange of information but, fundamentally, a different analytical perspective is called for.

Sometimes, the term 'knowledge-based economy' has been used as a substitute for 'the learning economy' and obviously there is a strong link between the two concepts. Learning (and forgetting!) may be regarded as the flow concept(s) corresponding to the stock of knowledge.[2]

There are two reasons to prefer the concept of *the learning economy*. First, it helps us to avoid an analysis where the focus is only on the institutions aiming directly at producing and distributing knowledge (schools, universities, R&D laboratories and so on) to the exclusion of routine-based learning. In the tradition of economic theory, the concept of learning has connotations of learning-by-doing (Arrow, 1962) and learning-by-using (Rosenberg, 1982), which emphasize knowledge creation as a by-product of routine activities.

Second, currently, there is a special need to focus on how economic structures and the institutional set-up affect the process of learning. To focus on the *stock of knowledge* is useful for understanding the long-term pattern of economic growth but it may imply a focus on allocation of existing resources (the stock of knowledge) rather than the formation of new resources (innovation). The general message in this chapter is that there is an urgent need to reassess structures and institutions in relation to how they affect learning and innovation rather than to evaluate them only in terms of static efficiency.

Different Kinds of Knowledge and Learning

In order to understand the role of learning it is necessary to make distinctions between different kinds of knowledge. In an earlier paper (Lundvall and Johnson, 1994), we proposed distinctions between four different kinds of knowledge: know-what; know-why; know-how; and know-who.

Know-what refers to knowledge about 'facts'. How many people live in New York, what are the ingredients in pancakes and the date of the battle of Waterloo are examples of this kind of knowledge. Here, knowledge is close to what is normally called information – it can be broken down into bits. There are complex areas where experts must have a lot of this kind of knowledge in order to fulfil their jobs – practitioners of law and medicine belong to this category. It is interesting to note that many of these experts will, typically, work in independent, specialized consulting firms.

Know-why refers to scientific knowledge of principles and laws of motion in nature, in the human mind and in society. This kind of knowledge has been extremely important for technological development in certain areas as, for example, chemical and electric/electronic industries. To have access to this kind of knowledge will often make advances in technology more rapid and reduce the frequency of errors in procedures of trial and error. Again, the production and reproduction of know-why is often organized in specialized organizations such as universities. To get access to this kind of knowledge, firms have to interact with these organizations either by recruiting scientifically trained labour or directly through contacts with university laboratories.

Know-how refers to skills – the capability to do something. It might relate to production but also to many other activities in the economic sphere. The businessmen judging the market prospects for a new product or the personnel manager selecting and training staff have to use their know-how and the same is true for the skilled worker operating complicated machine tools. It is important to realize that it is not only 'practical people' who need skills, however. One of the most interesting and profound analyses of the role and formation of know-how is actually about the need for skills among scientists (Polanyi, 1958/1978). Know-how is typically a kind of knowledge developed and kept within the border of the individual firm. But as the complexity of the knowledge base is increasing, a mix of a division of labour and cooperation between organizations tends to develop in this field. One of the most important rationales for the formation of long-term interorganizational relationships and of industrial networks is the need for firms to be able to share and combine elements of know-how.

This is why know-who becomes increasingly important. It refers to a mix of different kinds of skills including what might be characterized as social skills. Know-who involves information about who knows what and who knows how to do what. But it especially involves the formation of special social relationships to the expertise involved, which makes it possible to get access to and use their knowledge efficiently. This kind of knowledge is important in the modern economy where there is a need to have access to many different kinds of knowledge and skills that are widely dispersed because of a highly developed division of labour among organizations and experts. For the modern manager and organization it is especially important to utilize this kind of knowledge as a response to the acceleration in the rate of change. The know-who kind of knowledge is internal to the organization to a higher degree than any of the three other kinds of knowledge. In principle it is possible to establish markets for this kind of knowledge – for instance in a corrupt economy where bribery gives privileged access to important people – but normally introducing markets would change and radically depreciate the usefulness and value of the relationships.

LEARNING DIFFERENT KINDS OF KNOWLEDGE

Learning to master the four kinds of knowledge takes place through different channels. While know-what and know-why can be obtained through reading books, attending lectures and accessing databases, the other two categories are rooted primarily in practical experience. Written manuals may help but in order to use them some basic skills in the field of application may be needed.

Know-how will typically be learnt in apprenticeship relations where the apprentice follows his master and relies upon him as his trustworthy authority (Polanyi, 1958/1978, p. 53 and *passim*). Know-how and the capability to act skilfully is what makes a good skilled worker and artisan. But, it is also what distinguishes the excellent from the average manager and scientist. Most natural sciences involve fieldwork or work in laboratories to make it possible for students to learn some of the necessary skills. In management science, the strong emphasis on case-oriented training reflects an attempt to simulate learning based on practical experience.

This kind of basically tacit knowledge is not easily transferred. It will typically develop into a mature form only through years of experience in everyday practice – through learning-by-doing. This is true for lawyers, doctors and businessmen as well as for connoisseurs and artists. *Wunderkinder* who seem to be born with a fully developed skill in a specific area do exist but they are exceptional.

Know-who is learnt in social practice and some of it is learnt in specialized education environments. Communities of engineers and experts are kept together by reunions of alumni and by professional societies, giving the participant access to information bartering with professional colleagues (Carter, 1989). Know-who also develops in day-to-day dealings with customers, subcontractors and independent institutes. One important reason why big firms engage in basic research is that it gives them access to networks of academic experts crucial for their innovative capability (Pavitt, 1991). Again, know-who is socially embedded knowledge that cannot easily be transferred through formal channels of information.

LEARNING AND THE RATE OF CHANGE

Is it really correct to say that the current society is a learning economy as compared to earlier stages of development? In a sense knowledge has always been a crucial resource in the economy. The natural resources and the pure, physical human effort put very strict limits on how much and what can be produced and consumed. Even so-called primitive economies have relied upon the know-how of producers. Knowledge was layered in traditions and routines passed on from generation to generation, and some learning took place and led to increased know-how and made population growth possible.

The most important consequence of the advent of industrialization was not that it involved the use of knowledge, but rather that it made learning a much more fundamental and strategic process than before. In traditional societies people lived their whole life on the basis of a rather narrow and constant set of skills. This is no longer the case in the industrial economy.

Early industrialization had an ambiguous effect on skills. On the one hand, it increased the demand for skill-intensive mechanical engineering for constructing machinery. On the other hand, the labour process for those using the machinery was often characterized by a low and narrowly defined demand for skills. But the main effect of entering the industrial era was that technical and organizational change became the order of the day both for engineers and workers. And there is a strong relationship between the rate of change and the rate of learning.

Change provokes learning. Without change little learning is needed. In a recent article by von Hippel (1994), 'learning-by-doing' is identified with problem-solving in connection with the introduction of new machinery. In this case learning in terms of problem-solving is forced upon workers and engineers by the R&D department responsible for developing and introducing the new machinery. But the change agent might as well have been external to the organization: for instance, a customer defining new needs, a supplier promoting new process equipment, or a competitor introducing new products.[3]

But learning also lies behind change. Experiences of the everyday activities of the firm form an agenda for change and they also help to direct the process of change and to speed it up. It has been increasingly recognized that change in the form of technical and organizational innovations is rooted in a process of interactive learning (OECD, 1992, p. 26 and *passim*). In the interaction between individuals and organizations new combinations of different pieces of knowledge take the form of product and process innovations. There is thus a dual relationship between learning and change.[4]

THREE STYLIZED FACTS

Recent empirical studies focusing on the composition of the demand for labour support the general perspective presented so far. This is true for long-term economic growth analysis as well as for studies of more recent trends.

1. Analytical work on long-term economic growth has demonstrated that in the twentieth century the factor of production which has been growing most rapidly has been human capital. And there are no signs that the growing intensity in the use of human capital has reduced the rate of return on investment in education and training. On this basis economists and economic historians have argued that technical progress has favoured the

productivity of skilled rather than unskilled labour (Abramowitz, 1989, pp. 27ff.).

2. Recently, the Canadian government pursued a number of studies of the degree of knowledge intensity in job creation and job destruction in the 1980s. Using two different definitions (R&D intensity and proportion of staff with a university degree), it was found that net job creation was predominantly taking place in the knowledge-intensive parts of the economy. This tendency was significant across regions, across firm sizes and in services as well as in manufacturing (Industry Canada, 1993, 1994).

3. One of the most striking and worrying results coming out of the OECD's Jobs Study is the strong tendency in the 1980s towards a polarization in labour markets. In the United States relative wages for less skilled workers dropped dramatically, leaving a substantial proportion (almost 20 per cent) of the workforce at a level of earnings below the poverty line. In Italy, Germany and France there was no polarization in terms of wages, but the employment situation worsened dramatically for the unskilled, leaving an increasing proportion excluded from the labour market. The United Kingdom combined these two negative characteristics. It is interesting to note that among the major OECD economies only Japan avoided an increase in polarization in both the pay and the job opportunity dimension in the 1980s (OECD, 1994a).

INTERPRETATION AND EXPLANATION

These three sets of observations illustrate the fact that knowledge and learning has become extremely important in determining the economic fate of individuals, firms and national economies. They have in common that they indicate increasing rather than decreasing returns to the investment in knowledge: the growing proportion of human capital has not reduced its rate of return, the movement of resources into more knowledge-intensive activities seems to be accelerating rather than decelerating, and the relative scarcity of skilled workers has increased in spite of a rapidly growing supply of skilled workers and a decrease in the proportion of unskilled labour. Finally, they indicate that the different forms of investments in knowledge are complementary rather than each other's substitutes: for instance, the introduction of new technology reinforces the demand for skilled labour.

Why did this polarization of the labour market take place and why did the process accelerate in the 1980s? At least three different hypotheses have been put forward in this context. Globalization, biased technological change and changes in firm behaviour are the major factors evoked in the debate.

Especially in connection with the establishment of the North American Free Trade Agreement (NAFTA), there was an intense debate about the impact of intensified international competition on the demand for less skilled workers in the United States. The main result coming out of the empirical work pursued in this context was that increasing imports from low-wage countries does contribute to the polarization but that the scale of the import increase is so limited that it could not possibly by itself explain more than a small part of the phenomenon (Katz and Murphy, 1992).

An alternative explanation, arguing in accordance with the Abramowitz analysis, is that technological change recently has become even more strongly biased in favour of skilled workers. The evidence is still scattered and weak but studies of the use of information technology indicate such a tendency. Both US and Danish data show that the polarization of wages and employment opportunities is most dramatic in firms which have introduced computers and other forms of information technology in the workplace (Krueger, 1993; Lauritzen, 1994).

Finally, some scholars are sceptical both about the globalization and the technology-bias theses and point to institutional change in the labour market and changes in firm behaviour as the main explanations of falling real wages for the low-skilled workers in the United States. According to these scholars, the weakening of trade unions has had a negative impact on the relative position of the least skilled workers because it has incited US employers to implement a low-wage strategy in which delocalization and out-sourcing are important elements (Howell, 1994).

One general problem with these proposed explanations is that most of the analysis is based on data from the United States and it is not always clear to what degree it applies to Europe. Another weakness which reflects the present state of economic methodology is that the three hypotheses have normally been tested separately and regarded as alternatives to each other. It is more plausible that they interact in their impact on jobs. In what follows we propose an interpretation which regards the three elements as factors which work together in promoting an acceleration in the rate of change and learning.

According to standard economics, the major policy response to the polarization of job opportunities should be to make sure that wages were flexible downwards. But in the United States this kind of flexibility has resulted in a growing proportion of 'working poor', while in the United Kingdom the increased wage differences imposed by Thatcherite policies have gone hand in hand with an even stronger polarization than before in terms of job opportunities. The kind of flexibility characterizing the Japanese economy, which avoided polarization, has little to do with textbook labour market flexibility. This is one area where a new understanding of the economy as a learning economy is fundamental in order to avoid misinterpretations and outdated and misdirected solutions.

ACCELERATION OF LEARNING AND CHANGE?

I propose that there is some truth in all three explanations but that their major impact is that together they have speeded up the rate of change and the demand for rapid learning has become intensified. Changes in technology, especially information technology, and changes in international competition have had an impact on the way firms organize themselves and the three factors combine in accelerating learning at all levels of the economy.

There is little doubt that over a longer time span there has been an acceleration in the rate of learning and change. We have only to go back a few generations to find ancestors who were doing the same things in the same ways as their grandparents, and normally they did it in the same locality. Change has accelerated enormously since the beginning of the industrial revolution and people have been forced to engage in learning to do things differently and to operate in new environments.

But what about the rate of change in the medium term? It is not easy to find reliable and valid indicators for the rate of change and learning. The number of scientific articles is growing exponentially but this might have more to do with the institutional context than with an increase in the rate of learning. The rate of growth of the economy is actually lower than in the 1950s and the 1960s. Indicators of structural change in terms of changes in the sectoral composition of production and employment do not give clear indications in this respect. While changes in the structure of employment seem to slow down in the 1980s, a slight acceleration seems to have occurred when sectors are measured in terms of output (OECD, 1994b, p. 15; 1994c, p. 143).

Some anecdotal evidence indicates an acceleration of change. In 1993 the theme of the annual conference of European R&D managers – EIRMA – was 'accelerating innovation' and among the experts present there was little doubt that there had been an acceleration of the rate of technical innovation in the 1980s (EIRMA, 1993).[5]

Another phenomenon which involves a much broader set of actors than the R&D-intensive firms is the movement towards flexible specialization where producers increasingly compete by responding rapidly to volatile markets. Organizational change in terms of 'just in time' and lean production strategies may be regarded as responses to the need to speed up change. Again rapid change will imply a strong demand for a capability to learn and respond to new needs and market opportunities.[6]

A third phenomenon has to do with the introduction of more intense competition in sectors which have been living a more protected life. Competition may come from the opening of national markets for services to imports or from deregulation and privatization of activities. In this process the rate of change will accelerate even more rapidly than in the sectors which have been used to competition.

Another way of indicating the growing importance of change and learning has been proposed by Carter (1994). She shows that there is a close connection between the proportion of non-production workers and the rate of change in a sector and actually she argues that the major function of non-production workers is to create or to react to change. On the basis of data on employment patterns in manufacturing in the United States, it is demonstrated that a growing proportion of costs are costs of change rather than costs of production.

CHANGES IN THE RELATIONSHIPS BETWEEN TACIT AND CODIFIED KNOWLEDGE

One of the important trends in our economies is the increasing importance of codified knowledge (David, 1994). In the wake of World War II, science became a major factor in economic development. Specialized R&D laboratories were established, first in firms belonging to the chemical and electrical industries, and later in a wider set of sectors. The Manhattan project resulting in the first nuclear bomb and the Cold War period including the space race between the Soviet Union and the United States contributed to the general idea that a strong science base is important for international competitiveness. The massive investments in education and training following the Sputnik-chock also gave a major impetus to the codification of knowledge.

The development of information technology may be regarded as a response to the need for handling codified knowledge more effectively. Conversely, the very existence of information technology and communications infrastructures gives a strong impetus to the process of codification of knowledge. All knowledge which can be codified and reduced to information can now be transmitted over long distances with very limited costs. The area of potential applications of codified knowledge is extended and it makes it more attractive to allocate resources to the process of codification.

Codification may be understood as a process of generalizing what is specific and translating messages into a common and shared language. It involves the establishment of technical standards and of basing technical development on general scientific principles. A special aspect relates to the design of the innovation process itself where information technology makes it possible to pursue developmental work on computers through virtual experiments rather than through real tests in real laboratories. Increasingly this takes place in the testing of new drugs and in the design of big and complex systems such as aeroplanes and ships.

This new step in the degree of codification of knowledge is important because it moves the border between tacit and codified knowledge. However, it does not necessarily reduce the relative importance of skills, competencies and other elements of tacit knowledge. The easier and less expensive access to information makes skills and competencies relating to the selection and efficient use of information even more crucial than before. In general, skills related to handling codified knowledge become more important in the labour markets. This shift in the demand for skills may be a further element reinforcing the polarization in labour markets. The case studies showing that the polarization is most strongly developed in firms using computers point in this direction.

The most fundamental aspect of learning is perhaps the transformation of tacit into codified knowledge and the movement back to practice where new kinds of tacit knowledge are developed. Such a spiral movement is, according to Nonaka (1991), at the very core of individual as well as organizational learning. Also, in the real world the distinction between the two is not always as clear-cut as is normally assumed. At any point in time a certain amount of knowledge is in the pipeline, in the process of codification. While some engineers and scientists are involved in producing innovations and inventions, a much larger proportion is engaged in standardization and in codifying and generalizing knowledge.

THE NEED FOR A NEW DEAL

One basic hypothesis of this paper is that the speed-up of the rate of change imposed by growing international competition, deregulation and new technological opportunities gives an incentive to firms to hire personnel with a high learning capability. The information technology and the codification of new kinds of technology reinforce the acceleration and lead to a preference for workers with general competencies in handling codified knowledge. These tendencies increase the proportion of workers promoting change and lead to a further acceleration in the rate of change. The process is thus characterized by cumulative causation, excluding a large and growing proportion of the labour force from normal waged work. If this hypothesis is correct, there is a need to develop a new perspective on policy-making and to look for a new kind of social compromise.

One alternative is, paradoxically, to further speed up the rate of learning in the sectors facing international competition in order to obtain a bigger share in the most rapidly growing markets. Another is to create a sheltered sector where learning takes place at a slower rate. A third, and perhaps the most important, is to redistribute the access to information networks and the capabilities to learn in favour of the potentially excluded. Finally, to slow down some kinds of change by installing rigidities in the system may be a way of channelling processes of learning in directions less disruptive to social cohesion. Some major private agents have already moved in this direction when confronted with situations where costs of change have become too high as compared to benefits.

Speeding up Change

In the OECD Jobs Study the basic message is that countries should try to remain at 'the head of the pack' in terms of innovation and change (OECD, 1994a, p. 3 and *passim*). It is true that national innovation systems where firms are able to move rapidly into new growth areas in world markets and into areas of new promising technologies are better off than systems where the firms get stuck in stagnating activities. They will increase their share of world markets and value added at the global level. The number of jobs and real wages can be increased simultaneously.

This model has certain characteristics in common with the Japanese post-war economy. In the highly productive, export-oriented part of the economy, learning has been extremely effective in promoting income generation through moving rapidly into the most promising markets and technologies.

The very success of the model now seems to undermine it, however. One general problem of this strategy is of course that not every country can lead the pack and it may be argued that the other side of the Japanese success is the crisis in the labour markets in the rest of the OECD countries (Lundvall, 1995). In the United States and Europe, the very strength of the Japanese capability in high-growth areas has forced firms to speed up learning and change in activities characterized by slower growth and in technologies where the cost–benefit ratio of accelerating change is less favourable. Attempts to correct for the uneven development of competitiveness through currency rate corrections and manipulations have proved quite ineffective and the resulting financial instability has further undermined growth and job creation.

In spite of what is said in the OECD Jobs Study, speeding up change in Europe and the United States might not be the most promising response, however, and especially if it is not combined with a change in the pattern of specialization. An important explanation of the unemployment problem is the uneven development within the triad and the polarization in labour markets in the United States and the major European economies reflects an acceleration of learning in low-growth areas.

Creating a Sheltered Sector

Even if the United States and Europe were more successful in entering areas where learning curves are steep and markets are growing fast, this might not by itself solve the problem of social exclusion. A rapid growth in the tradeables sectors would give rise to a high and rapidly growing income level but only for a shrinking part of the potential labour force. To keep the living standard of the growing proportion of excluded workers at what has been established as a minimum to avoid poverty would include a dramatic increase in income transfers.

One way to reduce the burden of redistribution for governments and at the same time to reduce the proportion of workers excluded from the labour market would be to stimulate the creation or conservation of *a private sheltered sector* where change took place more slowly and the rate of learning and productivity were lower.

Again this corresponds to the Japanese development where the rate of change and learning in the tradeables sector has been very high while agriculture and parts of the services sector have remained sheltered from competition. The rate of change has been slowed down in the sheltered sectors not primarily through open protectionism but rather through complex informal institutional mechanisms. It should be pointed out that it might be misleading to call this a Japanese *strategy* since it is far from clear to what degree conscious choices were made to establish and reproduce such a dual system.

Today the international pressure to break up the sheltering institutions is mounting, however. From the point of view of the rest of the OECD countries they appear to be trade barriers efficiently blocking the entrance of foreign competition. There are also domestic forces working in the same direction emanating from the tradeable sector, which experiences an increasing pressure on its profits when confronted with high currency rates and protectionist responses abroad.

Network Access and Skill Formation as Social Policy

A third kind of policy response which is supplementary to the other two is one where the focus is on the development of human resources in a broad sense. Primary and secondary education of a high quality reaching all citizens and giving special attention to those having the greatest difficulties in learning would be an important part of such a strategy. But even more important and more difficult would be to establish incentives for firms and individuals to engage in upgrading the learning capability of the adult population and, again, with special attention to those who run the biggest risk of being excluded.

The further development of information infrastructures may, if it is not consciously managed, reinforce exclusion. To give workers and the unemployed a chance to learn and develop their cognitive skills and to give them skills specifically related to the use of computers would be another important part of this strategy. On the other hand, the very advent of information infrastructures and the growing political attention it attracts could be used to focus on these kinds of problems. Information infrastructures can be regarded both as something which threatens to aggravate the polarization in labour markets and as one element of the solution. Giving the weaker persons and groups privileged access to networks and using the networks to develop on-line learning would be a solution that increased the capability to cope with rapid learning without exclusion.

The traditional approach to social exclusion has been, *ex post*, and through governments, to organize income transfers from the employed to the unemployed and unemployable. There are signs that this way of attacking the problem does not work any more, for a number of reasons. The very scale of the problem and the limited willingness to pay taxes is one problem. The fact that exclusion tends to become chronic rather than temporary in this kind of regime is another. In the new context, strategies which attack the problem *ex ante* and which limit the creation of polarization and exclusion through a different distribution of access to learning and networking become correspondingly more adequate. This implies among other things the need for a new division of labour and new forms of cooperation within governments. Policies focusing on industrial development, technology, and especially information technology, have to be coordinated more strongly with economic and social policies.

Slowing down Change

An alternative to increasing the capability to cope with rapid change and accelerating the rate of learning would be to slow down change. Is it possible to do so? It is a difficult question since we have got so used to connecting change with economic growth and growth with increasing welfare. But it is possible that rates of change have become too high – that hyper-acceleration of change and learning may take place. 'Hyper-acceleration' refers to a situation where all parties would gain from slowing down the rate of learning but where the rules of the game are such that they give incentives to continuously accelerate the rate.

In order to illustrate that this is not completely far-fetched, two examples may be evoked. The first refers to the Japanese automobile industry, where some years ago the leading producers realized that the product life cycle of car models was becoming too short. The amount of resources which had to be allocated to product development, the coordination problems with subcontractors, and the sales and services organizations and the quality control were becoming such a heavy burden that it gave an incentive for the major firms to enter into an agreement to avoid a further shortening of the product life cycle.

The second example refers to the sector producing information technology and computers, where experts and management tend to agree that the acceleration of technology and supply-driven change was a major factor in undermining the market. The rate of learning imposed on final users became too high and the resulting disappointments when applying the technologies backfired, taking the form of a stagnation in demand.[7]

These two examples do not tell us how to slow down change and learning in the economy as a whole. They indicate, however, that hyper-acceleration of learning may develop but also that there might be major players in the economy who would be willing to support a certain slow-down in the rate of change.

The Ethical Dimension in the Learning Economy

The production and distribution of all kinds of knowledge is strongly rooted in the social system. It is generally accepted that information is not easily transacted in the market. One of Arrow's paradoxical statements is that you cannot know the full value of information if you do not have full access to it. And if you have full access to it there is no reason to pay for it. Property rights are not easily defined. On the one hand it is true that the one who sells information will not lose access to it while the one who buys it can reproduce it and distribute it to all potential customers (Arrow, 1973).

It is also obvious that trade in information by definition involves information impactedness and an asymmetrical distribution of information. Accordingly, transaction costs will be high when opportunistic behaviour is part of the game. These statements are, I believe, generally accepted.

What is perhaps less obvious is how these circumstances force the social context into the centre of economic analysis. Arrow has stated another paradox in this connection. He says that 'you cannot buy trust – and if you could buy it, it would be of no value whatsoever' (Arrow, 1971). This simple statement is radical in its implications. First, given that trust is necessary in order to make the economy work – and this is true for any trade in information and it is even more true in connection with processes of interactive learning – it becomes clear that there must be something outside the pure instrumental rationality of individual agents to keep the economy together.

Some social scientists have tried to overcome this kind of problem by introducing social exchange as an instrumental process (Blau, 1964). The basic idea is that if you are nice and honest to me, I will be nice and honest to you and as time goes by both parties will be willing to invest more and more trust in the relationship. There is some truth in these models but there is something lacking. If there were nothing but instrumental calculations behind cooperation it is difficult to see how any kind of stable and trust-based relationships could develop. If you knew that your partner was continuously calculating the utility of being honest to you, you would not give away too much sensitive information.

Another implication is that the level of transaction costs involved in connection with selling and buying information will reflect the degree of trust and the relative frequency of opportunistic behaviour in the local context. The learning capability would be even more dependent on the presence of trust. Tacit knowledge and know-how will typically be transferred and shared not through market operations but through a process of interactive learning. Such processes are extremely vulnerable to opportunistic behaviour and cheating.

This implies that the more an economy becomes dependent on the formation and efficient use of knowledge the more important its ethical foundations become. This points to a fundamental contradiction in the modern economy.

There are strong tendencies towards generalizing the market and letting it penetrate more and more deeply into all kinds of relationships. Today this is reinforced especially by the globalization and deregulation of financial markets, which tend to undermine all kinds of non-market regulations and relationships at the national level.

But economies where the market loses its roots in the social system and where all agents act exclusively on the basis of strategic and instrumental rationality will find that their capacity to learn and innovate will become undermined. Russia and some of the Eastern European countries illustrate what happens when the market is given free play and where trust is absent in the relationships between economic agents. Building formal institutions and introducing new laws will not help much if the social foundations are absent.

There are serious warning signals indicating that we are now in the midst of a process threatening the very social foundations which made rapid economic growth possible over a long period. The social exclusion of growing segments of the population is one factor pointing in this direction. A society which does not care for its weaker citizens will have difficulties in maintaining and fostering a social climate of trust and acceptance. This problem is aggravated by the fact that the financial sector increasingly offers rapid profits to young brainy people who get their living from financial speculation. A third factor is the growing number of scandals involving the economic and political elite in economic criminality.

On the other hand, it may be argued that the increasing importance of learning for economic performance in itself forms a countervailing power against these tendencies. The more advanced layers of management realize that it would be impossible to keep up with the rapid rate of change in the economy were the personnel to act exclusively on the basis of individual economic incentives and threats of losing their jobs. Without a minimum of loyalty to the organization, employees have all the opportunities to slow down processes of organizational learning. The same is true for interfirm relationships and networks of firms. Without a minimum of social trust, transaction costs become too high and interactive learning too difficult.

One of the dramas which we will be witnessing during the coming decades is the struggle between a financial and individualistic logic and a logic more compatible with the increasing importance of interactive learning.

INTERNATIONALIZATION AND THE CHANGING ROLE OF NATION STATES

These general tendencies reflecting changes in the role of knowledge are further reinforced by the internationalization of certain economic activities. Historically, the nation state has been the most important institutional framework for learning and innovation. This is obviously true for the legal system and for social policies compensating losers in the overall game of creative destruction. But it has also been true for informal and formal institutions (such as reputation mechanisms, professionals sharing, and self-imposed codes of conduct), reducing the scope for opportunistic behaviour.

Today, these elements of the national system are challenged by internationalization of economic activities and most forcefully by the internationalization of financial markets. National systems which have been extremely successful in building trust and promoting learning – such as Japan's – have come under increasing pressure to move towards 'pure' market relationships and to weaken some of the social institutions which have been the pillars of the innovation system.

Since the new institutional frameworks at the global level are not built at the same rate as the national ones are undermined, more and more economic activities take place in a social void and without the support of institutions of trust. What seems to happen in this situation is that regional, transnational or local networks establish their own specific rules of the game which are valid inside but not necessarily outside the network. We are witnessing a movement towards what one might call intellectual tribalism.

Networks or tribes engage in interactive learning in competition with other networks or tribes. Inside the network they share knowledge and build trust relationships. But in their interaction with individuals and organizations belonging to other tribes they remain opportunistic, and when it is to their advantage they break the rules of decency.

NATIONAL SYSTEMS OF INNOVATION

In spite of a far-reaching process of internationalization, national systems still play a major role in determining how common global trends affect economic performance. Japan is the only major OECD economy character-ized neither by high rates of unemployment nor by polarization in labour markets. Some of the most rapidly growing Asian economies have in com-mon with Japan a strong emphasis on education and training as well as an egalitarian income distribution. These countries have handled the accelera-tion in the rate of change differently from most of the OECD countries. The smaller OECD countries and especially the Nordic ones have also been more successful in avoiding social exclusion than the major OECD countries.

This reflects systemic features that distribute the social pressure emanating from an acceleration of change and innovation differently across nations. In the US model, learning is done the hard way – individuals carry most of the burden of change in a kind of lottery where both the losses and the potential gains are high. Learning takes place through job changes and through moving between firms.

The Japanese model is one where learning to a higher degree takes place internally as organizational learning. The degree of flexibility within firms is high and the firms – at least the big and advanced ones – share the risk of negative change with the individual.

Some of the European systems such as in the United Kingdom and France have old and established elitist education and training systems based on a mix of plutocracy, aristocracy and elitocracy. The education system fosters rigidities in the workplace both vertically as barriers to upward mobility and horizontally between job functions (especially in France) and the flexibility will mainly be interfirm. Rigidities give fewer incentives for learning new skills than both the US and the Japanese system. Following Thatcherite prescriptions and imposing more of the US kind of flexibility in these sys-tems results in dramatic increases in social inequality – it weakens the losers while keeping their chances for upward mobility low.

The Nordic countries are also characterized by a high rate of mobility between firms and jobs but they combine it with a welfare state system aimed at sharing the costs of change between winners and losers.

Each of these systems has its own comparative advantages and disadvan-tages when it comes to coping with the acceleration in the rate of change. In the United States most of the increasing pressure is put on the weakest segments of the population; in the Nordic countries it is the welfare state and its institutions that come under pressure; and in Japan it is the institutions providing a shelter for certain labour-intensive activities. None of the systems can cope with the acceleration of change without running into problems, reflecting the fact that the predominant institutional set-up is not fully adapted to the context of the globalized learning economy. In the longer term we believe that systems providing solutions based on solidarity will come out as the strongest but in the short term free-riding and playing on people's egoistic motives seem to flourish.

CONCLUSION

In standard economics it is generally recognized that information cannot easily be transacted in markets and that market failure is present in connection with both the production of and the trade in knowledge. From this recognition to understanding the full implications of the learning economy is, however, still a long way. This is illustrated most clearly by the present overstatement of what market forces can do in connection with solving the problems of unemployment and social exclusion. The assumption that more competition and wage flexibility is the key to solving the problem of unemployment neglects the fact that learning is a social process that can prosper only if society remains cohesive. The impact on the social and moral foundations of society must be taken into account by any policy aiming for long-term economic efficiency.

The alternative to the flexibilization strategy recommended by mainstream economists is not necessarily just to speed up the rate of innovation and learning, however. There are indications that currently the rate of change tends to outgrow the capacity to learn. The idea of slowing things down may seem alien to most of us but we still need to consider it seriously. The Japanese example shows that it might be quite efficient to introduce some specific rigidities that work as brakes on those processes of change and are the most socially disruptive. The alternative is a polarized society with little cohesion and such a society is not viable in the long run. Under all circumstances there is a need to redefine policies relating to technical change, industrial development, education and training, as well as information infrastructures, so that they take into account the distributional impact of policy alternatives. Traditional policies trying to correct income distributions *ex post* have reached their limits and an *ex ante* approach is called for.

NOTES

* This chapter is based on a talk given at the European Association for Evolutionary Political Economy conference in Copenhagen, March 1995. It was then revised and published in Nielsen and Johnson (1998). The content reflects the confrontation of ideas developed in academic work in the period 1990–92 (Lundvall and Johnson, 1994) with my experience from involvement in the OECD Jobs Study as deputy director for the Directorate for Science, Technology and Industry. I have left the original text without changes. Since then I have pursued the ideas related to the polarization in the labour market in a major project on the Danish innovation system (Lundvall and Nielsen, 1999), those on the economics of knowledge and learning in collaboration with CERI–OECD (OECD, 2000) and those on the need for new policy perspectives (Archibugi and Lundvall, 2001).

1. These are points I have made before in papers produced together with colleagues from Aalborg. They are at the core of the argument in Lundvall (1992). They have been further developed in Lundvall and Johnson (1994).

2. The concept of 'the knowledge-based information economy' has played a major role in several of the contributions by Eliasson, who emphasizes the role of micro-based economic competence in the process of economic growth (Eliasson, 1990). An early and interesting contribution to the role of learning in the process of innovation is Cantley and Sahal (1980).

3. Some learning may take place also in a technically stable environment, however. See for instance Lundberg (1961) regarding the so-called Horndahl effect where productivity was increased continuously through several decades in spite of very limited investments and very little change in the production technology.

4. This perspective should be confronted with von Hippel's (1994) analysis of 'sticky data'. According to von Hippel, the normal outcome of a situation where it is difficult to codify and transfer information is not cooperation and interactive learning but rather that the different parties establish a division of labour in a sequential mode. The process of innovation is regarded as one where the locus of innovation shifts back and forth between agents according to their special competencies. A similar perspective is immanent when applying theories of industrial organization emphasizing specialized assets to the process of innovation (Christensen, 1995). An interesting research agenda would be to test empirically the perspective of interactive learning with this division-of-labour approach.

5. It is interesting to note the introductory remarks to the conference by the EIRMA president, Dr E. Spitz:

> In a time of intensive global competition, speeding up the innovation process is one of the most important ingredients which enable the company to bring to the market the right product for right prices at the right time. …
>
> *We know that it is not only the R&D process which is important; we have to put emphasis on integration of technology in the complete business environment, production, marketing, regulations and many other activities essential to commercial success. These are the areas where the innovation process is being retarded.*
>
> *This subject is a very deep seated one which sometimes leads to important, fundamental rethinking and radical redesign of the whole business process. In this respect, especially during the difficult period in which we live today, where pressure is much higher, our organisations may, in fact, need to be changed.* (EIRMA, 1993, p. 7; emphasis added)

6. For an interesting collection of case studies illustrating the change in organizations responding to the need for flexible specialization, see Andreasen *et al.* (1995).

7. This was one of the main conclusions of the OECD High Level Seminar on Information Technology held in Paris in 1993.

REFERENCES

Abramowitz, M. (1989), *Thinking about Growth*, Cambridge: Cambridge University Press.

Andreasen, L.E. *et al.* (eds) (1995), *Europe's Next Step: Organisational Innovation, Competition and Employment*, London: Frank Cass.

Archibugi, D. and Lundvall, B.-Å. (eds) (2001), *The Globalising Learning Economy: Major Socio-economic Trends and European Innovation Policy*, Oxford: Oxford University Press.

Arrow, K.J. (1962), 'The economic implications of learning by doing', *Review of Economic Studies*, 29(2), pp. 155–73.

Arrow, K.J. (1971), 'Political and economic evaluation of social effects and externalities', in M. Intrilligator (ed.), *Frontiers of Quantitative Economics*, North Holland.

Arrow, K.J. (1973), *Information and Economic Behaviour*, Stockholm: Federation of Swedish Industries.

Arrow, K.J. (1994), 'Methodological individualism and social knowledge', Richard T. Ely Lecture, *AEA Papers and Proceedings*, 84(2), May, pp. 1–9.

Blau, P.M. (1964), *Exchange and Power in Social Life*, New York: John Wiley.

Cantley, M. and D. Sahal (1980), *Who Learns What? A Conceptual Description of Capability and Learning in Technological Systems*, Laxenburg: IIASA.

Carter, A.P. (1989), 'Know-how trading as economic exchange', *Research Policy*, 18(3), pp. 155–63.

Carter, A.P. (1994), 'Production workers, metainvestment and the pace of change', paper prepared for meeting of the International J.A. Schumpeter Society, Munster, August.

Christensen, J.F. (1995), 'The innovative assets and inter-asset linkages of the firm', revised version of paper presented at the EUNETIC Conference on Evolutionary Economics of Technological Change, Strasbourg, 1994.

David, P. (1994), 'Technological change, intangible investments and growth in the knowledge-based economy: the US historical experience', paper presented at the OECD conference on Employment and Growth in the Knowledge-based Economy, Copenhagen, November.

EIRMA (1993), *Speeding up Innovation*, conference papers for the EIRMA Helsinki conference, May.

Eliasson, G. (1990), 'Innovation, industrial competence and the micro-foundations of economic expansion', in E. Deiaco, E. Hornell and G. Vickery (eds), *Technology and Investments: Crucial Issues for the 1990s*, London: Pinter Publishers.

Freeman, C. (1991), 'Networks of innovators: a synthesis of research issues', *Research Policy*, 20(5), pp. 499–514.

Howell, D.R. (1994), 'Information technology and the demand for skills: a perspective on the US experience', paper presented at the OECD conference on Employment and Growth in the Knowledge-based Economy, Copenhagen, November.

Industry Canada (1993), 'Knowledge, technology and employment trends', memo by Pat Murray, July, Ottawa, Ministry of Industry.

Industry Canada (1994), 'Employment growth in Canada', memo by N. Stephens Ottawa, Ministry of Industry.

Katz, L.F. and K.M. Murphy (1992), 'Changes in relative wages 1963–1987: supply and demand factors', *Quarterly Journal of Economics*, February pp. 35–78.

Krueger, R.B. (1993), 'How computers have changed the wage structure: evidence from micro-data, 1984–89', *Quarterly Journal of Economics*, February pp. 33–60.

Lauritzen, F. (1994), 'Technology, education and employment', paper presented at the OECD conference on Employment and Growth in the Knowledge-based Economy, Copenhagen, November.

Lundberg, E. (1961), *Produktivitet och Räntabilitet: Studier i Kapitalets Betydelse inom Svenskt Näringsliv*, Stockholm: Studieförbundet Näringsliv och Samhälle.

Lundvall, B.-Å. (ed.) (1992), *National Systems of Innovation: Towards a Theory of Innovation and Interactive Learning*, London: Pinter Publishers.

Lundvall, B.-Å. (1995), 'The global unemployment problem and national systems of innovation', in D. O'Doherty (ed.), *Globalisation, Networking and Small Firm Innovation*, London: Graham and Trotman, pp. 35–45.

Lundvall, B.-Å. and B. Johnson (1994), 'The learning economy', *Journal of Industry Studies*, 1(2) December, pp. 23–42.

Lundvall, B.-Å. and P. Nielsen (1999), 'Competition and transformation in the learning economy – illustrated by the Danish case', *Revue d'Economie Industrielle*, 88, pp. 67–90.

Nielsen, K. and B. Johnson (eds.) (1998), *Institutions and Economic Change: New Perspectives on Markets, Firms and Technology*, Cheltenham: Edward Elgar Publishers.

Nonaka, K. (1991), 'The knowledge creating company', *Harvard Business Review*, Nov.–Dec., pp. 96–104.

OECD (1992), *Technology and the Economy – The Key Relationships*, Paris: OECD.

OECD (1994a), *The OECD Jobs Study – Facts, Analysis, Strategies*, Paris: OECD.

OECD (1994b), *The OECD Jobs Study – Evidence and Explanation, Part I*, Paris: OECD.

OECD (1994c), *Manufacturing Performance: A Scoreboard of Indicators*, Paris: OECD.

OECD (2000), *Knowledge Management in the Learning Society*, Paris: OECD.

Pavitt, K. (1991), 'What makes basic research economically useful?', *Research Policy*, 20(2) pp. 109–19.

Polanyi, M. (1958/1978), *Personal Knowledge*, London: Routledge and Kegan Paul.

Rosenberg, N. (1982), *Inside the Black Box: Technology and Economics*, Cambridge: Cambridge University Press.

von Hippel, E. (1994), 'Sticky information and the locus of problem solving: implications for innovation', *Management Science*, 40, pp. 429–39.

3. The meaning and role of power in economic theories

David Young

INTRODUCTION

The meaning and significance of power in economic analysis has seldom been a subject that has engaged the efforts of mainstream neoclassical theorists. That is not to say that the term 'power' is never used or that it does not play a significant role in certain models. But, it tends to be used in a very specific and narrow way and its alternative meanings and wider significance are seldom acknowledged.

In 1971 Rothschild commented that as 'in other important social fields we should expect that individuals and groups will struggle for position; that power will be used to improve one's chances in the economic "game". Power should, therefore, be a recurrent theme in economic studies of a theoretical or applied nature. Yet if we look at the main run of economic theory over the past hundred years we find that it is characterized by a strange lack of power considerations' (Rothschild, 1971, p. 7). This state of affairs has fundamentally changed very little. To a large extent, this neglect has continued almost uninterrupted as mainstream economists refine and extend the basic model postulated by neoclassical theory. Despite more common usage of the term 'power' in mainstream game-theoretic analysis, its meaning is still constrained by the conception of neoclassical competition, and so the general neglect of 'power' in mainstream analysis remains.

The main objectives of this chapter are to consider the alternative meanings of 'power' and to assess the different interpretations and roles of power in different types of economic theory. It will be argued that all the main schools of thought in economics adopt a particular view of power and that this reflects fundamental differences in the nature of the theories. It will also be suggested that it is difficult to ignore the significance of power in general for economic theory, and that attempts to examine the nature and role of power more explicitly may lead to a more satisfactory analysis of market interactions between individual agents, firms and other institutions.

DIFFERENT SCHOOLS OF ECONOMIC THOUGHT AND DIFFERENT NOTIONS OF POWER

The relative neglect (at least until recently) of the notion of power in mainstream economics is not shared by alternative schools of thought. In general, economic theorists of a Marxist or 'radical' persuasion have long emphasized the importance of 'power' for explaining economic phenomena. Similarly some other heterodox economists (whom we might refer to as institutionalists), such as those works collected in Samuels (1979), have also discussed various aspects of power, although from a somewhat different standpoint and in very diverse ways. By contrast, Austrian economists have long denied the importance of power for explaining the workings of competitive market economics.

Neither the Marxist nor the Austrian view of power accord with mainstream theory. To attempt to elucidate the different meanings of power and its general importance to economic theory, it is helpful to consider the different conceptions of power adopted by these three schools of thought: Marxian, Austrian and neoclassical. Although there are a number of different alternative approaches, it may be contended that these three bodies of theory can be regarded as the most clearly defined and distinctive approaches to economic theory. They have different philosophical presumptions and give rise to distinct policy prescriptions. Other approaches (and there are many) may be regarded as less than distinct schools of thought. They do not have such clearly defined foundations, either philosophically or in terms of their historical roots, and some have emerged specifically as a criticism of particular aspects of mainstream theory rather than being grounded in a different tradition or mode of thought. This may be so with respect to the institutionalist approach, which is clearly the most relevant in the present context.

Institutional economics encompasses a variety of different theoretical perspectives (based on correspondingly different philosophical foundations) united by an emphasis or an explicit discussion of institutions and institutional change. The three schools identified here may be regarded as having different views about the role and importance of institutions, and much of the content of what is often described as being an institutionalist approach may be regarded as being influenced by one or another of these schools. So the nature of power, which varies so much within institutionalist theories, may be clarified by considering the meaning of power as it relates to these three schools of thought. This is not to say that there are no important alternative ideas and that these do not provide some basis for future progress but, for the moment, the three schools we have identified may be taken to represent the basis of competing contemporary theories.

Before examining the views of power inherent in these different schools of thought, it is necessary to consider the meanings, which we might attach to the term 'power', and to consider some basis for comparing the different views of power that have emerged in economic theory.

THE MEANINGS OF POWER

As noted in the introduction, the term 'power' has been used in numerous ways and can be taken to involve a number of diverse dimensions. Within economics specifically, the term has been applied to 'power' over resources (for example, the means to produce), purchasing power, monopoly power and the power of the state. More generally it is also used with reference to natural powers (wind, waves) and to coercion or violence. The two latter meanings are normally not the concern of social theory and will not be of concern here, except inasmuch as some reference will be made to coercion in the discussion of economic power.

The issue of power has been widely discussed in social theory over a number of years, and particularly since Dahl (1957) has received considerable attention in sociological studies. One study, which is widely regarded as having provided an important approach to considering power is Lukes (1974), which argued for a more 'radical' approach. Though there are problems involved with this view, which have subsequently been discussed in sociological theory, Lukes does still provide a framework for thinking about different types or dimensions of power, which have generally not been recognized by economists in their modelling of problems which utilize some conception of power.

Lukes (1974) provides a detailed account of the dimensions of power that are often mentioned but largely neglected by liberal analysts. In particular we are offered a more 'radical' analysis which considers some of the more subtle and indirect ways in which power may be exercised. Lukes specifies three principal dimensions of power. The one-dimensional view concerns the ability to win in overt conflict through sheer 'weight'. This is the most obvious and most widely recognized dimension of power, although there may still be difficulties in modelling such conflicts. The two-dimensional view includes consideration of cases where, say, A has power over B if A can prevent B's wants from reaching the stage of overt conflict and decision, that is, rigging the 'game' before it starts or setting the agenda. This is clearly a less direct but potentially very important aspect of power, and continuing in this vein a three-dimensional view is defined, which involves situations where A can manipulate B's preferences in such a manner that they are then contrary to B's interests. This is perhaps the most controversial dimension, and in practice (as Lukes, 1974, discusses) involves establishing the appropriate counterfactuals in order to establish that such power has been exercised.

In addition we may also wish to draw a clear distinction between wants or preferences and interests. If this is so, then one may wish to divide Lukes's three-dimensional view into two categories, one involving the manipulation of wants and the other the manipulation of wants in the subversion of that agent's interests. Following Hollis (1987), we may then distinguish four clear categories which may be useful in thinking about what is meant by 'power' and the ways in which we might consider its significance. These categories may be summarized as follows. Consider two individuals (agents), A and B. A has power over B if:

1. A has the ability to win in overt conflict with B;
2. A is able to divert B's wants;
3. A is able to reconstitute B's wants;
4. A is able to reconstitute B's wants against B's interests.

Although not uncontroversial, such a classification does seem to capture most of the important aspects or dimensions of power that we might wish to discuss in economic theories. It should be acknowledged, however, that there are a number of desirable characteristics which any conception of power might involve, namely a positive as well as a negative dimension and a more dynamic or process quality. Although these aspects are not developed here, it should be emphasised that power may be an enabling as well as a restraining relation and the ways in which it emerges is within the context of an evolving process of relations between agents and institutions. These aspects of power may also be important in distinguishing between different economic theories but in general some Lukes-type classification will suffice for the purpose of examining the views of power adopted within the different schools that have been specified.

THE DISTINCT VIEWS OF 'POWER' INHERENT IN DIFFERENT SCHOOLS OF THOUGHT

Having sketched the different attitudes to 'power' adopted by the three principal schools of thought which we have identified, and having considered what we might mean by 'power', we may begin to develop a categorization of the different views of power embedded in each approach and to illuminate the key differences between them.

If we begin by considering mainstream neoclassical analysis, then it is clear that the term 'power' has long been in common usage but has seldom been explicitly considered; its meaning has often been specific but very narrow, arising out of the particular models within which it appears. As noted by

Rothschild (1971), much of early microeconomic analysis was built around the model of perfect competition. As is well known, this model (contestability aside) still forms the basis of welfare judgements with respect to monopolistic and oligopolistic markets. Game theory has developed models of firms' strategic behaviour but the conception of 'power' is linked to the old idea of monopoly or market power which is itself conceived of in terms of a departure from a competitive state. Similarly the neoclassical conception of dominance relies heavily on the concept of market power and price leadership.

For example, the standard dominant firm-price leadership model is based on the idea that a particular firm or group of firms has a sufficiently large market share to set prices as a monopolist would, but subject to a demand condition given by exogenous market demand minus the supply of the other 'fringe' producers. This is clearly a simplistic notion of power that is essentially seen in terms of a producer's ability to determine price. But there is really little analysis of the process by which such power is established or explanation of what exactly allows the dominant firm to continue to exert such market power. Of course, mainstream theory has developed more sophisticated models to attempt to model firms' use of market power by examining strategic behaviour in a game–theoretic setting. Nonetheless the conception of power remains similar.

An example of the attitude to 'power' adopted in modern mainstream theory is given in Skaperdas (1992) where it is commented that 'an agent's equilibrium win probability (or the share of total product) represents a clear index of the agent's power'.

> [Power is,] however, a notoriously difficult concept to define and investigate. When it is defined, it is frequently viewed as an exogenous parameter with unspecified determinants. (Skaperdas, 1992, p.721)

This indicates both the view of power typically adopted in mainstream analysis and the scepticism involved in trying to incorporate it into the analysis in a more general way. It is essentially a one-dimensional view of power, and therefore, although specific and analytically useful, it is too narrow to capture other dimensions of power relations. This is generally true of the type of 'power' discussed in mainstream game theory, which whilst bringing 'power' to a more prominent position has severely restricted its dimensions.

One issue in game theory, which is of importance for considering the role of power is what is usually known as 'cheap talk', that is, any communication that takes place between players prior to the beginning of a particular game, which incurs no cost to any of the players. This is often 'disallowed' on the grounds that if it were permitted it would give rise to an unmanageable number of potential outcomes. (The possible equilibria would clearly be significantly expanded.) This is not to say that some games do not take account of cheap talk, less still that the outcomes are influenced by cheap talk, but once we allow such pre-play communication there is no possibility of guaranteeing that an agreement/solution can be reached, or of predicting what the outcome might be. However, the pre-game environment and inter-play between the players is of great significance in that the initial conditions are crucial to the games solution. Moreover, consideration of the pre-game stage may give rise to a two-dimensional view of power (Lukes's category 2).

One obvious problem of analysing this within a standard game-theoretic framework is that we can always imagine a prior game to the game being specified, and therefore something qualitatively different has to be offered in order to find some alternative explanation of the initial conditions and the environment of the game under analysis. This would be a problem (although clearly not so severe) even in the absence of cheap talk given that the out-come of games is generally sensitive to the initial conditions. That game theory is characterized by multiple equilibria suggests in itself that something more needs to be said about the environmental, institutional and historical conditions in which the game takes place, which might limit the plausible solutions and outcomes.

Another feature of game theory where 'power' is important involves the fact that the solution to certain games appeal to some 'folk theorem'. These involve the following idea. If we consider a repeated game in general, then any feasible expected pay-off can be sustained in equilibrium as long as each player's expected pay-offs are greater than or equal to the pay-off that player is guaranteed if all the other players were to 'gang up' on him or her. If this is so, then if a player is told by the other players to stick to an agreement under threat of all the other players 'ganging up', then no single player has any incentive to deviate and a Nash equilibrium can be sustained. (On this see, for example, Kreps, 1990.) Now this idea clearly must involve some conception of power. How else are we to interpret the threat of players continuing to force a player to conform to an agreement? But although such threats seem to involve a simple one-dimensional view of power, it is far from clear what form such power may take. Is it just a version of market power? Even if it is, the crux of the problem for neoclassical theory is that it does not really have a full theory of market or monopoly power. It has a theory of monopoly, of course, but this is quite different. That no complete theory of monopoly power exists is acknowledged by some mainstream theorists. For example, Kreps (1990) sums up the situation by commenting that a firm's ability to stick to a monopoly price involves a fundamental problem of credibility and reputation, and that 'as long as we avoid … institutional details, it is hard to say much about whether a monopoly can muster credibility' (p. 317).

There is clearly scope therefore for a two-dimensional view of power within mainstream theory, but the nature of such power would be limited by the assumptions made regarding the nature of agency. That is to say, the standard assumption that agents are rational instrumental utilitarians influences the nature and outcome of the game. It is also possible in principle that some type of three-dimensional view of power might be possible within a broad neoclassical framework, although here there are much greater problems. There has been much work in recent years attempting to consider the problem of enforcement within organizations and firms endogenously but that has fallen short of considering endogenous preferences as well. Of course the possibility of endogenous preferences poses severe problems for neoclassical analysis.

As we shall discuss further in a later section, the idea of endogenous preferences is subversive of the welfare basis of mainstream theory and calls into question the foundational assumptions needed to generate virtually all the results of mainstream economics.[1] This is not to say that such an approach is necessarily incorrect (much less that it is not worthwhile) but it does emphasize that mainstream theory adopts a particular perspective which may not be the most useful. It may actually be the case that it is not correct to treat preferences as exogenous and make that the basis of demand theory. Similarly neoclassical production theory may be severely limited by excluding the social relations of production. It would also be the case that the types of neoclassical solution to situations involving one- and two-dimensional views of power would be undermined. However, it would be possible to a degree to introduce the endogeneity of preferences into a framework which adopts views of agency and equilibrium characteristic of neoclassical analysis.

The prominence of power in Austrian economics is quite different to its role in mainstream theory. Austrian writers almost invariably dismissed the idea that power is inherent in 'free' market economies. This does not mean that there is no reference to or discussion of power in Austrian theory. On the contrary, there have been a number of discussions and comments on power by most prominent Austrians, but all have been in an attempt to deny its importance. Although it is not feasible here to consider the Austrians' views on power in depth, the main ideas and issues of contention may be illustrated by considering the main lines of thought that have influenced contemporary views. There are a number of different approaches within Austrian economics, which reach similar conclusions regarding the issue of power but for importantly different reasons. An early example of the dismissal of 'power' is Böhm-Bawerk's well-known essay on 'Control or economic law' (1962/1914). The main thesis of this work is that although power or control[2] may be important in influencing the broader environment, economic laws still apply to market transactions. By this it is meant, for example, that the 'laws' determining price behaviour will apply even in cases of monopoly. This is entirely a neoclassical position. It is important to note that Böhm-Bawerk explicitly excluded cases of robbery, extortion and slavery from his discussion, believing that these belong to a different category of economic problems.

The term 'power' does appear in the Austrian literature even before this time, indeed 'power' quite frequently appears in Menger's *Gründsätze* (1950, 1871).[3] As noted by Vaughn (1990), for example, Menger generally uses the term in the sense of power over resources or enabling powers rather than power relations between individual agents. This is similar to the aforementioned uses by Böhm-Bawerk, but it should be noted that Menger was certainly concerned with the exercise of economic power which threatened the proper functioning of the market. There are examples in the *Gründsätze* where Menger is critical of situations in which power is exercised over certain resources and land (see Young, 1992). This concern, however, is again largely similar to neoclassical concerns regarding market power. Nevertheless, it is important to emphasise the concern for the issue of 'power' particularly in the case of Böhm-Bawerk, who considered it to be threatening to his version of economic theory. This view has remained important in Austrian economics but, as indicated, there are different views as to why power should be expunged from economic theory. To explain these we may briefly consider the main propositions relating to the ideas of Hayek, von Mises and Rothbard.

In Hayek (1960, and most notably 1944) there is a clear reliance on the notion of competitive capitalism when discussing power and coercion. Virtually all of Hayek's claims about the absence of power from market capitalism are with reference to a competitive market. For example, in Hayek (1944), in arguing his central thesis that it is the state which wields power and that this is an 'evil' which is to be contained, he writes:

> to believe that power which is thus conferred on the state is merely transferred to it from others is erroneous. It is a power which is newly created and which in a *competitive* society nobody possesses. So long as property is divided among many owners,[4] none of them acting independently has exclusive power to determine the income and position of particular people – nobody is tied to him except by the fact that he may offer better terms than anybody else. (Hayek, 1944, p. 77; emphasis added)

The idea that there is no power relation inherent in voluntary exchanges is crucial and runs throughout Austrian literature. However, given the reliance on competitive competition in dismissing the importance of power, we then must consider cases where there is some degree of monopoly over resources or source of employment which, it might be argued, is often found in practice. Obviously such cases are of concern in mainstream theory, but the Austrian line generally is to argue that exchange (contracts) is still voluntary in such situations. The problem here for the Hayek view is that when considering certain 'extreme' cases he appears to draw back from the strong subjectivist liberal argument and introduces rather *ad hoc* utilitarian ideas. Hayek (1960), for instance, gives a number of cases where government intervention is justified or where the 'normal' principles of the market are modified (for example, in the case of compulsory purchase orders when the national interest is at stake, or a doctor providing free service to a dying person). Once such 'modifications' or qualifications are introduced, of course, then we are entitled to question the wholly voluntary nature of exchange.

The von Misean position is somewhat different, reflecting perhaps the methodological differences that exist between von Mises and other Austrian theorists.[5] Broadly, the position articulated in von Mises (1949) is that power is connected with the state and is generally absent from free-market economies. This gives rise to the well-known policy view that the state should retreat from economic interventions. Von Mises however did develop a view of monopoly power based on the exclusive ownership of natural resources and limited-space monopoly (among several other conditions), which has been criticized by Austrians of a more radical subjectivist position on the grounds that even in these cases consumer sovereignty is not infringed (see O'Driscoll, 1982).

One proponent of this strong subjectivist line is Rothbard (1962). Rothbard (1970) develops these views with specific reference to power, again indicating the longstanding antipathy of Austrians to the intrusion of power into economic analysis. Rothbard defines 'economic power' as 'simply the right under freedom to refuse to make an exchange. Every man has this power. Every man has the same right to refuse to make a preferred exchange' (1970, p. 229). The state on the other hand wields political power and at various points Rothbard refers to 'violent' state intervention and to the 'coercive monopoly' position of state enterprises. Thus, as with Hayek and von Mises, exchange is wholly voluntary and the problem of 'power' and monopoly originate with state intervention. In elaborating these claims Rothbard emphasizes the distinction between 'power over nature' and 'power over man', which parallels and perhaps extends the distinction between economic and political power. Power over nature, it is argued, is essential for the advancement of mankind whereas the power of one person over another does not contribute to progress.

Although Rothbard's views are clearly related to the ideas expressed by von Mises (particularly in von Mises, 1949), there would appear to be a critical difference between the two on the precise role of power.[6] As indicated, Rothbard (1970) effectively dismisses the importance of power to market transactions, but he is prepared to admit that there may be some coercive behaviour by individuals. This, however, is outside the scope of market transactions; it might involve, for example, acts of violence or threats of violence by one agent on another and such problems are subject to legal restraint and not part of the economic domain. This, however, is not the view that is taken by von Mises (1949). Von Mises denies the relevance of 'power', not by restricting it to another (non-economic) domain but by arguing that it is of no particular significance *why* an agent decides to transact at a particular price. That is to say, even if 'power' takes the form of coercion and such coercion is employed by one agent over another in determining the price of a particular transaction, it is of no relevance for a theory of prices. In Misean terminology the motives are of no significance for catallactics. This view is difficult to sustain given that we would generally consider assumptions regarding the nature of agents' behaviour as an important determinant of economic outcomes (see Hollis, 1987). Similarly, a view which limits all aspects of power to wholly non-economic domains may be regarded as a less than satisfactory approach to market interactions.

In contrast to neoliberal approaches, Marxist or 'radical' theorists have always emphasized the importance of power in economic and social theory and have offered a distinctive view of the meaning and role of power. Again, it is impossible to consider all aspects of the Marxist view of power here, but some of the main perspectives may be indicated. The idea that power is of great significance in economic life was recognized in early Marxist thought including in many aspects of the works of Marx and Engels (for example, Marx and Engels, 1846). Generally speaking, modern Marxian and radical theorists have tried to develop certain aspects of their approach. This has involved the perception of power as a broader and more multidimensional concept than in mainstream analysis. Indeed, it should be recalled that the Lukes-type categorization which has been adopted here is in itself an attempt to put forward a broader, more 'radical' view of power.

An illuminating example of this more radical conception of power is contained in Tucker (1980), who contrasts the work of C.B. MacPherson with the liberal tradition. MacPherson regards power as the ability to exercise human capacities. This involves much more than the standard approach of liberal writers, who in their concern for freedom and choice typically deal with a narrower conception involving an 'absence of constraints imposed by others' (Tucker, 1980, p. 112). Tucker notes that although liberal writers have often acknowledged wider aspects of power, they have normally failed to include these in their own analyses. This would certainly seem to be true of mainstream economists.

As Tucker points out, however, there is a tricky problem with MacPherson's view in that the ability to do something might refer either to the manifestation of power or to a precondition for the exercise of power. Following Tucker (1980), we might regard power as being less 'passive' than ability. Power involves the ability to *change* prevailing conditions. In this context economic actors may be viewed as fulfilling strategic rather than passive roles. This is in contradistinction to the view of agency adopted in traditional neoclassical analysis (and still applies to the competitive model) and also in Austrian theory where an agent's behaviour (somewhat ironically perhaps) is of a passive manner not unlike individual agents under conditions of perfect competition.

As with other schools of thought, there are of course a number of divisions within Marxist-inspired theory and the precise meaning and role of power may differ not unsubstantially. For example, structuralist Marxist approaches differ in important respects from modern radical economic approaches. The structural approach to power is exemplified by Poulantzas (1986), who treats power as 'the capacity of a social class to realise its specific objective interests'. As Lukes (1986) notes, 'for Poulantzas, power identifies the ways in which the system (the ensemble of structures) effects the relations of practices of the various classes in conflict'. In this view class becomes not only a locus but the only locus of power operating through individuals (the 'bearers' or 'supports' of the structure) and its effects are understood solely in terms of the pursuit of class interests' (p. 4). As is well known, structuralist (and functionalist) Marxist theories have been much criticized, not least for their particular view of individual agency. In this context the structuralist view imposes a very specific interpretation of all dimensions of power.

Other radical approaches have been less emphatically concerned with notions of power that relate specifically and only to class struggle (at least in a structuralist interpretation). For example, some radical economists have been concerned to develop theories involving endogenous preferences in an attempt to move towards an analysis which considers the social relations of production. Contributions to this development notably include work by Bowles and Gintis, who have provided new arguments in favour of the 'radical' contention that even competitive capitalism involves a particular set of power relations. In doing so, they adopt a definition of power that concerns 'the capacity of some agents to influence the behaviour of others to their advantage through the threat of imposing sanctions' (Bowles and Gintis, 1992, p. 325).

The claim that there is an unequal relationship between capital and labour in the production process is of course a central Marxian position which distinguishes it from mainstream theory and which gives rise to a completely different welfare view of competitive capitalism. In this sense, Bowles and Gintis and indeed other modern radicals are following in a Marxian tradition, but they are departing from the traditional Marxian view in certain important respects. For example, the emphasis on the nature of *class* relations is less pronounced and most certainly the historical character of these radical critiques is more muted or sometimes absent. (This may be less so with regard to Marglin, 1984, though here too substantial criticisms of the historical character of such an approach have been made.)

Whatever the particular style and emphasis of Marxian and radical analyses, it is clear that the role of power is more significant, wide-reaching and fundamental than in all forms of neoliberal theory. In general, radicals would include all four categories of power outlined previously in their analysis of power relations. It should be recalled, however, that our purpose here is to illuminate and compare different approaches to power in different economic theories and no attempt has been made to assess the superiority of one approach over any other. Therefore, the fact that power often plays what seems to be a more significant role in Marxian theory than in mainstream or Austrian theories does not, of itself, invite the conclusion of its superiority.

CONCLUSION

The general proposition of this chapter is that all the types of economic theory which we have dealt with take a particular view of power either explicitly or implicitly, and that the recognition and discussion of this will furnish a better understanding of the principles/foundations of different economic theories and the ways in which they generate their conclusions.

Our deliberations have shown that the type of 'power' considered in mainstream and Austrian theories has in the main been of a one-dimensional type whereas those within a radical/Marxian framework have included two- and three-dimensional views of power. This is, of course, to be expected. The discussion of power by Lukes on which the three dimensions are based is itself a radical analysis. But, this approach has been helpful in distinguishing between different types of theory and, moreover, it appears that there is scope within mainstream analysis for moving towards a two-dimensional (and in a particular/limited manner, three-dimensional) view of power.

It may be suggested therefore that mainstream theory could be improved by making the particular view of power which is adopted more explicit and by considering wider dimensions of the concept of power. In doing so, of course it would not be necessary to move towards a Marxian position of power. It is clearly possible to maintain an essentially individualist approach while accepting, for example, a two-dimensional view of power. If, however, more radical ideas such as the endogeneity of preferences are embraced by the mainstream then the current formulation of the neoclassical approach would be undermined and a greater similarity with some modern radical approaches would ensue. Here again, the fundamental conflict between individualist and class-based analysis remains. With regard to Austrian theories, there seems less scope for developing multidimensional views of power, although it may be argued that in an attempt to deny the importance of power, the Austrians have in fact demonstrated its potential significance. Indeed, overall, power appears to be of considerable significance with regard to the behavioural foundations of most economic theories. An explicit analysis of its dimensions may therefore be useful in constructing more convincing theories, including those attempting to explain the evolution of institutions.

NOTES

1. Stiglitz (1993) argues that mainstream theory has long recognized certain aspects of endogenous preferences, particularly with respect to advertising and 'subjective utility theory', but there has never been a general acceptance of the idea of endogenously formed preferences and it is clearly the case that all of neoclassical welfare economics is based on exogenous preferences.
2. The original title is 'Macht oder ökonomishes Gesetz'. *Macht* clearly means power, so although control is seen as more appropriate in a certain sense there is little doubt as to Böhm-Bawerk's meaning.
3. Menger's work is usually regarded as the origin of Austrian economics. Though some of his ideas were developed along neoclassical lines, Menger's work is distinctively different to neoclassical theorists in some important respects and has not been regarded as adopting so neoclassical a position as Böhm-Bawerk.
4. It should be noted that by a wide distribution of property rights Hayek is not advocating an equal distribution across individuals throughout the economy. His arguments elsewhere make clear his view that great inequality may at times be consistent with a competitive market economy in which differentials between individuals are necessary from a motivational/incentive standpoint.
5. Philosophically, von Mises adopted a neo-Kantian position (see Parsons, 1990) while Menger had explicitly tried to develop an Aristotelian position. Hayek, though clearly influenced by both, attempted what he believed to be a classical liberal approach.
6. This point is developed in some detail in Young (1993).

REFERENCES

Böhm-Bawerk, E. (1914), 'Macht oder ökonomisches Gesetz?', *Zeitschrift für Volkswirtschaft, Socialpolitik und Verwaltung*, 23(3–4), pp. 205–71. Translated into English as 'Control or economic law?', *Shorter Classics of Böhm-Bawerk*, South Holland, IL: Libertarian Press, 1962.

Bowles, S. and H. Gintis (1992), 'Power and wealth in a competitive capitalist economy', *Philosophy and Public Affairs*, Fall, pp. 71–90.

Dahl, R. (1957), 'The concept of power', *Behavioral Science*, 2, pp. 201–15.

Hayek, F.A. von (1944), *The Road to Serfdom*, London: Routledge.

Hayek, F.A. von (1960), *The Constitution of Liberty*, London: Routledge.

Hollis, J.M. (1987), *The Cunning of Reason*, Cambridge: Cambridge University Press.

Kreps, D. (1990), *Microeconomic Theory*, Hemel Hempstead: Harvester, Wheatsheaf.

Lukes, S. (1974), *Power: A Radical View*, London: Macmillan.

Lukes, S. (ed.) (1986), *Power*, Oxford: Basil Blackwell.

Marglin, S. (1984), 'Knowledge and power', in F. Stephen (ed.), *The Economics of Organisation and Labour*, London: Macmillan, pp. 146–64.

Marx, K. and F. Engels (1964) [1846] *The German Ideology*, Moscow: Progress Publishers.

Menger, C. (1871), *Grundsätze der Volkswirtschaftslehre*, Vienna: Braumülter. Reprinted in F.A. von Hayek (ed.) (1968), *Menger, Gesammelte werke*, Vol. 1, Tübingen: Mohr. English translation in J. Dingwall and B.F. Hoselitz (eds) (1950), *Principles of Economics*, Glencoe, IL: Free Press.

Mises, L. von (1949), *Human Action: A Treatise on Economics*, New Haven, CT: Yale University Press. Based on L. von Mises (1940), *Nationalökonomie: Theorie des Handelns und Wirtschaftens*, Geneva: Editions Union. Reprinted 1980, Munich: Philosophia Verlag.

O'Driscoll, G. (1982), 'Monopoly in theory and practice', in I. Kirzner (ed.), *Method, Process and Austrian Economics*, Washington: Lexington Books, pp. 189–213.

Parsons, S. (1990), 'The philosophical roots of modem Austrian economies: past problems and future prospects', *History of Political Economy*, 22(2) pp. 295–319.

Poulantzas, N. (1986), 'Class power', in S. Lukes (ed.), *Power*, Oxford: Basil Blackwell, pp. 144–55.

Rothbard, M. (1962), *Man, Economy and State*, Vols. 1 and 2, Princeton, NJ: Van Nostrand Reinhold.

Rothbard, M. (1970), *Power and Market*, Kansas City: Sheed Andrews and McNeel.

Rothschild, K. (1971), *Power in Economics*, Harmondsworth: Penguin.

Samuels, W. (ed.) (1979), *The Economy as a System of Power*, New Jersey: Transaction Books.

Skaperdas, S. (1992), 'Cooperation, conflict and power in the absence of property rights', *American Economic Review*, 82(4), September, pp. 720–39.

Stiglitz, J. (1993), 'Post Walrasian and post Marxian economics', *Journal of Economic Perspectives*, 7(1) pp. 109–14.

Tucker, D.F.B. (1980), *Marxism and Individualism*, Oxford: Basil Blackwell.

Vaughn, K. (1990), 'The Mengerian roots of the Austrian revival', *History of Political Economy*, Vol. 22, pp. 379–407.

Young, D. (1992), 'Austrian views on monopoly: insights and problems', *Review of Political Economy*, 4(2).

Young, D. (1993), 'Power and Austrian economics', Department of Economics, University of Manchester, mimeo, pp. 203–25.

4. Discovery versus creation: implications of the Austrian view of the market process

Sandye Gloria-Palermo

The Austrian tradition can hardly be described as a unified paradigm. The divergences between the foremost exponents are striking. Consider for instance the following controversies: Menger explicitly rejects the Böhm-Bawerkian theory of capital and interest; Wieser develops interventionist advice that contrasts with the liberal ideology of the whole tradition; Hayek refuses Misesian apriorism; Lachmann and Kirzner sharply disagree on the role of the equilibrium concept in economic analysis.

Nevertheless, there seems to be a ground upon which modern Austrians (from Hayek, 1937, onwards) are relatively unified: the view of the market as a process.[1]

In this chapter, we will stress in a first step that beyond this apparent agreement, there is no unity at all. Indeed, it is possible to define two distinct conceptions of the market process within the realm of the Austrian tradition itself, namely the one of Hayek–Kirzner and that of Lachmann. We will in a second step investigate the origins of this divide. We will show that the cleavage lies in the exclusion of the creative dimension of the human mind from the Kirzner–Hayek conception: by contrast with Lachmann's view, agents are limited to discovery, discovery of profit opportunities and discovery of knowledge.

The distinction between discovery and creation implies much more than a mere intellectual curiosity about historical and analytical linkages between authors. More precisely, one of the issues at stake concerns the normative level: an analysis limited to discovery can attempt to prove the efficiency of unhampered markets, whereas the introduction of creation leads to the recognition of the coexistence of equilibrium and disequilibrium market forces.

A SYNTHETIC REPRESENTATION OF THE AUSTRIAN MARKET PROCESS

Within the Austrian logic, the market is viewed as a process; its thrust results from the interaction among individual plans. Agents are conceived of as dynamic actors by contrast with the orthodox definition of *homo economicus*, a mere reactor to external stimuli. The market process is more precisely the outcome of the succession of three sequences:

- confrontation of individual plans: the market configuration is the result of the confrontation of the effective individual actions that took place in the past;
- revision of plans: if inconsistencies between plans occur, that is, if plans are not well coordinated, it means that some individuals failed to reach their objectives; they will be led to modify their original plans;
- consequences of the adjustments: the interaction of the new plans leads to a new market configuration.

From this very general framework, it is possible to distinguish between three distinct views of the market process within the Austrian tradition itself: the views of Kirzner, Hayek and Lachmann. In order to delineate the specificities of each one, we propose the following conceptualization (see Figure 4.1).

This diagram is useful for two reasons. First, it provides a synthetic overview in which it is possible to position, despite their diversity, the three authors and their conception of the market process. Second, starting from this framework, we can determine precisely what are the splitting points between the authors.

THE KIRZNERIAN MARKET PROCESS

The Kirznerian view of the market process flows from the theory of entrepreneurship. Kirzner introduces a new dimension in the concept of human action inherited from Mises: entrepreneurship. Entrepreneurship expresses itself through the quality of alertness. An alert individual is able to find unexploited profit opportunities. Profit opportunities consist in price discrepancies between sellers and buyers in the same market and reflect the imperfection of the economic configuration: in a perfectly coordinated world, all profit opportunities have been exploited and there is no room for entrepreneurship; in a disequilibrium world, discoordination is the consequence of imperfect knowledge, and imperfect knowledge is precisely the source of profit opportunities. The alert agent is not an individual possessing more knowledge than others

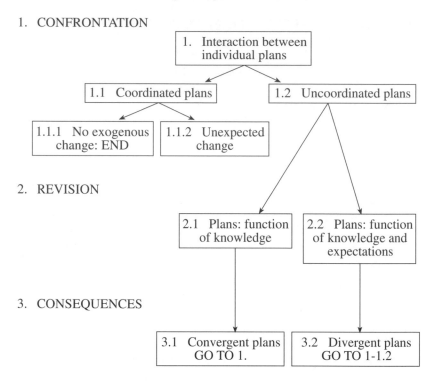

Figure 4.1   A general representation of the Austrian market process

but an individual whose incentive is, through the existence of profit opportunities, to find new knowledge. Entrepreneurship consists in the exploitation of the profit opportunities discovered through alertness. This category of action has an equilibrating effect on the economic configuration: entrepreneurs contribute to the diffusion of the new knowledge their alertness allows them to discover. The exploitation of a profit opportunity renders available for all agents the existence of a punctual disadjustment on the market. They can revise their plan on the basis of this new knowledge. The degree of coordination depends precisely on the amount of knowledge available to agents. From that perspective, entrepreneurship is considered to be the propeller of the adjustment towards equilibrium. The role of the entrepreneur is to reduce the initial ignorance of the economy through the discovery and diffusion of new knowledge that is revealed by the exploitation of profit opportunities.

> For me the changes the entrepreneur initiates are always toward the hypothetical state of equilibrium; they are changes brought about in response to an existing

pattern of mistaken decisions, a pattern characterised by missed opportunities. The entrepreneur, in my view, brings into mutual adjustment those discordant elements which resulted from prior market ignorance. (Kirzner, 1973, p. 73)

The Kirznerian market process stemming from entrepreneurship theory is given the following conceptualization (see Figure 4.2).

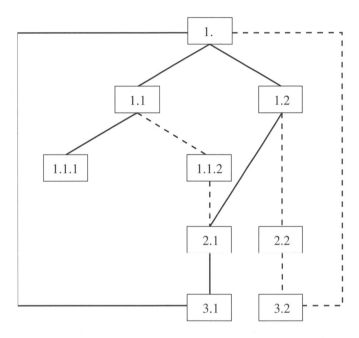

Figure 4.2   The Kirznerian view of the market process

Suppose that the initial market configuration is one of ignorance, that is, a situation in which individual plans are not coordinated (1.2); discoordination means existence of unexploited profit opportunities. Alert entrepreneurs notice these possibilities and take advantage of profitable arbitrages between price discrepancies on markets. This kind of action conducive to reducing ignorance in the decision-making environment (2.1).

The process converges towards equilibrium as profit opportunities are found and exploited (3.1). The equilibrium configuration is reached when the whole set of knowledge which defines the economic configuration is made available to individuals, through entrepreneurship ($1 \rightarrow 1.1 \rightarrow 1.1.1$). Such an adjustment mechanism is based on the implicit assumption of the existence of an underlying reality to be discovered. Equilibrium is reached only when the set of knowledge is made fully explicit for agents; entrepreneurship is the element of change from ignorance to perfect knowledge of the data that defined the given and stable economic configuration.

THE HAYEKIAN MARKET PROCESS

The Kirznerian conception represents a specific instance of the Hayekian market process. The specificity stems from two circumstances:

1. On the one hand, Hayek does not rely on the assumption of an immutable reality that is out there and waiting to be discovered once and for all. His world is one of continual change. Unexpected change results from changes in exogenous variables; consequently, and unlike Kirzner, Hayek sees no use in focusing ' ... on a long-term equilibrium which in an ever changing world can never be reached' (Hayek, 1946, p. 101). The set of knowledge to be discovered through competition is not immutable and plans have to continuously adapt to this circumstance. Nevertheless, both of the authors have the same objective: to stress the efficiency of the market process, defined as a coordinating device.

2. On the other hand, the argumentation provided by Hayek is much more general than the theory of entrepreneurship: the author develops a conception of competition as a discovery procedure. The price system resulting from individual confrontations in an unhampered market provides relevant signals for agents to adjust their plans. These prices are not equilibrium prices (in an ever-changing world) but the market order is built precisely from the negative feedbacks that agents extract from them (see Hayek, 1946, p. 184). Discoordination stems from the diffuse nature of knowledge upon which agents rely to form their plan; competition, through the role of the price system, is a procedure of discovery and diffusion of knowledge and thus plays a coordinating function. According to Hayek, competition represents the most efficient procedure for knowledge discovery. This assertion is indeed a strong hypothesis. The author justifies the existence of a tendency towards equilibrium on the basis of empirical evidence:

> It is only with this assertion [the supposed existence of a tendency towards equilibrium] that economics ceases to be an exercise of pure logic and becomes an empirical science; ... In the light of our analysis of the meaning of a state of equilibrium it should be easy to say what is the real content of the assertion that a tendency towards equilibrium exists. It can hardly mean anything but that under certain conditions the knowledge and intentions of the different members of society are supposed to come more and more into agreement ... In this form the assertion of the existence of a tendency towards equilibrium is clearly an

empirical proposition, that is, an assertion about what happens in the real world which ought, at least in principle, to be capable of verification. (Hayek, 1937, p. 44)

The Hayekian procedure thus unrolls as follows (see Figure 4.3). In an inefficient configuration (1.2), market prices act as signposts for agents, providing new knowledge about the direction in which plans have to be modified (2.1). In that perspective, competition is by assumption an efficient device of knowledge discovery and entails the convergence of plans (3.1). The occurrence of unexpected change prevents the economy from reaching a long-term equilibrium (1.1.2). Competition permits the adaptation to the new configuration via its capacity to diffuse the new relevant knowledge (2.1 and so on).

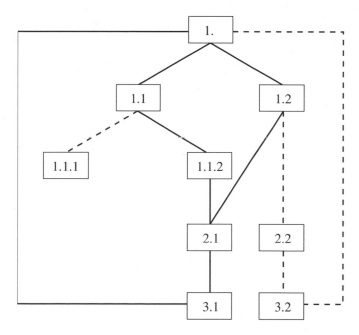

Figure 4.3   The Hayekian conception of the market process

THE LACHMANNIAN MARKET PROCESS

The logical founding of Lachmann's view of the market process is similar in all points but one to the Kirzner–Hayek conception. The splitting point concerns precisely the definition of individual plans. According to Hayek, plans are conceived on the basis of the subjective interpretation of past experience. Lachmann introduces a second dimension, namely that plans are the outcome of the interaction of two elements:

- knowledge as Hayek puts it, that is, a diagnostic of the economic situation understood as interpretation of experience;
- expectations, that is, an interpretation of the future situation, understood as imagination.

> ... plans are products of mental activity which is oriented no less to an imagined future than to an experienced past. (Lachmann, 1969, p. 95)

Given this enlargement of the concept of plan, the resulting view of the market process contrasts sharply with the traditional one – a true butterfly effect![2] Market is described as a continuous process, characterized by unexpected change and inconsistency of plans. This latter feature is the direct consequence of the introduction of subjective expectations. Plans are divergent because subjective expectations are based on the image agents form about an 'unknown though not unimaginable' future (Lachmann, 1976a, p. 59). Competition could be conducive to the diffusion of relevant knowledge, but good expectations cannot be diffused by any ways, for once they have revealed themselves as relevant they are already obsolete and need to be revised; no *ex ante* criterion of success exists. Inconsistency of plans challenges the traditional view of a tendency towards equilibrium. Market is an undetermined process governed by the interaction of equilibrium *and disequilibrium forces*.

The representation of the Lachmannian market process concerns only the right branch of our diagram (see Figure 4.4). Inconsistency of plans is the rule and reflects the fact that plans are built up not only from subjective knowledge but also from subjective expectations (2.2 → 3.2). As a result, the economic configuration emerging from the interaction of individual plans is definitely one of discoordination (3.2 → 1. → 1.2). In that perspective, there is no more reason to emphasize the equilibrating function of the market. Divergence of plans is the consequence of the extension of the subjective dimension to expectations and represents, within the Lachmannian view, the propeller of change.

> The market process consists of a sequence of individual interactions, each denoting the encounter (and sometimes collision) of a number of plans, which, while coherent individually and reflecting the individual equilibrium, are incoherent as a group. The process would not go otherwise. (Lachmann, 1976b, p.131)

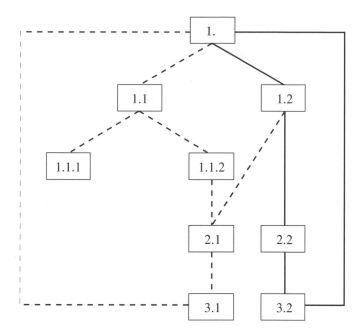

Figure 4.4   The Lachmannian view of the market process

DISCOVERY VERSUS CREATION

The cleavage between the traditional and the Lachmannian view of the market process proceeds from a different conception of the individual agent. Both lines consider the agent as an actor, in continuity with Mises' developments on human action (Mises, 1949). However, the subjective dimension of the human mind is extended to creativity within Lachmann's view, as opposed to the Hayek–Kirzner one, which limits itself to discovery. The creative agent builds plans upon his or her imagination of the future whereas the discoverer elaborates plans exclusively on the basis of the knowledge at his or her disposal. In that perspective, the degree of coordination of individual plans, that is, the degree of efficiency of the market process, depends on the stock of knowledge it allows agents to discover and to use. Competition is analysed as an efficient – the most efficient – discovery procedure and the role of the entrepreneur consists in finding unnoticed profit opportunities and diffusing the knowledge they reveal through their exploitation.

The sharp distinction between discovery and creation is never made explicit by the authors concerned. Nevertheless, there is no doubt that the thorough-going choice in the words of Hayek gives evidence for a conscious recognition of the existence of an issue; the term 'creation' is carefully avoided. Maybe Kirzner makes it more explicit when he recognizes the relevance of the criticisms addressed to his theory of entrepreneurship:

> My theory of entrepreneurship has sometimes been criticised as viewing the future as a kind of tapestry waiting to be unfolded: it is already there it is simply behind the screen; it only has to be unrolled and then the future will come into the field of vision, whereas the truth surely is, the critics point out, that the future does not 'exist' in any philosophically valid sense. It must be created so that the notion of alertness in the sense of seeing what is out there in the future is a mistaken notion. I recognise the philosophical validity of this kind of criticism. (Interview in Boehm, 1992)

Beyond the conflict under analysis, the distinction between discovery and creativity appears also to contribute to a large extent to the tensions characterizing the odd relationships between traditional Austrians and Schumpeter.

Consider first of all their opposition regarding the theory of the trade cycle and the role of credit: according to Hayek, economic fluctuations are initiated by the reduction of the monetary rate of interest below its natural rate, through credit creation; such a reduction is analysed as an erroneous signal provided by the banks, without real counterpart (increase in monetary savings). This signal acts as an incentive to investment for entrepreneurs. Crisis is precisely the consequence of the lengthening of the production period in a context where intertemporal preferences stay the same. In this analysis, banks appear to deteriorate the ability of the free market to provide good signals for investment. In the Schumpeter perspective, the role of credit is exactly drawn the other way round: credit represents a necessary condition for the system to evolve from one configuration to another. The impulsion of change comes from the creative behaviour of entrepreneurs who, instead of being limited to the discovery and interpretation of the relevant market signals, introduce innovations in the system: new ways of doing things and new things. The entrepreneur is a disrupter of stability and the credit system is indispensable for the viability of the transition he initiates.

This consideration leads to a second circumstance in which traditional Austrians stand in stark opposition to Schumpeter: precisely the role of the entrepreneur. According to Kirzner, the entrepreneur fills an equilibrating function through the discovery of unnoticed profit opportunities, bringing the economy from ignorance towards equilibrium, that is, a configuration in which all profit opportunities have been discovered and where the whole stock of knowledge is available to agents. In the Schumpeterian analysis, the well-known expression of creative destruction synthesizes the extent of the gap: the entrepreneur is the agent of change and disequilibrium. Creativity means the break in continuity towards a disequilibrium dynamic. The contrast between the Kirzner–Hayek view and that of Schumpeter is perfectly well drawn by Kirzner himself:

> For Schumpeter the essence of entrepreneurship is the ability to break away from routine, to destroy existing structures, to move the system away from the even, circular flow of equilibrium. For us, on the other hand, the crucial element in entrepreneurship is the ability to see unexploited opportunities whose prior existence meant that the initial evenness of the circular flow was illusory – that, far from being a state of equilibrium, it represented a situation of disequilibrium inevitably destined to be disrupted. For Schumpeter the entrepreneur is the disruptive, disequilibrating force that dislodges the market from the somnolence of equilibrium; for us the entrepreneur is the equilibrating force whose activity responds to the existing tensions and provides those corrections for which the unexploited opportunities have been crying out. (Kirzner, 1973, p.127)

The Schumpeterian actor creates profit opportunities whereas the Kirznerian entrepreneur is limited to the discovery of existing opportunities.

Harking back to the present issue, a set of questions arises. Why do not traditional Austrians follow Lachmann in his extension of the subjectivist dimension to expectations? Why is the Austrian theory of the trade cycle based on an implicit assumption of perfectly elastic expectations, and why do not Mises and his followers deepen the implications of the speculative dimension inherent in every human action? All these questions are a symptom of the same phenomenon and call for the same answer: the rejection of the creative dimension of the human mind from the analysis.

According to us, Lachmann does not go far enough in his analysis. More precisely, he wonders why

> Austrians fail to grasp with both hands this golden opportunity to enlarge the basis of their approach and, by and large, treated the subject [of subjective expectations] rather gingerly? (Lachmann, 1976a, p. 58)

However, the author does not come to grips with the problem. He dodges the question simply by saying that at this point there seems to be a real conundrum, or referring in his deepest argument to the strict adhesion of Mises to a neo-Kantian rationalism that impeded him from taking into account the full consequences of the very idea of time. In that perspective, Lachmann quotes Shackle, according to who in 'time is the denial of the omnipotence of reason' (Shackle, 1972, p. 27); Mises deals with the dimension of time and more precisely with a Bergsonian conception of time; he therefore acknowledges the speculative aspect inherent in every human action but never went further in this recognition, for instance through the development of an analysis of the subjective nature of expectations. No reason is given for Hayek's limitation to knowledge discovery, despite the fact that the adhesion of the author to the subjectivist paradigm is by and large recognized. The following well-known quotation appears numerous times in both Kirzner's and Lachmann's works:

> It is probably no exaggeration to say that every important advance in economic theory during the last hundred years was a further step in the consistent application of subjectivism. (Hayek, 1952, p. 31)

Why then are traditional Austrians reluctant to extend the subjectivism of tastes and preferences to expectations? This attitude may appear curious given that their adhesion to the subjectivist paradigm is beyond doubt and the introduction of the creative dimension of the human mind through imagination seems to follow the natural course of progress described by Hayek in the foregoing quotation. There seems to be no logical reason for this neglect. Moreover, the limitation of human action to discovery contradicts the emphasis Austrians put on time and its implications, namely uncertainty and error.

Ultimately, there seems to be only one reason that justifies such disregard. We are here referring to an ideological reason; the fact is that the introduction of imagination, that is, of the creative dimension, would have overwhelming consequences for the representation of the market process. Consider precisely the results reached by Lachmann: we stressed above that the definition of plans in terms of knowledge – discovery dimension – and expectations – creative dimension – leads to the recognition of the influence of both equilibrating and disequilibrating forces. The existence of a tendency towards equilibrium brought about by competition and market activities is theoretically questioned; theory can do no more than describe the market as an indeterministic process, the efficiency of which (in terms of plan coordination) can no longer be established.

This result stands in sharp conflict with the normative objectives of traditional Austrians, oriented towards an unconditional defence of *laissez-faire* and the free market. Oakeshott (1962, p. 21) characterizes in one expression the unifying feature of Hayek's works: it is 'a plan to resist all planning'. This applies to the whole Austrian tradition … except Lachmann.

The attitude of traditional Austrians towards Lachmann is rather ambivalent. This stems from the fact that the results of his analysis, quite embarrassingly for anti-interventionist supporters, are built upon a deductive framework the foundations of which are the expression of the purest Austrian essence: the enlargement of the subjectivist dimension cannot be criticized for it represents an improvement, in Hayek's sense, towards a deeper understanding of complex socio-economic phenomena, and the introduction of expectations in the definition of plan does nothing more than make explicit Mises' assertion of the speculative dimension inherent in every human action. As a result, what is criticized is not the issue of subjective expectations, that is, the full recognition of freedom of choice, but its logical implications, namely the view of market as a non-convergent process. More precisely, critics typically accuse Lachmann of theoretical nihilism. Traditional Austrians underline the indeterminist result of his approach: the market is the outcome of a constellation of divergent forces and this is strictly speaking all that can be deduced theoretically from the analysis.

However, such critics ignore the endeavour of the author to show that the alternative does not stand between determinism and chaos. The strict indeterminacy of market process is evidence of the limits of pure abstraction. However, the task of the theoretician does not finish at this point. The pure theory of the market process as we presented it in Figure 4.1 cannot go beyond the relatively general assertion of indeterminacy, *unless the decision-making environment is specified*. According to Lachmann (1986, ch. 6), economists should aim to provide not an abstract and general theory of the market process but different theories of market processes. The author refers to an ideal-typical method of analysis as it is advocated in the works of Max Weber. More precisely, the general framework of Figure 4.1 should be enriched through the specification of the institutional set-up that characterizes the typical process under analysis. Our framework thus needs to be completed by a general theory of institutions. Such a theory should make level 2 of our general diagram more precise. In that perspective, Lachmann's theory of institutions, as he developed it in his 1970 book, is an attempt to investigate the role of institutions in the formation and revision of individual plans. Institutions, described as reference points in a world of radical uncertainty, serve as benchmarks, guides to the elaboration of plans.

> An institution provides means of orientation to a large number of actors. It enables them to coordinate their actions by means of orientation to a common signpost. ... [Institutions] enable us to rely on the actions of thousands of anonymous others about whose individual purposes and plans we can know nothing. They are nodal points of society, coordinating the actions of millions whom they relieve of the need to acquire and digest detailed knowledge about others and form detailed expectations about their future action. (Lachmann, 1970, pp. 49–50)

The theory of institutions fills a different part in Lachmann's approach to the market process compared with the Hayekian logic. Hayek's theories of cultural evolution and spontaneous order are oriented towards a different end, namely the establishment of the superior efficiency of spontaneous phenomena over planned ones. The Hayekian theory of institutions constitutes another set of arguments for justifying the assumption of the existence of a market tendency towards equilibrium. On the contrary, Lachmann's theory of institutions constitutes more than an implicit assumption that underlines the view of the market process.

We reach here the real limit of Lachmann's developments: he lacks a general and unified theory of institutions to complete the exposition of the market process, and without such a theory, his view of the market process is indeed subject to the criticism of theoretical nihilism. Nevertheless, the orientation is given and maybe we could find here the ground for a fruitful cooperation with the institutionalist logic.

NOTES

1. See Dolan (1976), especially the articles from Lachmann (1976b), 'On the central concept of Austrian economics: market process' and Kirzner (1976), 'Equilibrium versus market process'.
2. From now on, the term 'traditional', when employed to characterize an Austrian proposition, will refer to the Kirzner–Hayek view of the market process.

REFERENCES

Boehm, S. (1992), 'Austrian economics and the theory of entrepreneurship: I.M. Kirzner interviewed by Stephan Boehm on 2 May 1989', *Review of Political Economy*, 4(1), pp. 95–110.

Dolan, E. (ed.) (1976), *The Foundations of Modern Austrian Economics*, Kansas City: Sheed and Ward.

Hayek, F.A. (1937), 'Economics and knowledge', *Economica*, (13).

Hayek, F.A. (1946), 'The Meaning of Competition', conference, Princeton University, 20 May, in Hayek (1949), p. 189.

Hayek, F.A. (1949), *Individualism and Economic Order*, London: Routledge and Kegan Paul.

Hayek, Friedrich A. (1952), *The Counter-revolution of Science: Studies on the Abuse of Reason*, 1st edn., Glencoe, IL: Free Press.

Kirzner, Israel M. (1973), *Competition and Entrepreneurship*, Chicago: University of Chicago Press.

Kirzner, Israel M. (1976), 'Equilibrium versus the market process', in E. Dolan (ed.), *The Foundations of Modern Austrian Economics*, Kansas City: Sheed and Ward, pp. 115–25.

Lachmann, L. (1969), 'Methodological individualism and the market process', in Eric Streissler (ed.), *Roads to Freedom,* Essays in Honour of Friedrich A. von Hayek, London: Free Press of Glencoe, pp. 89–103.

Lachmann, L. (1970), *The Legacy of Max Weber*, London: Heinemann.

Lachmann, L. (1976a), 'From Mises to Shackle: an essay on Austrian economics and the kaleidic society', *Journal of Economic Literature*, 14, pp. 54–62.

Lachmann, L. (1976b), 'On the central concept of Austrian economics: market process', in E. Dolan (ed.), (1976), pp. 126–33.

Lachmann, L. (1986), *The Market as an Economic Process*, Oxford: Basil Blackwell.

Mises, L. von (1949), *Human Action, a Treatise on Economics*, London: William Hodge and Company Limited.
Oakeshott, M. (1962), *Rationalism in Politics and Other Essays*, London: Methuen.
Shackle, G.L.S. (1972), *Epistemics and Economics: A Critique of Economic Doctrines*, Cambridge: Cambridge University Press.

5. Determinants of supplier dependence: an empirical study

Hans Berger, Niels G. Noorderhaven and Bart Nooteboom*

INTRODUCTION

According to transaction cost economics (TCE), as formulated by Oliver Williamson (1975, 1979, 1985, 1991), the governance of vertical interfirm relations is determined predominantly by the degree to which assets are specific to the transaction relation. In the absence of safeguards, asset specificity leads to vulnerability to opportunistic rent-seeking by the other party (Klein, *et al.* 1978). Therefore the alignment of the level of asset specificity and the configuration of safeguards is important. The basic explanatory scheme of TCE is given in Figure 5.1.

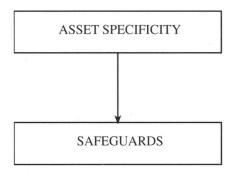

Figure 5.1   A simple model based on TCE

At low levels of asset specificity arm's-length market relations are expected because, in the absence of relation-specific assets that need to be protected, this governance structure is efficient and offers strong incentives. At high levels of asset specificity, on the other hand, market relations break down because the firm incurring the specific investments finds insufficient protection. Therefore, integration of both firms under common ownership and hierarchical control of transactions is to be expected.

At intermediate levels of asset specificity, full integration would not be efficient, but a governance structure offering more protection than a pure market relation will have to be erected. In this case the relationship is more durable and tight than the typical market relationship, but at the same time looser than the relationship between parts of one and the same firm, and can be called a 'hybrid, compared with the pure forms of market and hierarchy' (Williamson, 1991).

The two most important mechanisms for safeguarding intermediate levels of asset specificity are legal ordering and private ordering. In the case of legal ordering, detailed, legally enforceable, long-term contracts are specified in which as many contingencies as possible are dealt with. However, no contract covering a transaction of some complexity and duration can ever be complete. Therefore in hybrid interfirm relations, formal contracts are often replaced by or complemented with other arrangements, aimed at establishing a better balance between the vulnerabilities of both parties.

These other arrangements go under the name of 'private ordering' because their efficacy does not depend on the use of legal courts. An example of private ordering is an arrangement according to which the assets that are specific to the production for a certain buyer are paid for and owned by that buyer, so-called 'quasi-integration' (see Monteverde and Teece, 1982, Blois, 1972). In this way the scope for opportunistic behaviour by the buyer in hybrid relationships is reduced.

In this chapter we focus on the market and hybrid relationships with suppliers of one particular buyer, a Dutch manufacturer of office equipment. The level of asset specificity may be assumed to vary between these relationships, and – following transaction cost reasoning – we expect parallel variations in supplier dependence and the kinds of safeguards (legal and private ordering) installed. Whereas most of the literature deals with a broadly defined market–hierarchy dichotomy or a market–hybrid–hierarchy trichotomy, we focus on the variation of specific safeguards within market and hybrid relationships.

PERCEIVED DEPENDENCE

In received TCE, the perception of managers is seen as relatively unimportant. The objective circumstances call for one or the other governance structure, and a manager who fails to interpret the signals correctly will bring his firm to bankruptcy.

In our view, received TCE does insufficient justice to the fundamental uncertainty managers of business firms face, and falls short of acknowledging the stringent boundaries to the rational capabilities of human decision-makers. For instance, Williamson (1985) assumes that the sometimes very complex private ordering arrangements proposed by TCE are completely designed *ex ante*. A very high strain is put on the rational faculties of parties if they are to design the private order that is to discipline the relationship before the actual start of the transactions. While TCE ostensibly employs a bounded rationality assumption as proposed by Simon, the theory is also characterized by a 'strong commitment to intended rationality' (Williamson, 1985, p. 387).

However, there is no unambiguous information, nor a simple algorithm, for managers deciding on the optimal governance structure for interfirm relations. Managers can only advance on the basis of their own imperfect perceptions, using trial and error, and making the most of an abundance of equivocal signs. Given the importance of these perceptions, they should explicitly be taken into account in a theory of interfirm relations (see Dietrich, 1994).

The insertion of perception in the causal chain between asset specificity and governance structure has several implications. In the first place, perception may dampen the effect of changes in asset specificity. A supplier's asset specificity may grow over time (for example, in the form of skills and knowledge) without the increase being perceived. Or a supplier may notice an increase of asset specificity, and perceive an increase in dependence, but nevertheless refrain from demanding a change in the governance structure. Threshold effects are likely to occur.

Secondly, the perception of dependence will be influenced not only by the level of asset specificity, but also by other factors. Some factors, like the proportion of total turnover made up by the sales to a particular buyer, will contribute positively to perceived dependence. Other factors, in particular those discussed in the following two subsections of this chapter, may have a negative effect on perceived dependence. In sum, the inclusion of perceived dependence in the model has the effect of opening up the analysis for factors not taken into consideration in received TCE.

Moreover, perceived dependence and governance structure may affect each other. A higher perceived dependence will cause a manager to demand more stringent safeguards, but once these safeguards have been installed, they have the effect of mitigating perceived dependence. Therefore the level of perceived dependence interpreted as independent from asset specificity and governance structure is hardly meaningful. In combination, however, these concepts can be very informative. To anticipate the discussion of the empirical investigation in the following sections, if for some reason or the other the governance structure is not adequately aligned with the level of asset specificity, this may result in a high level of perceived dependence on the part of the party that has incurred the investments in these assets. In this way perceived dependence can serve as a thermometer for the adequacy of the safeguards installed.

We will now turn to the discussion of the factors that should in our view be incorporated into a theory of vertical interfirm relations.

NETWORK EMBEDDEDNESS

Parties in a particular transaction relation normally also maintain relations with many other firms. In some instances all these relationships may be completely self-contained. If this is the case a theory isolating a particular transaction relation from all other relations does not neglect valuable information. Most of the time, however, there will exist multiple relations between buying and selling firms in a certain industry and in a certain region. When this is the case, the focal relation is said to be 'embedded' in a network of social relations. The implications of this condition have to be taken into account (Granovetter, 1985, 1992).

Network embeddedness may influence the relationship between asset specificity and governance structure, leading to the installation of safeguards that on the face of it are either too weak or too strong. The direction of this influence depends on the relative network positions of the parties. Two cases with relatively straightforward implications will be reviewed here: 'positive' and 'negative' network embeddedness (as seen from the position of the supplier).

In the case of positive network embeddedness, the supplier uses inputs from several subcontractors that are in no direct relationship with the buying firm. Ibis means that the supplier performs a coordinating function for the buyer. An example of this network configuration is the Japanese automobile industry, in which main suppliers coordinate the inputs of second- and third-tier subcontractors that are not directly in contact with the automobile manufacturers (see Asanuma, 1989).

In the opposite case of negative network embeddedness, the supplier does not only sell to a particular buyer directly, but also indirectly. That is, part of the total turnover of the supplier consists of deliveries to third firms, which use these inputs in their production for the same buyer firm. In this situation the supplier is more dependent, for not only the direct but also the indirect sales to the buyer firm are at risk in the case of a conflict. At least this is the case if the buyer firm is assumed to be able to persuade the third firms to discontinue buying from the supplier in question.

In the case of positive network embeddedness the supplier can be somewhat less easily disposed of, for the buyer would also have to replace the network of contacts it maintains. Therefore, other things being equal, a supplier in a position of positive network embeddedness can be expected to demand less stringent safeguards and/or express a lesser sense of dependence. Negative network embeddedness, all other things equal, makes us expect more stringent safeguards, or a greater sense of dependence in their absence.

THE TIME DIMENSION

Transaction relations are embedded not only in networks of relationships, but also in time. Temporal embeddedness refers to the history of the transaction relationship, and to associated expectations with regard to future transactions. If two parties have been doing business together for a long time, and if this relationship is relatively satisfactory, the expectation grows that they will be doing business together in the future.

Ibis expectation is not necessarily based on rational considerations, but may largely be unconscious. Repeated interactions lead to the forming of habits and the institutionalization of behaviour (Berger and Luckmann, 1966; Zucker, 1987). Both processes have as their effect that patterns of behaviour are shielded from rational decision-making in the pursuit of efficiency. Case study research has borne out that in industrial buying relations buyers display a strong tendency to persist in the use of existing suppliers (Woodside and Möller, 1992). This kind of inertia has to be reckoned with in a theory of vertical interfirm relations.

Other things being equal, we expect that in a relationship that is temporally embedded, that is, in which habitualization and institutionalization of interactions have taken place, a given level of asset specificity will lead to a lower perceived dependence. At least the risk associated with dependence will be smaller, as the relationship is assumed to continue indefinitely. The negative relationship between temporal embeddedness and perceived dependence will in turn, *ceteris paribus*, lead to less stringent safeguards.

TRUST

The third concept we propose to add to the analysis is trust. To 'trust' another party means to engage voluntarily in a course of action the outcome of which is contingent on choices made by that other party (Barber, 1983; Deutsch, 1973; Gambetta, 1988). The view on trust expounded here is consistent with our emphasis on bounded rationality. Trust is pre-eminently an expedient for reducing complexity (Luhmann, 1979). If one feels that the other party can be trusted to honour his or her part of the letter and the spirit of a deal, many thorny questions that might increase the dangers of opportunism regarding future developments can be avoided.

The urge to bring the concept of 'trust' into TCE stems from the finding in various empirical studies that trust is often the glue that keeps business partners together (Barber, 1983; Lorenz, 1988; Palay, 1984). However, incorporation of the concept of trust constitutes a breach with the explanatory strategy of received TCE.[1]

Williamson assumes that 'some individuals are opportunistic some of the time and that differential trustworthiness is rarely transparent *ex ante*. As a consequence, *ex ante* screening efforts are made and *ex post* safeguards are created' (Williamson, 1985, p. 64). However, the main thrust of TCE is to explain existing safeguards in transaction relations as a response to the problems of opportunism. The possibility of screening successfully for opportunism and consequently of being able to renounce safeguards is hardly worked out. The line of reasoning is that if it is very difficult or impossible to recognize an opportunistic actor *ex ante*, those who design a governance form must reckon with opportunism all the time.

We propose that managers, at least in transaction relations of some duration, *can* successfully screen for opportunism. In the process of exchange, opportunities for opportunistic rent-seeking will inevitably occur, and the behaviour of the other party can be monitored closely. Every time he renounces an opportunity for opportunism, trust grows.

Trust, just like temporal embeddedness, will tend to mitigate the perceived dependence stemming from asset specificity, or at least the perceived risk associated with this dependence. Therefore trust may be expected to lead to less stringent safeguards, other things being equal.

The three factors discussed above, both network and temporal embeddedness as well as trust, may under some circumstances be highly correlated. For one thing, as the development of trust takes time, higher levels of trust are to be expected in older relationships. Furthermore, if business relations are a part of a dense network, they will presumably on average be longer-lived, and are more likely to be governed by social norms. Consequently trust, temporal embeddedness and network embeddedness may in many cases come as a complex of variables rather than as isolated factors.

The model based on our version of TCE is represented in Figure 5.2. Perceived dependence can be measured independently, but can be interpreted only in the context of the independent variables and of the safeguards installed. Various tests of hypotheses based on received TCE and our changes and additions to the theory will be discussed in the next section.

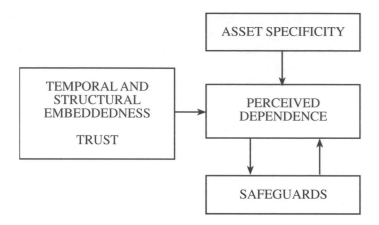

Figure 5.2   Model based on extended TCE

DATA COLLECTION AND ANALYSIS SCHEMES

In order to test the hypotheses that can be derived from (our version of) TCE, we are conducting a series of empirical investigations. In the first study we analysed the supplier relations of one particular firm, a manufacturer of office equipment ('Buyer'). Buyer has a turnover of $1.4 billion and a net profit of $54 million, and employs 12 000 people (1991).

In the first phase of this study, we interviewed the managers who were responsible for maintaining relationships with Buyer's suppliers, as well as their counterparts at 12 suppliers. The purpose of these interviews was the drafting and testing of a written questionnaire. In the second stage, we sent this questionnaire to 80 of Buyer's largest suppliers. The response was a total of 67 returned questionnaires (84 per cent). For some suppliers, supplementary information relating to legal ordering was derived from internal Buyer sources.

Questions in the questionnaires pertained among other things to asset specificity as incurred by suppliers, legal and private order safeguards installed, perceived dependence of Buyer and supplier, trust, length of the supply history, the development of the supply relationship in terms of sales volume, and the occurrence of positive and negative network embeddedness of the supplier. Most items had the format of five-point Likert-type scales. On the basis of the individual items a number of additive scales have been constructed.[2]

First, we attempted a direct test of the causal scheme of TCE, according to Figure 5.1. Here, asset specificity is seen as a (the?) cause of safeguards.

Regressing different measures of safeguards on measures of specificity, we found no statistically significant results. But on second thought, we should see safeguards as being constructed into an integrated, coherent governance scheme, and perhaps it makes little sense to regress individual items of such a scheme on asset specificity. But it is not clear how individual items of governance should be combined to reflect the overall design, as tailored to each individual case. Thinking further, it seemed to make most sense not to look at safeguards as dependent variables, but at perceived dependence. Our causal scheme for this is given in Figure 5.2. Here, dependence is seen as providing the incentive to institute means of governance, and as resulting from measures already instituted.

Safeguards are instruments to reduce a dependence that results from causes such as asset specificity, enhanced or attenuated by embeddedness in networks and time, trust, percentage of sales involved in the transaction relation and so on. By taking perceived dependence as the dependent variable, we are looking at the crucial end result of the entire scheme, and we can test for all factors simultaneously. Hence, we focus on perceived dependence of suppliers, since in the present study of a large number of suppliers to a single buyer that is where interesting variation occurs.

Another reason for this focus of the analysis was the remarks made by purchasing managers at Buyer. According to these informants, standard contractual clauses were widely used. Whatever variation of contractual terms occurred was seen as coincidental rather than a meaningful parameter of relationships with suppliers. The same would be true for private ordering. Relation-specific tools were routinely paid for and owned by Buyer, and the provision of technical knowledge depended on the technical expertise of the supplier, and not on considerations of governance.

As a result, the variation in safeguards observed in our sample would at best very imperfectly reflect the risk of dependence incurred by suppliers that have invested in relation-specific assets. According to our restated model of transaction cost economics (Figure 5.2), this would result in an increased net perceived dependence for these suppliers. The results of the regression analysis confirm this expectation (see Table 5.2).

OPERATIONALIZATION OF VARIABLES

From the perspective of TCE, the variables explaining dependence are asset specificity and safeguards. A scale of asset specificity was constructed by adding items pertaining to location specificity (one item), physical asset specificity (two items), dedicated capacity (four items) and knowledge specificity (two items).[3]

For the safeguards we require measures of legal and private ordering. With regard to legal ordering, five questions were answered by Buyer pertaining to the question of whether all transactions with the supplier in question were governed by a 'master contract'; the term of notice in the contract; whether or not security stocks of components of materials were specified; whether or not the terms of delivery on order diverged from the standard formulation; and whether or not the technical specifications of the products to be delivered diverged from the standard formulation.

On the basis of these variables we hoped to be able to construct a scale of contractual extensiveness, with taken-for-granted standard contracts at one extreme of the scale, and carefully negotiated contracts at the other.

Our premise was that parties seeking protection in legal ordering will spend more effort in negotiating and drafting the agreement, resulting in a non-standard contract. However, the correlations between the first two variables and the other three proved to be very low. Factor analysis of the five variables revealed two distinct factors, with master contract and term of notice loading high on one factor, and terms of delivery and technical specifications on the other. The fifth variable, security stocks, showed intermediate and opposite loadings on both factors.

On the basis of these observations it was decided to construct one additive scale of contract extensiveness on the basis of the items pertaining to terms of delivery, technical specifications and security stocks only.[4]

Two dichotomous items were considered for the measurement of private ordering. The first item pertained to the question of whether specific tools were paid for and owned by Buyer; the second item pertained to the question of whether Buyer provided technical knowledge to the supplier. Both arrangements can be seen as mitigating the risk of asset specificity borne by the supplier. If specific tools are paid for by the buying firm, the supplier has to incur lower specific investments. And if the buying firm provides technical knowledge, this helps create a balance of dependencies, for in case of opportunistic rent-seeking by the buying firm the supplier can now retaliate by using this technical knowledge in a way that would be harmful to the buyer.[5] The summative scale of the two items was rejected for a too low value of Cronbach's alpha. The first item was extremely skewed: as almost all suppliers used tools owned by Buyer, the item does not discriminate. This left us with the second item as a sole measure of private ordering.

ON THE OPERATIONALIZATION OF ADDITIONAL VARIABLES

Two kinds of embeddedness were distinguished, both measured on a dichotomous scale: positive network embeddedness, if the supplier extensively used the input of third parties in the production for Buyer; and negative network embeddedness, if the supplier also delivered to Buyer indirectly.

The time dimension was included by constructing a variable measuring the number of years the supply relationship had existed. The natural logarithm of this number was used in the analysis, because the influence of this factor was assumed to be non-linear. Not only the age of the supply relationship, but also its development is important. Therefore another variable was added, reflecting the growth or decline of sales to Buyer during the past five years, on the hypothesis that growth might mitigate perceived dependence.[6]

A scale was also constructed for the trust of the supplier in the goodwill of the buyer.[7] The sales of the supplier to Buyer as a percentage of its total turnover was considered as an additional determinant of dependence as perceived by the supplier. Annual total turnover of the supplier was also considered, on the basis of the hypothesis that larger firms are better able to handle risks and reduce transaction costs (Nooteboom, 1993).

For both variables the logarithm was taken on the assumption that the effect may be subject to diminishing returns. Means, standard deviations and intercorrelations of the various measures are shown in Table 5.1.

FINDINGS

Two approaches to the explanation of perceived dependence were used. One approach was to take the supplier's perceived dependence as the dependent variable, and to take the dependence of the buyer, as perceived by the supplier, as one of the explanatory variables (with the hypothesis of a negative effect). The alternative was to take net perceived dependence as the dependent variable, defined as the excess of the dependence the supplier perceives for himself over the dependency he perceives for the buyer. Our hypotheses are as follows:

1. There are positive effects on dependence from: asset specificity, percentage of total sales to buyer, negative network embeddedness.
2. There are negative effects on dependence from: contractual extensiveness, total turnover of the supplier (as a measure of firm size), positive network embeddedness, trust in goodwill of the buyer, information pro-

Table 5.1 Means, standard deviations and correlations

Variables	Means	S.D.	1	2	3	4	5	6	7	8	9	10	11	12	13
1. Not perceived dependence by supplier	−1.86	1.46													
2. Supplier dependency perceived by supplier	2.07	1.14	+0.746***												
3. Buyer dependency perceived by supplier	3.93	0.97	−0.626***	−0.052											
4. Asset specificity	22.53	6.05	+0.437***	+0.557***	+0.051										
5. Contractual extensiveness	3.79	1.09	+0.106	+0.097	0.066	+0.001									
6. Natural logarithm of length of supply history	2.48	0.54	+0.114	+0.237**	+0.054	+0.078	+0.154								
7. Growth of sales to buyer	11.39	2.41	+0.159	+0.221**	+0.025	+0.242**	+0.111	+0.096							
8. Knowledge exchange	1.29	0.46	−0.114	−0.226**	−0.111	+0.118	−0.259**	−0.205**	−0.111						
9. Negative network embeddedness	1.71	0.46	+0.273**	+0.102	−0.285**	−0.030	−0.167	−0.056	+0.163	−0.039					
10. Positive network embeddedness	2.35	0.69	−0.062	−0.171*	−0.126	−0.349***	−0.390***	−0.016	−0.118	+0.214**	+0.079				
11. Trust in goodwill buyer	24.57	4.12	−0.216*	−0.185*	+0.071	+0.004	−0.053	−0.005	+0.206*	−0.024	−0.166	+0.086			
12. Trust in competence buyer	8.81	1.37	−0.104	−0.068	+0.091	+0.030	−0.103	+0.177*	+0.404***	+0.118	−0.141	+0.073	+0.558***		
13. Natural logarithm of total turnover supplier	7.82	1.49	−0.343***	−0.323***	+0.170	−0.032	+0.146	−0.277**	+0.154	+0.089	+0.054	−0.014	−0.091	+0.038	
14. Natural logarithm of sales to buyer as % of total sales	1.75	1.10	+0.376***	+0.515***	+0.031	+0.180*	+0.368***	+0.242*	+0.027	−0.249**	−0.275**	−0.210*	+0.008	−0.099	+0.470**

Notes: *** p < 0.01; ** p < 0.05; * p < 0.10.

vided by the buyer to the supplier, length of supply history, growth of sales to buyer.

The empirical results are given in Table 5.2. The coefficients are standardized regression coefficients, labelled beta.[8] For missing observations in explanatory variables, means substitution was applied. Cases with missing variables in the dependent variable were deleted. The left column gives the results for net perceived dependence as the dependent variable (supplier dependence minus buyer dependence, both as perceived by the supplier). The right column gives the results for (gross) perceived supplier dependence. The results in the left column are based on fewer observations due to the policy of deleting cases with missing values in the dependent variable (there are missing values in buyer dependence as perceived by supplier).

Table 5.2 shows that in both models the effect of asset specificity is highly significant, and in the expected direction. For both models negative network embeddedness has the expected positive effect, and this effect is fairly to moderately significant. In the model for net dependence the only additional variable with an expected significant effect is total turnover (firm size of supplier). This effect is not significant in the model for perceived dependence. But in that model we see significant expected effects for trust in goodwill buyer, knowledge exchange and percentage of total sales sold to buyer.

In neither model do we find the expected effects for length of supply, contractual extensiveness and positive network embeddedness. Nor do we find the expected negative effect of buyer dependence on (gross) supplier dependence.

DISCUSSION

In this study no direct relationships between asset specificity and individual elements of governance structure are found. In retrospect this is reasonable. The findings of our study suggest that items of governance structure are composed into a coherent whole, in order to meet the specific configuration of conditions and requirements of a given situation. Significant results, which are to a large extent in accordance with our theoretical expectations, are found when we consider the joint, simultaneous effect on perceived dependence of causes and conditions of dependence, together with measures of governance taken to influence dependence.

The analysis of the net perceived dependence of suppliers (Table 5.2, column 1) indicates an incomplete alignment of asset specificity and safeguards; suppliers perceive themselves as more dependent on Buyer than the other way around. Hence, no balance of dependence is achieved. However,

Table 5.2   Results of a regression analysis[a]

	Net Perceived Dependency by Supplier	Supplier Dependency Perceived by Supplier
Buyer dependency perceived by supplier		0.089664
		(0.3566)
Length of supply history	–0.073882	0.015654
	(0.5417)	(0.8761)
Trust in goodwill buyer	–0.211940	–0.238367**
	(0.1246)	(0.0317)
Asset specificity	0.444565***	0.490929***
	(0.0008)	(0.0000)
Contractual extensiveness	0.178780	0.010070
	(0.1883)	(0.9282)
Growth of sales to buyer	0.106631	0.091941
	(0.4146)	(0.3937)
Knowledge exchange	–0.114951	–0.202502**
	(0.3659)	(0.0486)
Total turnover supplier	–0.306616**	–0.164452
	(0.0316)	(0.1577)
Negative network embeddedness	0.294782**	0.182140*
	(0.0177)	(0.0790)
Positive network embeddedness	0.195393	0.127083
	(0.1354)	(0.2340)
Sales to buyer as % of total sales	0.170351	0.358378***
	(0.2608)	(0.0042)
Trust in competence: buyer	0.081062	0.081285
	(0.6033)	(0.5030)
R squared	0.47539	0.58792
F-statistic	3.87191	6.30143
Significance *F*	0.0005	0.0000
N	59	66

Notes:
[a]Coefficients are standardized. T-significance in parentheses.
*** $p < 0.01$; ** $p < 0.05$; * $p < 0.10$.

the analysis of (gross) perceived dependence does not show any significant effect of perceived dependence of the other party (the buyer), which indicates that suppliers may not think in terms of a balance of dependence. We focus now on the results for the second model (gross dependence). Contractual extensiveness shows no effect, which is difficult to explain on the basis of the hypothesis that legal safeguards are used to neutralize (imbalanced) dependencies. However, if the degree of contractual extensiveness cannot be used to compensate for supplier dependence, or is unilaterally imposed by Buyer, this finding is understandable. Information exchange does show the expected effect, and this can be considered as an element of private ordering. As pointed out above, the effect of asset specificity is positive and highly significant, and thus confirms this aspect of TCE.

Negative embeddedness shows the expected effect. So does trust in goodwill of the buyer. These results confirm part of our extension to TCE. Also as expected, percentage of sales to buyer contributes to dependence, while firm size of the supplier reduces it. However, positive network embeddedness fails to show the expected effect. Neither of the two variables reflecting the temporal dimension of the transaction relation contributes significantly to the explanation of perceived dependence. This contradicts our expectation. This could be taken as an indication that habitualization and institutionalization do not play an important role in the relationships investigated.

However, perhaps allowance should be made for the possibility that time reduces the probability of discontinuity of the relation, but increases the penalty incurred when discontinuity occurs, so that the net effect on dependence is ambiguous. Another consideration is that perhaps these two variables fail to reflect the most relevant aspects of the temporal dimension of transaction relations. For instance, perhaps the expectation of future exchange should be measured directly, instead of being inferred from the length of the supply history (see Heide and John, 1990; Heide and Miner, 1992). Habitualization and institutionalization could also be measured directly, using questions that probe the degree of conscious decision-making in the context of a specific exchange relation, and the use of procedures and routines.

Our data refer to only one buying firm, and hence we must be modest in our conclusions. Specifically, with regard to factors like embeddedness and institutionalization of behaviour, firm- and industry-specific factors may play a quite important role. Larger samples, encompassing several industries and many buyers, can help us to distinguish between general tendencies and firm- and industry-specific phenomena. Nevertheless, some conclusions can be drawn.

CONCLUSIONS

Our most important finding perhaps is the strong positive association between asset specificity and perceived dependence of suppliers. In the first place, this finding confirms that asset specificity is an important factor. Secondly, it endorses our suggestion that the perceptions of the parties to a transaction relation have to be included in the analysis. Inclusion of this variable allows us to apply transaction cost reasoning also in cases in which governance structure is more of a constant than a variable. It also opens up the analysis to factors that are excluded from received TCE, such as negative network embeddedness and trust. In this study these factors had significant effects. The dynamic dimension of transaction relations, represented in our analysis by the variables pertaining to the length of the supply history and the development of sales volume, did not make an interpretable contribution to the explanation of the dependent variables. There is an obvious limitation in including a time effect in a cross-sectional study. However, given this limitation, we still think that the time dimension can be captured more adequately. Suggestions for improvement have been made.

APPENDIX

Transaction cost economics and extensions of this theory guided the development of the scales employed in the study. Most items had the format of five-point Likert-type scales. Individual scale items were factor analysed and items with factor loadings exceeding 0.30 and contributing positively to each scale's reliability (Cronbach's alpha) became part of each construct. The Cronbach's alpha coefficients for the scales range from 0.59 to 0.82, which is satisfactory for exploratory research. A respondent's score for a particular construct was the sum of his response over the number of items from which the scale was constructed. For missing observations in independent variables, means substitution was applied. Cases with missing variables in the dependent variable were deleted.

NOTES

*   This chapter is a product of a research project sponsored by the Economics Research Foundation, which is part of the Netherlands' Organization for Scientific Research (NWO). Berger and Nooteboom work at the University of Groningen; Noorderhaven works at Tilburg University. The authors gratefully acknowledge valuable comments made by Celeste Wilderom.
1.   Ibis is worked out more systematically in Noorderhaven (1995).
2.   The questionnaire items are available from the authors. The adequacy of the scales was tested by means of Cronbach's alpha, taken to be satisfactory when >0.5.
3.   Cronbach's alpha for the asset specificity scale is 0.7493. However, it can be reasoned that the scale is formative rather than reflexive and that Cronbach's alpha is irrelevant.
4.   Cronbach's alpha for this scale is 0.7329.
5.   The fact that specific tools are owned by the buyer can also increase the vulnerability of the

supplier, in the absence of other specificity (for example, human asset specificity), as the buying firm can now more easily shift business to another firm (see Semlinger, 1991).

6. A scale was constructed (Cronbach's alpha 0.5918) from three five-point Likert items: (1) the relation between our firm and buyer has improved in the course of time; (2) the relation in the course of time has encompassed more areas; and (3) how has your sales to buyer evolved in the past five years?

7. The scale was constructed from six items, with a Cronbach alpha of 0.8246. An alternative dimension of trust considered in the study is trust of the supplier in the competence of the buyer. This was neither expected nor found to have a significant effect on perceived supplier dependence.

8. Regression coefficients multiplied by the ratio of the standard deviation of the independent variable to the standard deviation of the dependent variable results in a dimensionless coefficient. The beta coefficient is the slope of the least squares regression line when both dependent and independent variables are expressed as z scores (deviation from mean in standard deviations).

REFERENCES

Asanuma, B. (1989), 'Manufacturer–supplier relationships in Japan and the concept of relation-specific skill,' *Journal of the Japanese and International Economies*, 3, pp. 1–30.

Barber, B. (1983), *The Logic and Limits of Trust*, New Brunswick, NJ: Rutgers University Press.

Berger, P.L. and T. Luckmann (1966), *The Social Construction of Reality*, Garden City, NY: Doubleday.

Blois, K.J. (1972), 'Vertical quasi-integration', *Journal of Industrial Economics*, 20, pp. 253–72.

Deutsch, M. (1973), *The Resolution of Conflict: Constructive and Destructive Processes*, New Haven, CT: Yale University Press.

Dietrich, M. (1994), 'The economics of quasi-integration', *Review of Political Economy*, 6, pp.1–18.

Gambetta, D. (ed.) (1988), *Trust: Making and Breaking Cooperative Relations*, Oxford: Basil Blackwell.

Granovetter, M. (1985), 'Economic action and social structure: a theory of embeddedness', *American Journal of Sociology*, 91, pp. 481–510.

Granovetter, M. (1992), 'Economic institutions as social constructions: a framework for analysis', *Acia Sociologica*, 35, pp. 3–11.

Heide, J.B. and G. John (1990), 'Alliances in industrial purchasing: the determinants of joint venture action in buyer–supplier relationships', *Journal of Marketing Research*, 27, pp. 24–36.

Heide, J.B. and A.S. Miner (1992), 'The shadow of the future: effects of anticipated interaction and frequency of contact on buyer–seller cooperation', *Academy of Management Journal*, 35, pp. 265–91.

Klein, B., R.G. Crawford and A.A. Alchian (1978), 'Vertical integration, appropriable rents, and the competitive contracting process', *Journal of Law and Economics*, 21, pp. 297–326.

Lorenz, E.H. (1988), 'Neither friends nor strangers: informal networks of subcontracting in French industry', in D. Gambetta (ed.), *Trust: Making and Breaking Cooperative Relations*, Oxford: Basil Blackwell, pp. 194–210.

Luhmann, N. (1979), *Trust and Power* (translated from German), Chichester: John Wiley.

Monteverde, K. and D.J. Teece (1982), 'Appropriable rents and quasi-vertical integration', *Journal of Law and Economics*, 25, pp. 321–8.

Noorderhaven, N.G. (1995), 'Trust and transactions: toward transaction cost analysis with a differential behavioral assumption', *Tijdschrift voor Economie en Management*, 15, pp. 5–18.

Nooteboom, B. (1993), 'Firm size effects on transaction costs', *Small Business Economics*, 5, pp. 283–95.

Palay, Th.M. (1984), 'Comparative institutional economics: the governance of rail freight contracting', *Journal of Legal Studies*, 13, pp. 265–87.

Semlinger, K. (1991), *Innovation, Cooperation and Strategic Contracting*, Paris: International Colloquium on Management of Technology.

Williamson, O.E. (1975), *Markets and Hierarchies: Analysis and Antitrust Implications*, New York: Free Press.

Williamson, O.E. (1979), 'Transaction-cost economies: the governance of contractual relations', *Journal of Law and Economics*, 22, pp. 233–61.

Williamson, O.E. (1985), *The Economic Institutions of Capitalism, Firms, Markets, Relational Contracting*, New York: Free Press.

Williamson, O.E. (1991), 'Comparative economic organization: the analysis of discrete structural alternatives', *Administrative Science Quarterly*, 36, pp. 269–96.

Woodside, A.G. and K. Möller (1992), 'Middle range theories of industrial purchasing strategies', *Advances in Marketing and Purchasing*, 5, pp. 21–59.

Zucker, L.G. (1987), 'Institutional theories of organization', *Annual Review of Sociology*, 13, pp. 443–64.

PART II

Pluralism and Comparative Paradigms

6.   The institutional embeddedness of economic change: an appraisal of the 'evolutionary' and 'regulationist' research programmes

Benjamin Coriat and Giovanni Dosi*

1.   INTRODUCTION

There are at least two complementary ways to present the ideas that follow. One is with reference to some 'grand' questions that have faced social sciences since their inception, namely, how do institutions shape the behaviour of individual agents, within and outside the economic arena? And what are institutions in the first place? How do they come about and how do they change? What are the relationships between 'agency' and structure? And also, nearer economic concerns, what is the role of institutions in economic coordination and change?

Another, more modest, way of tackling some of these grand issues is to see how this is done in practice by different research programmes which nonetheless share a common preoccupation with understanding economic change as a historical, institutionally embedded process.

This is what we shall attempt to do in this work, by discussing the links, overlaps, tensions and possible interbreedings between an emerging evolutionary theory of economic dynamics and various strands of institutionalist theories, with particular attention to the regulation approach.

Some definitions of what we mean by those terms and of where we put the boundaries of different theories are in order. We shall introduce these, in a rather telegraphic fashion, in sections 2–4. In section 5 we sketch, as an illustration, interpretations of the growth process in general and, in particular, the case – very familiar to institutionalist macroeconomists – of the so-called 'Fordist' phase of development experienced by Western countries after World War II, and we assess the different 'styles' of explanation of evolutionary and regulation theories, respectively. In turn, these differences in 'style' partly hide different levels of observation – hence, probably, entailing fruitful

95

complementarities – and partly also reveal genuine differences in the choice of explanatory variables and causal relationships. We shall discuss some of these issues with respect to the nature of institutions and behavioural microfoundations in section 6. Finally, in section 7 we propose a sort of taxonomy of potentially complementary levels of descriptions and analytical methodologies and, together, we suggest some items that in our view are high on both evolutionist and institutionalist research agendas.

2. EVOLUTIONARY THEORIES: SOME DEFINITIONS

For the purposes of this work we will restrict our discussion to evolutionary theories of *economic* change. In brief, a sort of 'archetypical' evolutionary model possesses, in our view, the following characteristics. (Much more detailed discussions of the state of the art are in Hodgson, 1993; Dosi and Nelson, 1994; Nelson, 1995; and Silverberg and Verspagen, 1995a.)

1. As Sidney Winter used to summarize it, the methodological imperative is dynamics first! That is, the explanation of why something exists rests intimately on how it became what it is. Or putting it in terms of negative prescriptions: never take as a good 'explanation' either an existence theorem or a purely functionalist claim (entity x exists because it performs function y ...).
2. Theories are explicitly microfounded, in the sense that they must involve or at least be consistent with a story of what agents do and why they do it.[1]
3. Agents have at best an imperfect understanding of the environment they live in, and, even more so, of what the future will deliver. Hence, 'bounded rationality' in a very broad sense is generally assumed.
4. Imperfect understanding and imperfect, path-dependent learning entails persistent heterogeneity among agents, even when facing identical information and identical notional opportunities.
5. Agents are always capable of discovering new technologies, new behavioural patterns and new organizational set-ups. Hence, also, the continuous appearance of various forms of novelty in the system.
6. Related to the last point, while (imperfect) adaptation and discovery generate variety (possibly in seemingly random fashion), collective interactions within and outside markets perform as selection mechanisms, yielding also differential growth (and possibly also disappearance) of different entities which are, so to speak, 'carriers' of diverse technologies, routines, strategies and so on.
7. As a result of all this, aggregate phenomena (for example, regularities in the growth process or in industrial structures and so forth) are 'ex-

plained' as emergent properties. They are the collective outcome of far-from-equilibrium interactions and heterogeneous learning. Finally, they often have a metastable nature, in the sense that while persistent on a time-scale longer than the processes generating them, they tend to disappear with probability one.[2]

This is not the place to review the growing number of contributions which share some or all of these seven broad methodological building blocks.[3] Suffice it to mention, first, the flourishing number of formal models and historical interpretations of economic growth as an evolutionary process propelled by technical change which have followed the seminal work of Nelson and Winter (1982): see, among others, Dosi *et al.* (1988), Day and Eliasson (1986), Silverberg and Verspagen (1994), Conlisk (1989), Chiaromonte and Dosi (1993), Silverberg and Soete (1993) and the discussion in Nelson (1995) and Silverberg and Verspagen (1995a).

Second, the diffusion of innovations has been fruitfully analysed, from different angles, as an evolutionary, path-dependent process (see, among others, David, 1985 and 1992; Silverberg *et al.*, 1988; Arthur *et al.*, 1987; Nakicenovic and Grübler, 1992; and Metcalfe, 1992).

Third, the very development of an evolutionary perspective has been deeply intertwined with the historical analysis of the processes by which technical change is generated, ranging from the microeconomic level all the way to 'national systems of innovation'. (Within an enormous literature, see Freeman, 1982; David, 1975; Rosenberg, 1976 and 1982; Basalla, 1988; Mokyr, 1990; Granstrand, 1994; Vincenti, 1990; Nelson, 1993; and the reviews in Dosi, 1988, and Freeman, 1994.)

Fourth, a growing number of industrial case studies and models of industrial change fits quite well the evolutionary conjectures outlined above. (Again, just as examples, see Pavitt, 1984; Utterback and Suarez, 1992; Klepper, 1993; Malerba and Orsenigo, 1994; Winter, 1984; and Dosi *et al.*, 1995.)

Fifth, one is starting to explore learning itself as an evolutionary process at the levels of both individuals and organizations. (Limiting ourselves to economic applications, see Marengo, 1992; Marengo and Tordjman, 1996; Lindgren, 1992; Dosi *et al.*, 1995; Levinthal, 1990; Warglien, 1995; and Palmer *et al.*, 1994.) This links also with a wide tradition of studies in the field of organizational economics which is impossible to review here (but see the remarks in Winter, 1986 and 1995).

Finally, there is a good overlap between the evolutionary perspective as we have defined it and various types of 'self-organization' models (see Lesourne, 1991), and also with the expanding field of evolutionary games (see for example Young, 1993; Kandori *et al.*, 1993; and Kaniovski and Young, 1995). Short of any detailed discussion of analogies and differences (which will be briefly mentioned below), let us just mention that certainly they have in common the emphasis on dynamics (point 1 above) and bounded rationality assumptions (point 3), but much less so the role of novelty (point 5) and the focus on non-equilibrium, finite-time properties (point 7).[4]

So, yes: indeed, we do have a rich and growing body of economic literature which at last tackles change and evolution, whereby increasing returns are the norm rather than the exception (and, with that, also the possibility of 'lock-ins'), history counts, and agents are presumed to be less than perfectly rational and knowledgeable. But where do institutions fit in this picture?

Let us now turn to this issue.

3.   INSTITUTIONS AND EVOLUTION

Again, for the sake of clarity, starting with some definitions helps.

Here we use the term 'institution' with a broad meaning to include:

(a)   formal organizations (ranging from firms to technical societies, trade unions, universities, all the way to state agencies);
(b)   patterns of behaviour that are collectively shared (from routines to social conventions to ethical codes); and
(c)   negative norms and constraints (from moral prescriptions to formal laws).

Distinctions between the three subcategories will be made in the following when necessary.

The proposition that in a sense 'institutions count' in shaping economic coordination and change is certainly shared by all breeds of 'evolutionists' mentioned earlier with various strands of 'neo-institutionalists' (see for example Williamson, 1985 and 1995, and North, 1990 and 1991), and also, of course, with 'old' institutionalism (drawing back to Veblen, Commons and so on). But, clearly, the tricky issue is *in which sense* they count.

Simplifying to the extreme, two archetypical, opposing views can be found in all this literature. At one end of the spectrum, the role of institutions can be seen as that of (i) parameterizing the environmental state variables (say the comparative costs of markets, hybrids and hierarchies in Williamson or, nearer to evolutionary concerns, technological opportunities and appropriability conditions); and (ii) constraining the menus of actions available to the agents (which in some game-theoretic versions reduces to 'the rules of the game'). Conversely, at the opposite end, let us put under the heading of embeddedness view all those theories which claim, in different fashions, that institutions not only 'parameterize' and 'constrain', but, given any one environment, also shape the 'visions of the world', the interaction networks, the behavioural patterns and, ultimately, the very identity of the agents. (In the contemporary literature, under this heading come, for example, Granovetter, 1985, and also March and Olsen, 1989, and DiMaggio and Powell, 1991, just to name a few, and has a close relative in the 'cultural theory': see Schwartz and Thompson, 1990, and Grendstad and Selle, 1995.) Note that where a theory is placed along this spectrum it has significant implications in terms of the predictions that it makes with respect to the collective outcomes of interactions and to the directions of change. On the grounds of the former view, the knowledge (by the analyst) of the (institutionally shaped) system parameters is sufficient to determine the collective outcomes (precisely, under 'perfect' rationality with the caveat of multiple equilibria; and approximately, under 'bounded' rationality). Conversely, the embeddedness view implies that in order to understand 'what happens' and the directions of change over time, much richer institutional details are needed. (First of all, one is likely to require to know much more about the multiple institutions of which the agents are part, and also much more of their histories.)

As discussed at greater length in Dosi (1995), three other dichotomies are relevant here. The first concerns the origin of the institutions. Briefly put, are institutions themselves a *primitive* of the theory or is *self-seeking rationality* the primitive and institutions a derived concept? Under the latter view, whatever institution one observes, one has to justify it, asking the question how self-seeking agents have come to build it (with an answer that could be either via forward-looking rationality or myopic adaptation). Conversely, under the former view, the existence of an institution is 'explained' relying much more heavily on the institutions that preceded it and the mechanisms that led to the transition. One is also entitled to ask why people embedded in certain institutions behave the way they do (that is, how institutions shape their specific 'rationality' and equally specific perceptions of their interests).

The second dichotomy regards the degrees of intentionality of institutional constructions, that is, whether they are purposefully built according to some sort of collective *constitutional* activity or, conversely, are mainly the outcome of an unintentional *self-organization* process.

The third dichotomy concerns the efficiency properties (and the equilibrium nature) of institutions themselves. Do they exist *because* they 'perform a function' and, thus, are the equilibrium outcome of some process that selected in favour of that function? Or conversely, paraphrasing Paul David (1994), are they mainly 'carriers of history', in the sense that they tend to path-dependently reproduce themselves well beyond the time of their usefulness (if they ever had one)?

The four dichotomies together define the distance between any one institutionalist view and the standard 'neoclassical' paradigm (institution-free, with

Table 6.1   Weak and strong varieties of institutionalism

		'Weak' Institutionalism	'Strong' Institutionalism
1.	Role of institutions	Parameterize system variables; contain menu of strategies	Also 'embed' cognitive and behavioural patterns; shape identities of actors
2.	'Primitives' of the theory	(Perfectly or boundedly) rational self-seeking agents; institutions as derived entities	Institutions as 'primitives'; forms of 'rationality' and perceptions of self-interest as derived entities
3.	Mechanisms of institution-formulation	Mainly intentional, 'constitutional', processes	Mainly unintentional self-organization processes
4.	Efficiency properties	Institutions perform useful coordinating and governance functions; may be considered equilibria in some selection space	Institutions as 'carriers of history'; reproduce path-dependently, often irrespectively of this functional efficiency

perfectly rational agents, well-formed and invariant preferences and so on). As shown in Table 6.1, one may identify different *gradations* of institutionalism, ranging from *weak* forms retaining a lot of the canonic microfoundations to *strong* forms wherein institutions have much more life of their own and also much more influence on what microentities think and do.

How does the evolutionary research programme (as we have defined it) relate to the various strands of institutionalism, if it does at all? It is our view that the links are indeed profound. (The famous plea for an evolution-ary approach to economic analysis by one of the founding figures of institutionalism, T. Veblen (1898), is a historical symbol of this intuitive relationship.) However, it seems to us also true that the linkages so far still are to a large extent implicit.

Certainly there are a lot of institutional assumptions in evolutionary rea-soning. So, for example, it is quite natural to assume that the particular behavioural rules, interaction mechanisms and learning patterns that one finds in evolutionary models are embedded in particular institutions. In fact, markets themselves are viewed as specific, history-contingent institutions.

Moreover, it is plain that *routines* – which play a prominent role in evolutionary theorizing of economic behaviours – are shaped by the history of the organizations in which they have developed and also by a broader institutional history. (For example, one is quite at ease with the idea that the routines and strategies of a firm from Victorian Manchester are likely to be quite different from those of American multidivisional corporations analysed by Alfred Chandler; that differences in the institutional contexts contribute to explaining the behavioural differences among contemporary Japanese, American, and European firms and so on).

Finally, a lot of effort has gone into the understanding of the specificities of the institutions supporting technological change (see, for example, Nelson, 1993; Lundvall, 1992; and the chapters by Nelson and Freeman in Dosi *et al.*, 1988).

However, it is fair to say that the institutional embeddedness of technological opportunities, routines, forms of market interactions and selection mechanisms, and so on, while abundantly acknowledged, has received little attention on its own (with the exception of those institutions more directly linked with innovative activities and notwithstanding the suggestions in Lundvall, 1992 aiming to provide a broader institutional meaning for the notion of 'national systems of innovation'). So, for example, one is still lacking any systematic mapping between classes of institutional arrangements of the economy and classes of interaction mechanisms/adjustment rules that one finds in evolutionary theories. As a consequence, one is equally still unable to map institutional arrangements into particular dynamic properties of aggregate variables such as income and productivity growth, employment and so on. (See, however, Chiaromonte *et al.*, 1993, for an initial, still quite preliminary, attempt.) Conversely, these types of mapping are precisely the *starting point* of 'strong' institutionalist approaches as defined above. As a term of comparison, let us consider in particular the 'regulation' school.

4. AN INSTITUTIONALIST VIEW OF THE ECONOMIC SYSTEM: THE 'REGULATION' APPROACH

For those who are not familiar with this tradition of studies, which originally developed in France (see Aglietta, 1982; Boyer and Mistral, 1978; Boyer, 1987, 1988a, 1988b and 1990; Coriat, 1991; Jessop, 1990; and Boyer and Saillard, 1995), first note that by '*régulation*', in French, one does not mean the legal regulatory apparatus as understood by the same term in English. Rather, its meaning is nearer the notion from system theory of different parts or processes that under certain conditions reciprocally adjust, yielding some orderly dynamics. Hence *regulation* stands for the relatively coherent socio-economic tuning of any one economic system, and different *regimes of regulation* capture the specificities in the 'mechanisms and principles of adjustment associated with a configuration of wage relations, competition, State interventions and hierarchisation of the international economy' (Boyer, 1987, p. 127).

In this perspective, and unlike evolutionary models, the description of the system is immediately institutional and taxonomic, attempting to identify some sort of archetypical structural forms which distinguish alternative socio-economic regimes.[5]

For our purposes here, let us define different regimes of accumulation in terms of the institutional arrangements concerning six domains, namely:

1. *The wage-labour nexus.* Under this heading come the nature of the social division of labour; the type of employment and the mechanism of governance of industrial conflict; the existence and nature of union representation; the systems of wage formation; and so on.
2. The forms of *competition* in the product markets (whether nearly competitive or oligopolist; the related mechanism of price formation; and so on).
3. The institutions governing *financial markets* and monetary management (including the relationships between banks and industry, the role of stock exchanges in industrial financing, the mechanisms of liquidity creation in the system and so on).
4. The norms of *consumption* (that is, the composition and changes in the baskets of consumption and their differences across social groups).
5. The forms of *state intervention* in the economy (for example, monetary and fiscal policies; 'state as arbiter' versus state as an active player with respect to social conflict, income distribution, welfare and so on).
6. The organization of the *international system* of exchanges (for example, the rules of international trade; the presence/absence of a single hegemonic power; the patterns of specialization; and so on).

The identification of discrete regimes implies, then, a sort of combinatorial exercise among these six domains; the historically informed identification of dominant ones in particular periods; the assessment of the conditions of their viability and eventual crises; and the specific realizations of a dominant regime in different countries. So a lot of work has been done in order to identify the nature of the 'classical' (or 'competitive') regime, which ran through most of the nineteenth century, as opposed to a 'Fordist' (or 'monopolistic') regime coming to maturity in the developed West after World War II (see Aglietta, 1982; Boyer and Mistral, 1978; and the works reviewed in Boyer and Saillard, 1995). The focus of the analysis is to a great extent the *long term*, influenced by Marxism and the French historical tradition of the *Annales*, and the emphasis is macroinstitutional: it is centred, for example, on the institutions governing 'social compromises' among major social groups (Delorme and André, 1983; Coriat, 1982 and 1990), educational institutions (Caroli, 1995), financial institutions and so on.

One could say that the regulation approach is an ambitious attempt – paraphrasing John Hicks – to develop a 'theory of contemporary history'. It has proved indeed to be a very rich source of heuristics and categories for historical analyses and comparative studies (a thorough survey of the state of the art is in Boyer and Saillard, 1995). But there are also a few exercises of formalization of types of reduced forms of the theory whereby the (institutionally shaped) regularities in the above six domains are summarized by some functional relations linking aggregate variables (for example, wages with prices, productivity and employment; productivity growth with the growth of output, investments and R&D; output growth with investment and exports: see in particular Boyer, 1988b, and the contributions by Billandot, Juillard and Amable in Boyer and Saillard, 1995). The models have a strong Keynesian–Kaldorian ascendency, but certainly expand upon the ancestors and, more important, attempt to capture the differences across regimes in terms of different parametrizations and functional specifications of those aggregate relationships. (For example, do wages depend mainly on unemployment, as in the 'competitive' regime, or are they basically linked to consumer prices and productivity, as in the 'Fordist' regime? Does some sort of 'Verdoorn–Kaldor law' apply to productivity growth? How sensitive are investments to profits as opposed to 'accelerator' effects? And so on.) In these reduced forms, the stability of 'regimes' is investigated in terms of the existence of stable steady states engendered by particular ranges of parameters. Moreover, by specifying dynamic couplings across these same aggregate variables one is able to identify quite rich long-term patterns including bifurcations (Lordon, 1993) and phase transitions.

At this point, readers not too familiar with both the evolutionary and the regulation approaches might reasonably wonder what they have in common. *Prima facie,* they do indeed share some methodological commitment to the understanding of dynamic patterns that do not simply involve 'more of the same'. They both also depart from the canonic view of the economy as a 'naturally' self-regulating system. Moreover, their microfoundations (explicit in most 'evolutionary' contributions, implicit in most of the 'regulationist' ones) imply much less than perfect rationality and foresight. And finally, they share a deep commitment to the idea that 'institutions matter'. But what else beyond that? Are they talking about the same objects of analysis? And, when they do, how do their interpretations overlap or diverge? In order to clarify these issues for the discussion, let us briefly check the two perspectives against an object of inquiry that both have abundantly addressed, namely growth, and in particular the observed patterns during the period after World War II.

5. SOME DIFFERENT THEORETICAL STORIES ON GROWTH, IN GENERAL, AND THE POST-WAR PERIOD, IN PARTICULAR

It is revealing to compare the bare bones of the interpretative stories that 'evolutionists' and 'regulationists' would be inclined to put forward about the basics of the growth process were they forced to summarize them in a few sentences.

Most likely, the story provided within an evolutionary perspective would start with a multitude of firms searching for more efficient techniques of production and better performing products, and competing in the markets for products and finance. Differential success in search, together with different behavioural rules and strategies (concerning, for example, pricing, investment and so on), would then determine their differential revealed performances (in terms, for example, of their profitability, market shares or survival probabilities) and hence their ability to grow in the next 'period'. Aggregate growth, in this view, is essentially driven by technological advances. Similarly, the eye of the analyst is naturally led to look for the origins, nature and accessibility of technological opportunities; the ease with which firms can imitate each other (that is, appropriability conditions); the ways firms are able to store and augment their knowledge (that is, the relationships between organizational routines and competences); and finally, the mechanisms and speed of market selection.

As already emphasized, such an evolutionary story is comfortable with complementary institutional factors. Most straightforwardly, for example, it is consistent with (and indeed demands) an institutionally grounded explanation of the mechanisms of generation of 'opportunities' to be tapped by private agents; of the legal framework contributing to shape appropriability conditions; of the origins of particular sets of corporate routines; of the nature of market interactions; of the ways wages react to the changes in the demand for labour induced by technical change and growth; and so on.

However, compare this story with the much more directly institution-based story within a regulation perspective. In the latter, plausibly, the starting point would be an analysis of the factors which render a particular regime of accumulation viable (note incidentally that while it was possible to tell a caricature of an evolutionary story of capitalist growth in general, here one needs history-contingent specifications from the start). One part of the story would concern the institutions governing wage formation, the labour process and income distribution – determining labour productivity and the surplus available for investment. Another part of the story would focus on the mechanisms of generation of aggregate demand (including the ways income distribution and social institutions affect the composition and dynamics of consumption baskets). Yes another part would address the ways the state intervenes in the economy (for example, is it a 'Keynesian'/welfare state or is it a *laissez-faire* one. Moreover, one would look at the ways products and financial markets are organized. In a nutshell, the answer to the question of 'what drives growth' is found in the consistency conditions among those major pieces of institutional organization of the socio-economic fabric. Hence, consistent matching fosters sustained growth, while mismatching engenders instability, crises and macroeconomic depression.

Having focused, *in primis,* on the institutional features of the system, the approach in manners somewhat symmetrically opposite to the 'evolutionary' interpretation is complementary to detailed specifications of the patterns of technological change. For example, it is easily acknowledged that technological innovation is a major determinant of the division of labour and work organization; of the importance of economics of scale (and thus of the aggregate relationships between productivity growth and income growth); of demand patterns, of international competitiveness, and so on. However, it is fair to say that what appears as the major driver of growth in the evolutionary account, here (in the regulation approach) it tends to feature more in the background among the necessary or constraining conditions for growth, while the opposite applies to the thread of country-specific and period-specific institutions.

A similar difference (which might be just a matter of emphasis or might be much more; see below) emerges when handling the interpretation of specific historical circumstances. Compare, as an illustration, Nelson and Wright (1992) and Aglietta (1982) on American performance in this century (notwithstanding the only partial overlap between the two, with the former focused on technological performance and the latter, more broadly, on growth patterns). In brief, the Nelson–Wright story reconstructs the origins of American leadership after World War II, tracing it back to

> two conceptually distinct components. There was, first of all, the longstanding strength in mass production industries that grew out of unique conditions of resource abundance and large market size. There was, second, a lead in 'high technology' industries that was new and stemmed from investment in higher education and in research and development, far surpassing the levels of other countries at the time. (Nelson and Wright, 1992, p. 1960)

The erosion of that leadership is then analysed in terms of the factors which allowed a more or less complete technological catching-up by other OECD countries over the last four decades (subject to the qualifications put forward by Patel and Pavitt (1994) on the long-term specificities in the patterns of technological accumulation by individual countries).

Nelson and Wright do not explicitly talk about the impact of technology on growth, but a strong evolutionary conjecture is that innovation and imitation have a major importance in explaining both trade patterns and growth patterns. (For some empirical tests, see Dosi *et al.*, 1990; Verspagen, 1993; Amendola *et al.*, 1993; and Fagerberg, 1994.) Conversely, the Aglietta story, directly concerning American (and international) *growth* patterns, is an archetypical application of the regulation framework sketched above. The conditions for a sustained regime of growth are identified into the 'virtuous' complementarity of (i) mechanization/automation/standardization of production (entailing also ample opportunities for the exploitation of economies of scale); (ii) the development of 'Fordist' patterns of management of industrial relations; (iii) mechanisms of governance of the labour market on the grounds of implicit or explicit conventions indexing wages on productivity and consumer prices (with the effect, among others, of smoothing business cycles and sustaining effective demand); (iv) symmetrically, relatively stable forms of oligopolistic organization of product markets (which, combined with the wage dynamics described above, sustained rather stable patterns of income distribution and easy 'accelerator-driven' investment planning); (v) the diffusion in consumption of mass-produced durables; (vi) 'welfare' and 'Keynesian' fiscal policies; and (vii) the development of an international monetary regime conducive to international exchanges (the Bretton Woods set-up) under the hegemony of one economic and technological leader (the United States).

Correspondingly, the end of the 'Golden Age' following World War II is seen as the outcome of 'mismatched dynamics', for institutional and technological reasons, at all the foregoing seven levels: the exhaustion of the potential for economies of scale; inflationary pressures amplified by the wage formation mechanism; the entry of new competitors, destabilizing cosy oligopolistic arrangements; increasing social conflict favoured by near-full-employment conditions; the collapse of the Bretton Woods regime; and so on.

Are these two basic stories essentially two complementary ways of looking at a broadly similar object? But in this case where does the complementarity precisely rest? Or do they entail competing explanations of the same phenomena? As we shall see, it is our conjecture that there is a bit of both – and sorting out what is what would be already a significant step forward.

6. DIFFERENT LEVELS OF ANALYSIS OR COMPETING INTERPRETATIONS?

Certainly, part of the difference in the 'building blocks' of the basic stories outlined above relates to different levels of observation and different primary phenomena to be explained (and this, of course, militates for a would-be complementarity). In many respects, the much greater parsimoniousness on institutional assumptions that one finds in evolutionary models is due to the higher level of 'historical abstraction' in which they are set. Metaphorically speaking, this is the level at which one investigates the properties of an (imperfect) Invisible (or oligopolistically visible) Hand operating in the presence of the Unbound Prometheus – as David Landes puts it – of technological change. In other words, evolutionary models – at least the first generation of them – start by addressing, in a first approximation, some stylized properties of capitalist dynamics in general, such as the possibility of self-sustained growth driven by the mistake-ridden search by self-seeking agents. Relatedly, the primary objects of interpretation are broad statistical regularities (or 'stylized facts') at aggregate level, such as exponential growth, the rough constancy of distributive shares, the secular increase in capital/labour ratios, the degrees of persistency in macrofluctuations and more generally the spectral density of time series; the broad patterns of divergence/convergence of per capita income in the world economy; and so on (see Nelson and Winter, 1982; Dosi *et al.*, 1994a; Silverberg and Verspagen, 1994; and the (far too modest!) overview in Silverberg and Verspagen, 1995a). Similarly, at 'meso' level – that is, that of single industries – evolutionary models have proved to be quite capable of interpreting statistical phenomena such as skewed distributions of firms by size, 'life cycle' patterns of evolution, intersectoral differences in industrial structures grounded in different 'technological regimes', and so on (see Dosi *et al.*, 1995).

With respect to this level of observation, in many ways, the degree of abstraction of regulation theories *is* much lower and the interpretative ambition is higher, in the sense that the aim goes well beyond the account of broad statistical invariances but points at the understanding of discrete forms of development and the transitions across them. Similarly, the degree of institutional specification is bound to be much higher and, as it happens, the 'microfoundations' much more implicit (when they are there at all).

So we have here a potentially fruitful complementarity concerning two different levels of description (see also below). As we see it, the aggregate functional and institutional regularities, which are the starting point of most regulation models[6], could possibly be shown to be emergent properties of underlying, explicitly microfounded, evolutionary models, appropriately enriched in their institutional specifications.

Take for example the Verdoorn–Kaldor functional form relating productivity growth and income growth which is postulated in regulation models. Evolutionary models are in principle suited to establishing the microeconomic conditions under which it emerges in the aggregate as a stable relation. For example what are the microlearning processes that sustain it? What happens to its form and parameterizations if one varies the underlying mechanisms of search and sources of technological opportunities? Under what circumstances can one identify phenomena of 'symmetry-breaking' engendered by microfluctuations and yielding the transition to different structural forms?

Similarly, with respect to wage formation mechanisms, the 'structural forms' in the regulation account tend to postulate aggregate invariances, say in the elasticities of wages to unemployment, prices and productivity. Conversely, evolution-inspired models of the labour market and labour processes (still to be built!) might well account for the conditions of their emergence, stability and crises. And the same could be said for most other primary building blocks of regulation models.

Of course we do not want to push the 'emergence philosophy' too far. It would be naive to think that straightforward links between levels of description can be made without resorting to a lot of further 'phenomenological', history-based specifications. Jokingly, we illustrate all this with the parallel of the cow. If anyone is asked to describe what a cow is, it would be silly to start from a quantum mechanics account of the atoms composing it, and then move on to the levels of atoms, molecules, cells … all the way to the morphological description of the cow. However, the example is handy because it illustrates, first, the consistency in principle between the different levels of description; second, the fact that a good deal of higher-level properties (for example, concerning cells' self-maintenance) can be understood as emerging properties from lower-level dynamics; and third, that without a lot of additional 'phenomenological' information, generic emergent properties are not enough to determine why that animal is a cow and not an elephant or a bird.

Admittedly, in economics we are very far from such a consistency across levels of descriptions (and certainly the compression to one single ahistorical level that the neoclassical tradition has taught us did not help). However, we want to suggest that a theory-informed dialogue between bottom-up (microfounded, and so on) evolutionary approaches and more top-down (aggregate, albeit institutionally richer) regulation ones is likely to be a formidable but analytically promising challenge.[7] Not only would it help to rigorously define the bridges between microbehaviours and entities at different levels of aggregation, but it would also highlight potential conflicts of interpretation which are currently often confused by level-of-description issues. Having said that, a few unresolved questions and areas of possible conflict come to mind.

The Descriptive Counterparts of Socio-economic Regimes

We have already mentioned earlier that, in a sense, the regulation approach sets itself the ambitious task of dissecting the anatomy of discrete regimes of growth. But then, it seems to us, an unavoidable task is the empirical *and statistical* identification of these regimes. Some work has been done in this direction, concerning especially long-term wage dynamics, but also labour productivity and demand formation (for surveys, see Chapter 10 by C. Leroy, Chapter 22 by M. Juillard and Chapter 23 by B. Amable in Boyer and Saillard, 1995, and also Boyer, 1988b). However, a lot remains to be done – difficult as it is. For example, if phases of development and crises are traced back to the properties of underlying regimes, how are they revealed by the dynamics of statistical aggregates? And which ones? And at which level of aggregation? (For example, are GDP series too noisy and imprecise so that one should look at sectoral data?) Or is one forced to the conclusion that current econometric methods are ill-suited to detect changes, which appear very important when inspecting qualitatively 'how the economy works', but are blurred by statistical noise in the reported series?

An answer to these questions will help a lot in pinning down the common objects of interpretation (and also in revealing the comparative merits of an institutionalist approach to macroeconomics as compared to more traditional ones). Moreover, a crucial part of the regulationist exercise involves the mapping of socio-economic regimes into dynamic properties of the system. But then a lot more work is required to find statistical proxies for those regimes themselves (this mirrors the effort that scholars in the evolutionary tradition have started putting into the statistical identification of 'technological regimes'; see Malerba and Orsenigo, 1994).

The Institutional Specifications of the Evolutionary Model

In a sort of complementary way, in order to start talking about (roughly) the same things, it is urgent that a new generation of evolutionary models begins experimenting systematically with variations in the institutional contexts in which evolutionary processes are embedded. One can think of different ways of doing it (corresponding also to different degrees of difficulty). First, holding constant the system parameters concerning, for example, notional technological opportunities, one may ask what happens to aggregate dynamics if one changes behavioural routines (an early example is in Chiaromonte *et al.*, 1993), and the constraints on those routines themselves (well expanding upon the exercise of Nelson and Winter, 1982, regarding different financial constraints on borrowed funds). Second, even holding routines constant, one should experiment with different interaction environments (for example, centralized versus pairwise forms of interaction; price-based competition versus selection based on multidimensional product attributes; bank-based versus market-based access to finance; and so on). In fact a major claim of both evolutionary and regulation theories is that markets are themselves institutional constructions whose organizational details deeply affect collective outcomes. However one knows very little of how markets actually work[8] and even less does one have taxonomies of the sort of 'archetypes' of markets that can thereafter be stylized and formally explored. Third, one might allow for routines themselves to be learnt in different institutional environments.[9] That would imply, in turn, the identification of distinct learning procedures in different environments. Fourth (and harder), it might be time to explore in an evolutionary perspective other domains of economic activity (for example, the labour market, financial markets, the endogenous dynamics of consumer preferences and so on).

Some Possible Misunderstandings: Microfoundations, Representative Agents and Methodological Individualism

In the argument so far, an implicit assumption has been that the degrees of 'bottom-up-ness' or 'top-down-ness' (including the presence and details of interactions among lower-level entities with emergence of higher-level properties) is essentially conditional on the levels and modes of description themselves.

So, for example, we do not have any problem in acknowledging the descriptive power of the now-discredited Keynesian 'income multipliers', as a concise way of accounting – under historical conditions to be specified – for a specific relationship between modal behaviours of 'firms' and 'consumers'. In turn, such an aggregate description implies, of course, that functional roles in society count. (Here there should be little disagreement between the evolutionary and regulation approaches.) The underlying idea is that an economic agent, Mr Jones – even when he is at the same time a worker at factory X, is a shareholder of company Y which owns that factory, and a consumer of the products of that factory and of many other ones – will behave according to modal patterns deriving from an institution-shaped logic of appropriateness, as James March puts it (how should Jones, as a consumer or as a worker, behave?). Most likely what Mr Jones does as a worker ought to be interpreted on the grounds of the collective history of many Mr Joneses, their experiences at the workplace, their successes and failures in industrial bargaining and so on. Analogously, the same should apply to his behaviour as a consumer or a shareholder. The basic point here is that a reduction of Mr Jones's behaviour to a coherent exercise of utility maximization in a largely institution-free environment misses the point and is interpretatively misleading or, at best, void of any descriptive content. Mr Jones might, for example, feel safe to buy shares of very conservative companies in order to ensure a rosy retirement age, fight in the meantime at the workplace against the very practices that these same companies try to implement, and buy Japanese products even when that endangers the wealth possibly stemming from the companies whose shares he bought.

Having said that, however, it seems to us that the hypothesis of institutional embeddedness of social behaviours – largely shared by the evolutionary and regulationist approaches – cannot be pushed to the dangerous borders of some renewed functionalism. There is some echo of all that when one finds a too cavalier use of sorts of 'functional representative agents' in regulationist interpretations ('the behaviour of the Fordist firm', 'the unionized worker' and so on). If anything, those stylized behavioural archetypes ought to be considered as rough first approximations, demanding further investigations into their microfoundations and the conditions of their sustainability over time. For example, under what context conditions will the behaviours of many Mr Joneses (or, for that matter, of many firms 'Jones Inc.') remain relatively invariant over time? What are the conditions on interactions and statistical aggregation that sustain relatively invariant mean behaviours? And, conversely, under what circumstances do non-average behaviours induce symmetry-breaking and, possibly, phase transitions? (Note that this last issue is particularly relevant when accounting for the dynamics across different regimes). Certainly, we share Boyer and Saillard's general conjecture that

a mode of *regulation* elicits a set of procedures and individual and collective behaviours which ought at the same time to reproduce [particular] social relations . . . and sustain the prevailing regime of accumulation. Moreover, a mode of regulation must assure the compatibility among a collection of decentralized decisions, without necessarily requiring the acknowledgment by the agents of the principles which govern the dynamics of the system as a whole. (Boyer and Saillard, 1995, p. 64, our translation)

Work to support this claim (at levels of both empirical investigations and formal modelling) is urgently needed, and in our view is also another area of fruitful complementarity between 'evolutionists' and 'regulationists'.

In this respect, a possible misunderstanding has to be dispelled. The requirement of microfoundations of aggregate statements (that is, foundations in what a multitude of agents actually do and, possibly, think), which we have emphasized throughout this work, must not at all be considered equivalent to any advocacy for foundations into any 'methodological individualism'. The latter, in its canonic form, requires, first, that any collective state of the system ought to be explained on the grounds of what people contributing with their actions to determine that state think and do; and, second, that these micro 'thoughts', strategies and actions are the primitives of the theory. Our claim is much weaker. We share, in principle, the first requirement,[10] but we strongly deny the second. So, for example, we are perfectly happy with 'microfoundations', which are themselves macrofounded, that is, where what 'people think and do' is *deeply but imperfectly* shaped by the organization and states of the system itself.

As an illustration consider the following toy model. Take a competitive world (as similar as possible to a temporary general equilibrium, of pure exchange – in order to make things simple). Suppose the state of the system, $s(0)$ at time $t(0)$ is defined by a price vector $p(0)$ and allocations $w_i(0)$ to each agent $i,(w_i e W(0))$. As usual, given prices and allocations, preference relations will determine the demand functions. If we specify a mechanism of exchange (which indeed the theory seldom does), this yields well-defined transition laws to the price sequence $p(1)$, $p(2)$ ... and $W(1)$, $W(2)$ ... (the subsequent allocations). This is obviously a microfounded story. However, add to the story that the *preference relations themselves* depend, imperfectly, on the lagged $p(\ )$ and $W(\ )$, for example, because of phenomena of reduction of cognitive dissonance (' ... don't desire what you were not able to get ... '), social imitation, learning-how-to-like-what-you-have, and so on. In this case, we still have a microfounded story, but of course (a) individual preferences stop being a 'primitive' of the explanation, and (b) we have here a sort of 'macrofoundation of the micro', in the sense that what microentities do is to a good extent determined by the collective history of the system itself.[11] This metaphor, we suggest, is of wide applicability, well beyond the foregoing caricatural example.

A Crossroad for Dialogue (or Conflict): The Nature of Economic Routines

We have mentioned earlier that both evolutionary and regulation approaches share the idea that a good deal of individual and collective behaviours are 'boundedly rational', context-dependent and relatively inertial over time, shaped as they are by equally inertial institutions in which they are embedded. In a word, both approaches share the view that a good deal of the reproduction of the socio-economic fabric rests on the development and implementation of organizational routines. However, as we discuss at much greater length in Coriat and Dosi (1998), most organizational routines entail a double nature: on the one hand, they store and reproduce problem-solving competences, while, at the same time, they are also mechanisms of governance of potentially conflictual relations.

As it happens, the evolutionary approach has focused almost exclusively on the 'cognitive' aspects of routines (and by doing that has begun to open interesting avenues of dialogue with disciplines like cognitive psychology and artificial intelligence), but it has largely neglected the dimensions of power and control intertwined into the routines themselves.[12]

Almost the opposite applies to the regulation approach, which has tended to emphasize the requirements of social coherence implied by routines, but has not paid much attention to their knowledge content.

All this might be alright again as a first approximation but it is clearly unsatisfactory as an end result in either approach. Pushing it to the extreme, in the former perspective, an answer to the question of 'how Renault (or GM or United Biscuits ...) behaves' is inclined to account for operating procedures, mechanisms of knowledge accumulation, learning strategies and so on, leaving in the background phenomena like the conflict between different social groups, the links that particular organizational rules bear to income distribution and the exercise of power (well beyond their knowledge content) and so on. Conversely, the regulationist answer, by putting most of the emphasis on the latter phenomena, tends to convey the idea that governance is the paramount role of routines, quite irrespectively of the fact that Renault or GM have to know how to produce cars, and United Biscuits cakes, and they have got to do it well, and better over time. The risks of one-sided accounts are particularly great when accounting for the *origins* of routines themselves, with an evolutionary inclination to trace them back to cognitive dynamics only, and the regulationists feeling a bit too comfortable with a reduction of the problem to a selection dynamics among well-specified menus of actions/strategies/conventions.[13]

We argue in Coriat and Dosi (1998) that the double nature of routines, and related to this the double marks on their origins, are challenging points of encounter between the evolutionist and institutionalist research programmes. Or, conversely, it could be the crossroad where the former take some sort of 'hypercognitive' route, whereby microeconomics and cognitive psychology tend to simply merge, and regulationists could well discover that 'methodological individualism' and weaker forms of 'neoinstitutionalism' (see Table 6.1) are not so bad after all.

7.   SOME CONCLUSIONS: TOWARDS A DEMANDING AND EXCITING INTERBREEDING?

Notwithstanding a series of important analytical issues – which might indeed be a source of serious interpretative conflict, and of which we have provided some illustrations – we do see an ideal sequence of modes of interpretation and levels of description in which both the evolutionist and regulationist programmes could ambitiously fit. As sketched in Table 6.2, they run from a

Table 6.2 Levels of analysis

		Objects of Analysis (some still to be explored)	Examples of 'Analytical Styles'
Level 0 – from nanoeconomics to microeconomics	(i)	Nature and origins of routines and, generally, behavioural norms	From H. Simon to Holland et al. (1986); microanalytic part of Nelson and Winter (1982); Cohen and Bacdayan (1994); Egidi (1994); organizational economic 'competences' and so on; Coriat (1994b); Dosi et al. (1994b); Marengo (1992); Warglien (1995); Marengo and Tordjman (1996); possible economic applications of Fontana and Buss (1994a and b); and a lot to be done
	(ii)	Learning processes	
	(iii)	Mechanisms of expectation formation	
	(iv)	Nature and evolution of micro-organizations (e.g. business firms)	
	(v)	Embedding mechanisms of individual behaviours into the institutional context	
	(vi)	The evolution of criteria of actions and 'visions of the world'	
Level 1 – from micro-economics to aggregate properties	(i)	Generic properties of growth fuelled by technical changes	Explicit microfounded models with aggregate emergent statistical properties, for example, Nelson and Winter (1982); Silverberg and Verspagen (1994); Lesourne (1991); Dosi et al. (1995)
	(ii)	Industrial evolution	
	(iii)	Self-organizing properties of labour markets	
	(iv)	The dynamics of consumption patterns	
Level 2 – aggregate dynamics	(i)	Functional relations among aggregate variables	More 'stylized' but (hopefully) institutionally richer macro models (necessarily microfounded): from Keynesian/ Kaldorian models to Boyer (1988a and b) and Silverberg (1987)
	(ii)	Socio-economic regimes: consistency conditions among processes of economic adjustment and institutions	
Level 3 – 'co-evolution'	(i)	Co-evolutionary patterns between technologies, corporate organizations and broader institutions	A lot of appreciative theorizing from historians but relatively little modelling (but see the suggestion in Nelson, 1994, on industrial dynamics); a vast regulation-inspired empirical literature (see Boyer and Saillard, 1995)
	(ii)	Coupled institutional dynamics	
	(iii)	'Political discretionality' and institutional inertias	
Level 4 – 'grand history'		General interpretative conjectures on long-term historical patterns	From Marx to … Schumpeter … to Freeman and Perez (1988) … to Aglietta (1982) and Boyer and Mistral (1978) (just to name the perspectives discussed in the work)

114

sort of 'nano-economics', wherein the abandonment of any magic of a perfect and invariant rationality forces a dialogue with cognitive and social psychology, organization theory and sociology, all the way to grand historical conjectures on the long-term destinies of contemporary forms of socio-economic organization. Even a quick look at the table highlights the enormous gaps between what we know and what such an ideal evolutionary–institutionalist research programme would demand. These gaps are high at all levels, but in our view four issues are particularly urgent on the agenda.

A first one concerns co-evolutionary processes. The essence of the co-evolutionary point is that what happens in each partly autonomous domain of the system (for example, technology or institutional structures) shapes and constrains what is going to happen in the other ones. Hence, the overall dynamics is determined by the ways each domain evolves but also by the ways the various domains are coupled with each other.[14] We have listed 'co-evolution' under a separate level or description in order to demarcate that broad area covering, for example, the interactions among the forms of economic organization, social and political institutions and technical change. However, co-evolutionary issues appear at all levels of description. For example, the emergence and development of each industry ought to be seen as a co-evolutionary process among technologies, corporate organizations and supporting institutions (Nelson, 1994). Analogously, the origins of organizational routines (see above) is intimately a co evolutionary process, shaped by diverse and probably conflicting selection criteria (that is, problem-solving versus governance requirements).

A second (and related) item which is high on the research agenda considers the transition across different socio-economic regimes of growth: for example, at which level can such transitions be detected? (This will probably be conditional on the type of transition one is talking about.) What are the effects of 'higher-level' changes (for example, in the institutional set-ups or in the policy environment) upon microeconomic behaviour? And, conversely, under what circumstances do non-average microbehaviours become 'auto-catalytic' and eventually induce higher-level phase transitions? What kind of co-evolutionary processes do particular classes of transitions entail?

A third priority item, in our view, concerns what could be called, in shorthand, the relationships between emergence and embeddedness, or, putting it another way, the role of 'bottom-up' processes shaping/generating higher-level entities (or at least aggregate statistical patterns) versus 'top-down' processes by which higher-level entities (for example, institutions, established mechanisms of interaction and so on) shape/generate 'lower-level' behaviours. One of the claims underlying this whole chapter is that the links work both ways and that one ought to account for 'macrofoundation of the micro' as well as 'microfoundations of the macro'. But how does one get beyond suggestive metaphors and elaborate more rigorous, albeit highly simplified, models which nonetheless capture the intuition? (Note that what we mean is something more than a feedback between a system-level state variable (say, a price or a market share) and the argument of an individual decision algorithm (say, pricing or investment rules): somewhat deeper, we think it is not beyond reach to develop models whereby micro decision algorithms themselves are shaped by macro states and, conversely, possibly non-linear interactions among the former change collective interaction rules/constraints/perceived pay-offs/perceived opportunities.) But in turn, all this involves difficult issues concerning, again, coordination; relative time scales of change; relative invariances of 'structures' and conditions of their stability.

Fourth, we suggest that the nature of learning processes, too, ought to deserve priority attention. As Lundvall (in this volume) emphasizes, the *objects of learning* ('know what', 'know why', 'know how', 'know who') are likely to discriminate among classes of learning processes. And, certainly, the competence gap between the intrinsic complexity of any one cognition/decision problem at hand and the pre-existing abilities of (individual or collective) agents fundamentally shapes learning processes (for a discussion, see Dosi and Egidi, 1991). But, in turn, it is only a weird twist of contemporary economic thought that gives credibility to the idea that incrementalist procedures, based either on sophisticated hypothesis testing (such as in Bayesian models) or stimulus–response reinforcements, are the general paradigm of learning (note that this applies to 'evolutionary games', but also to most evolutionary models in general) that one has developed so far.[15]

As a way forward, we suggest, possibly building upon preliminary (and still very rudimentary) attempts by, among others, Marengo (1992), Egidi (1994), Cohen and Bacdayan (1994), Marengo and Tordjman (1996) and also Dosi *et al.* (1994c), a priority task is to account for the formation and collective establishment of cognitive categories, problem-solving procedures (routines?) and expectations about the identities and behaviours of other social actors.[16]

Yes, all this is an enormous task. Very fascinating and extremely difficult. The way we see it pursued, it involves tight and troublesome interchanges among empirical investigations, 'appreciative theorizing' and formal modelling efforts. It is likely also to involve major adjustments in the building blocks of institutionalist–evolutionary theories themselves.

We are probably now witnessing a rare window of opportunity for fulfilling the promise of making economics an 'evolutionary/institutionalist discipline'. The blame for failing to do so will fall mainly on ourselves, rather than the sectarian attitudes of chair committees or international journal editors.

NOTES

* Support for this research from the Italian Ministry of Universities and Research (MURST, 'Progetti 40%') and from the International Institute for Applied Systems Analysis (IIASA), Laxenburg, Austria, is gratefully acknowledged. An earlier version of this chapter appeared in French in Boyer and Saillard (1995). The current version is republished in Dosi (2000) where the reader will find several other applications of evolutionary theory.

1. Note, however, that there are a few 'aggregate' (that is, non-microfounded) models which are nonetheless 'evolutionary' in spirit (for a survey, see Silverberg and Verspagen, 1995a).

2. On the notions of 'emergence' and 'metastability' see the discussion in Lane (1993).

3. Note that, given the above quite broad definition of the evolutionary research programme, it may well describe also the contributions of authors who would not call themselves 'evolutionist' in any strict sense.

4. To repeat, this is not meant to be a thorough review but just an approximate roadmap. Moreover, at least a partial overlap with the evolutionary archetype can be found in quite diverse fields of economic theory: see for example Aoki (1995) and Stiglitz (1994).

5. A related perspective, which it is not possible to discuss here, pursued especially by 'radical' American economists, is known as the theory of 'social structures of accumulation'. See for example Bowles and Gintis (1993) and the references therein.

6. Note that we do not mean only formal, mathematically expressed, 'models', but also rigorous, albeit verbally expressed, theory-based propositions about whatever phenomena.

7. Broad historical interpretations building upon a *lato sensu* evolutionary microeconomics, such as Freeman and Perez (1988), might be considered as another point of departure for this dialogue.

8. A noticeable exception is Kirman and Vignes (1991) on the fish market in Marseilles (!).

9. A simple adaptive learning mechanism nested in a macro model is presented in Silverberg and Verspagen (1995b). Much more constructive models of behavioural learning are in Marengo (1992), Marengo and Tordjman (1996) and Dosi *et al* (1994c), but they are far from any macro model. Moreover, they, too, lack experiments on different institutional specifications.

   Note that, here, by routines we specifically mean those rules of thumb concerning such things as pricing, R&D, investments and so on. It is a fundamental point of evolutionary theories that different techniques are intimately associated also with different production routines. And, indeed, the models provide a representation of the dynamics of the latter via a low-dimensional representation of search outcomes in the technology space. However, a major step forward would be an explicit account of the dynamics of the underlying problem-solving routines (see also below).

10. We also want to emphasize the fact that we share the requirement *in principle*, even if it might turn out that in many circumstances the micro–macro link turns out to be practically impossible. It is a circumstance familiar also to natural sciences, where it is often the case that one can write the aggregate statistical properties (say, in a thermodynamic problem) without being able to derive them from an underlying micro description (say, detailed balance equations).

11. We have repeatedly stressed the *imperfect* adaptation of agents to the macro configurations of the system. A perfect adaptation would indeed imply a strong functionalist conjecture ('people do and think what they are supposed to do, given the functional requirements of the system itself'). In our view, on the contrary, it is precisely imperfect adaptation which is an important source of dynamics.

12. This notwithstanding the acknowledgement of their importance: see for example, Nelson and Winter's (1982) definition of routines as truces among conflicting interests.

13. In turn, as known, once the problem is posed in these terms it can be formally handled by means, for example, of 'evolutionary games' (see Boyer and Orlean, 1992, for such an attempt). Far from denying the usefulness of such exercises as sorts of *gedankenexperiment* on collective adaptation under potential conflict of interests (or conflicts between individual incentives and collective good), they still deliver a quite partial picture of the object

of inquiry. For example, in the current state of the art we do not know of any model allowing for adaptation on preferences themselves (that is, in game terms, endogenously evolving pay-off matrices). Neither is there the discovery of new 'strategies' (with the exception of Lindgren, 1992). And finally, 'learning' tends to neglect any cognitive/ problem-solving aspect and be reduced to a stimulus–response mechanism of reinforcement (possibly mitigated by stochastic search or mistakes).

14. A co-evolutionary view runs against, for example, 'technological determinism' (that is, technology proceeds exclusively according to its inner logics, and institutions ought simply to adjust, with varying lags) but also 'social determinism' (for example, technology is purely a 'social construction'). On the contrary, the co-evolutionary view does accept that technological change and social change have their own inner logics (possibly conflicting with each other) and does attempt to explain, for example, the emerging trajectories of technical change as the outcome of such a coupling.

15. Incidentally, 'Bayesian' and 'Pavlovian' learning have most characteristics in common since both claim (i) what Savage would have called a 'small world' hypothesis (the notional set of events and response strategies is given from the start); and (ii) there is a striking transparence of the links between actions and consequences. Hence, ultimately, the difference between the two just rests on what the theorist assumes the agent to consciously know, without much influence on the ultimate outcomes. So, for example, it is easy for biologists overwhelmed by economists' fascination to build models of rats who behave in equilibrium 'as if' understanding strategies involving first-order conditions and Lagrange multipliers, or conversely, respectable economists claiming 'Pavlovian' convergence to sophisticated rational expectation equilibria.

16. By way of a comparison, recall that even in the most sophisticated state-of-the-art accounts, in economics, of behaviours and interactions (even under conditions of imperfect information) agents are assumed to *obviously* have the correct 'transparent' understanding of the causal links of the environment, and to *obviously* know how to solve the technical problems at hand.

REFERENCES

Aglietta, M. (1982), *Regulation and Crisis of Capitalism*, New York: Monthly Review Press.

Amendola, G., G. Dosi and E. Papagni (1993), 'The dynamics of international competitiveness', *Weltwirtschaftliches Archiv*, 129(3) pp. 451–71.

Aoki, M. (1995), 'Unintended fit: organisational evolution and government design of institutions in Japan', Working Paper, Department of Economics, Stanford University, Stanford, CA.

Arthur, B., Y. Ermoliev and Y. Kaniovski (1987), 'Path-dependent processes and the emergence of macrostructures', *European Journal of Operations Research*, 30, pp. 294–303.

Basalla, G. (1988), *The Evolution of Technology*, Cambridge: Cambridge University Press.

Basle, M., J. Mazier and J.F. Vidal (1984), 'Quand les crise durent ... ', *Economica*, Paris.

Bowles, S. and H. Gintis (1993), 'The revenge of homo economicus: contested exchange and the revival of political economy', *Journal of Economic Perspectives*, 7, pp. 83–102.

Boyer, R. (1979), 'La crise actuelle une mise en perspective historique', *Critiques de l'Economie Politique Revue*, Paris, No. 7/8 pp. 5–113.

Boyer, R. (1987), 'Régulation', in *The New Palgrave*, London: Macmillan, 4, pp. 126–8.

Boyer, R. (1988a), 'Technical change and the theory of "Regulation"', in Dosi *et al.* (1988), pp. 67–94.

Boyer, R. (1988b), 'Formalizing growth regimes', in Dosi *et al.* (1988), pp. 608–30.

Boyer, R. (1990), *The Regulation School: A Critical Introduction*, New York: Columbia University Press.

Boyer, R. and J. Mistral (1978), *Accumulation, Inflation et Crise*, Paris: Puf.

Boyer, R. and A. Orlean (1992), 'How do conventions evolve?', *Journal of Evolutionary Economics*, 2, pp. 165–77.

Boyer, R. and Y. Saillard (eds) (1995), *Théorie de la Regulation: L'Etat des Savoir*, Paris: La Découvert.

Caroli, E. (1995), *Formation, Institutions et Croissance Economique*, Paris: These IEP.

Chiaromonte, F. and G. Dosi (1993), 'Heterogeneity, competition and macroeconomic dynamics', *Structural Change and Economic Dynamics*, 4, pp. 39–63.

Chiaromonte, F., G. Dosi and L. Orsenigo (1993), 'Innovative learning and institutions in the process of development: on the microfoundations of growth regimes', in R. Thomson (ed.), *Learning and Technological Change*, London: Macmillan, pp. 117–149.

Cohen, M. and P. Bacdayan (1994), 'Organizational routines as stored procedural memory: evidence from a laboratory study', *Organization Sciences*, 5, pp. 554–68.

Conlisk, J. (1989), 'An aggregate model of technical change', *Quarterly Journal of Economics*, 104, pp. 787–821.

Coriat, B. (1982), *L'Atelier et le Chronomètre*, Paris: Bourgeois.

Coriat, B. (1990), *L'Atelier et le Robot*, Paris: Bourgeois.

Coriat, B. (1991–94), *Penser à l'Envers – Travail et Organisation dans la Firme Japonaise*, Paris: C. Bourgois; 2nd revised edition, Bourgeois/Choix 1994.

Coriat, B. (1992), 'La spécificité de l'économie japonaise à la lumière de la théorie de la régulation. L'hypothèse du compagnie-isme', *Mondes en Développement Revue*, 4 Paris, No. 79–80, pp. 109–19.

Coriat, B. (1994), 'La théorie de la régulation: origines, spécificités, perspectives', in Michael Aglietta *et al.*, *Ecole de la Regulation et Critique de la Raison Economique*, Paris: Futur antérieur-L'Harmattan, pp. 101–52.

Coriat, B. (1995), 'Variety, routines and networks: the metamorphosis of the Fordist firms', *Industrial and Corporate Change*, 4(1), pp. 205–28, Oxford University Press.

Coriat, B. and G. Dosi (1998), 'Learning how to govern and learning how to solve problems: on the coevolution of competences, conflicts and organisational routines', in A. Chandler, P. Hagström and Ö. Sölvell (eds), *The Dynamic Firm: The Role of Technology, Strategy, Organization, and Regions*, Oxford: Oxford University Press, pp. 103-33.

David, P. (1975), *Technical Choice, Innovation and Economic Growth*, Cambridge: Cambridge University Press.

David, P.A. (1985), 'Clio and the economics of QWERTY', *American Economic Review, Papers and Proceedings*, 75, pp. 332–7.

David, P.A. (1992), 'Heroes, herds and hysteresis in technological change: Thomas Edison and the battle of the systems', *Industrial and Corporate Change*, 1, pp. 139–80.

David, P.A. (1994), 'Why are institutions the carriers of history?', *Structural Change and Economic Dynamics*, 5(2), pp. 205–20.

Day, R. and G. Eliasson (eds) (1986), *The Dynamics of Market Economics*, Amsterdam: North Holland.

Delorme, R. and C. André (1983), *L'Etat et l'Economie*, Paris: Seuil.

DiMaggio, P.M. and W.W. Powell (1983), 'The iron cage revisited', *American Sociological Review*, 48, pp. 147–160.

Dosi, G. (1988), 'Sources, procedures and microeconomic effects of innovation', *Journal of Economic Literature*, 26, pp. 126–73.

Dosi, G. (1995), 'Hierarchies, markets and power: some foundational issues on the nature of contemporary economic organisations', *Industrial and Corporate Change*, 4, pp. 1–19.

Dosi, G. (2000) *Innovation, Organization and Industrial Dynamics*, Cheltenham: Edward Elgar.

Dosi, G. and M. Egidi (1991), 'Substantive and procedural uncertainty: an exploration of economic behaviours in changing environments', *Journal of Evolutionary Economics*, 1(2) April, pp. 145–68.

Dosi, G. and R.R. Nelson (1994), 'An introduction to evolutionary theories in economics', *Journal of Evolutionary Economics*, 4, pp. 153–72.

Dosi, G., K. Pavitt and L. Soete (1990), *The Economics of Technological Change and International Trade*, Brighton: Wheatsheaf; New York: New York University Press.

Dosi, G., S. Fabiani, R. Aversi and M. Meacci (1994a), 'The dynamics of international differentiation: a multi-country evolutionary model', *Industrial and Corporate Change*, 3, pp. 225–42.

Dosi, G., C. Freeman and S. Fabiani (1994b), 'The process of economic development: introducing some stylized facts and theories on technologies, firms and institutions', *Industrial and Corporate Change*, 3, pp. 1–46.

Dosi, G., L. Marengo, A. Bassanini and M. Valente (1994c), 'Norms as emergent properties of adaptive learning: the case of economic routines', Working Paper, WP-94-73, Laxenburg, Austria.

Dosi, G., O. Marsili, L. Orsenigo and R. Salvatore (1995), 'Learning market selection and the evolution of industrial structure', *Small Business Economics*, 7(6), pp. 411–36.

Dosi, G., C. Freeman, R.R. Nelson, G. Silverberg and L. Soete (eds) (1988), *Technical Change and Economic Theory*, London: Francis Pinter; New York: Columbia University Press.

Egidi, M. (1994), 'Routines, hierarchies of problems, procedural behaviour: some evidence from experiments', IIASA Working Paper WP-94-58, Laxenburg, Austria.

Fagerberg, J. (1994), 'Technology and international differences in growth rates', *Journal of Economic Literature*, 32, pp. 1147–75.

Fontana, W. and L.W. Buss (1994a), '"The arrival of the fittest": Toward a theory of biological organization', *Bulletin of Mathematical Biology*, 56, pp. 1–64.

Fontana, W. and L.W. Buss (1994b), 'What would be conserved if "the tape were run twice!"', Proceedings of the National Academy of Science, USA, 91, pp. 757–61.

Freeman, C. (1982), *The Economics of Industrial Innovation*, 2nd edn, London: Francis Pinter.

Freeman, C. (1994), 'The economics of technical change', *Cambridge Journal of Economics*, 18, pp. 463–514.

Freeman. C. and C. Perez (1988), 'Structural crises of adjustment', in Dosi *et al.* (1988), pp. 38–66.

Granovetter, M. (1985), 'Economic action and social structure: the problem of embeddedness', *American Journal of Sociology*, 91, pp. 481–510.

Granstrand, O. (ed.) (1994), *The Economics of Technology*, Amsterdam: Elsevier/ North Holland.

Grendstad, G. and P. Selle (1995), 'Cultural theory and the new institutionalism', *Journal of Theoretical Politics*, 7, pp. 5–27.

Hodgson, G. (1993), *Economics and Evolution*, Cambridge: Polity Press; Ann Arbor: Michigan University Press.

Holland, J.H., K.J. Holyoak, R.E. Nisbett and P.R. Thagaro (1986), *Induction*, Cambridge, MA: MIT Press.

Jessop, B. (1990), 'Regulation theories in retrospect and prospect', *Economy and Society*, 19(2), pp. 153–216.

Kandori, M., G.J. Mailath and R. Rob (1993), 'Learning, mutation and long run equilibria in games', *Econometrica*, 61, pp. 29–56.

Kaniovski, Y. and P. Young (1995), 'Learning dynamics in games with stochastic perturbations', *Games and Economic Behaviour*, 11(2) pp. 330–63.

Kirman, A.P. and A. Vignes (1991), 'Price dispersion: theoretical considerations and empirical evidence from the Marseille fish market', in K.G. Arrow (ed.), *Issues in Contemporary Economics*, London: Macmillan.

Klepper, S. (1993), 'Entry, exit, growth and innovation over the product cycle', Working Paper, Carnegie-Mellon University, Pittsburg, PA.

Lane, D. (1993), 'Artificial worlds and economics', Parts I and II, *Journal of Evolutionary Economics*, 3, pp. 89–107 and 177–97.

Lesourne, J. (1991), *Ordre et Désordre*, Paris: Economica.

Levinthal, D. (1990), 'Organizational adaptation and environmental selection: interrelated processes of change', *Organization Science*, 2, pp. 140–45.

Lindgren, R. (1992), 'Evolutionary phenomena in simple dynamics', in C.G. Langton (ed.), *Artificial Life II*, Redwood City: Addison-Wesley, pp. 295–312.

Lordon, F. (1993), 'Endogenous structural change and crisis in a multiple time-scales growth model', CEPREMAP Working Paper 9324, Paris.

Lundvall, B.-Å. (ed.) (1992), *National Systems of Innovation*, London: Francis Pinter.

Malerba, F. and L. Orsenigo (1994), 'The dynamics and evolution of industries', IIASA, Laxenburg, Austria. Working Paper, WP-94-120.

March, J.G. and J.P. Olsen (1989), *Rediscovering Institutions: The Organizational Basis of Policies*, New York: Free Press.

Marengo, L. (1992), 'Coordination and organisational learning in the firm', *Journal of Evolutionary Economics*, 2, pp. 313–26.

Marengo, L. and H. Tordjman (1996), 'Speculation, heterogeneity and learning – a model of exchange rate dynamics', *Kyklos*, 49(3), pp. 407–38.

Metcalfe, S. (1992), 'Variety, structure and change: an evolutionary perspective on the competitive process', *Revue d'Economie Industrielle*, 65, pp. 46–61.

Mokyr, J. (1990), *The Lever of Riches*, Oxford: Oxford University Press.

Nakicenovic, N. and A. Grübler (eds) (1992), *Diffusion of Technologies and Social Behaviour*, Berlin, Heidelberg and New York: Springer Verlag.

Nelson, R.R. (ed.) (1993), *National Innovation Systems: A Comparative Analysis*, Oxford and New York: Oxford University Press.

Nelson, R.R. (1994),' The co-evolution of technology, industrial structure, and supporting institutions', *Industrial and Corporate Change*, 3, pp. 47–63.

Nelson, R. (1995), 'Recent evolutionary theorizing about economic change', *Journal of Economic Literature*, 33, pp. 48–90.

Nelson, R. and S. Winter (1982), *An Evolutionary Theory of Economic Change*, Cambridge, MA: Bellkap Press of Harvard University Press.

Nelson, R.R. and G. Wright (1992), 'The rise and fall of American technological leadership: the post-war era in historical perspective', *Journal of Economic Literature*, 30, pp. 1931–64.

North, D. (1990), *Institutions, Institutional Change and Economic Performance*, Cambridge: Cambridge University Press.

North, D. (1991), 'Institutions', *Journal of Economic Perspectives*, 75, pp. 264–74.

Palmer, R.G., W.B. Arthur, J.H. Holland, B. LeBaron and P. Taylor (1994), 'Artificial economic life: a simple model of a stockmarket', *Physica D*, 75, pp. 264–74.

Patel, P. and K. Pavitt (1994), 'Uneven (and divergent) technological accumulation among advanced countries: evidence and framework of explanation', *Industrial and Corporate Change*, 3(3), pp. 759–87.

Pavitt, I. (1984), 'Sectoral patterns of innovation: toward a taxonomy and a theory', *Research Policy*, 13, pp. 343–75.

Powell, Walter W. and Paul J. DiMaggio (eds) (1991), *The New Institutionalism in Organizational Analysis*, Chicago and London: University of Chicago Press.

Rosenberg, N. (1976), *Perspectives on Technology*, Cambridge: Cambridge University Press.

Rosenberg, N. (1982), *Inside the Black Box*, Cambridge: Cambridge University Press.

Schwartz, M. and M. Thompson (1990), *Divided We Stand: Redefining Polities, Technology and Social Choice*, Brighton: Harvester Wheatsheaf.

Silverberg, G. (1987), 'Technical progress, capital accumulation and effective demand: a self-organization model', in D. Batten, J. Casti and B. Johansson (eds), *Economic Evolution and Structural Adjustment*, Berlin and New York: Springer Verlag, pp. 116–44.

Silverberg, G. and L. Soete (eds) (1993), *The Economics of Growth and Technical Change: Technologies, Nations, Agents*, Aldershot: Edward Elgar.

Silverberg, G. and B. Verspagen (1994), 'Learning, innovation and economic growth: a long-run model of industrial dynamics', *Industrial and Corporate Change*, 3, pp. 199–223.

Silverberg, G. and B. Verspagen (1995a), 'Evolutionary theorizing on economic growth', IIASA Working Paper WP-95-78j; forthcoming in K. Dopfer (ed.), *The Evolutionary Principles of Economics*, Boston: Kluwer.

Silverberg, G. and B. Verspagen (1995b), 'From the artificial to the endogenous: modelling evolutionary adaptation and economic growth', IIASA Working Paper, WP-95-, Laxenburg, Austria.

Silverberg, G., G. Dosi and L. Orsenigo (1988), 'Innovation, diversity and diffusion: a self-organisation model', *Economic Journal*, 98, pp. 1032–54.

Stiglitz, J.E. (1994), 'Economic growth revisited', *Industrial and Corporate Change*, 3, pp. 65–110.

Utterback, J. and F. Suarez (1992), 'Innovation, competition and market structure', *Research Policy*, 21, pp. 1–21.

Veblen, T. (1898), 'Why is economics not an evolutionary science?', *Quarterly Journal of Economics*, 12, pp. 373–397.

Verspagen, B. (1993), *Uneven Growth Between Independent Economics: The Evolutionary Dynamics of Growth and Technology*, Aldershot: Avebury.

Vincenti, W. (1990), *What Do Engineers Do and How Do They Know It?*, Baltimore: Johns Hopkins University Press.

Warglien, M. (1995), 'Hierarchical selection and organisational adaptation', *Industrial and Corporate Change*, 4, pp. 161–86.

Williamson, O.E. (1985), *The Economic Institutions of Capitalism*, New York: Free Press.

Williamson, O.E. (1995), 'Hierarchies, market and power in the economy: an economic perspective', *Industrial and Corporate Change*, 4, pp. 21–50.

Winter, S.G. (1984). 'Schumpeterian competition under alternative technological regimes', *Journal of Economic Behaviour and Organization*, 5, pp. 287–320.

Winter, S.G. (1986), 'The research program of the behavioral theory of the firm: orthodox critique and evolutionary perspectives', in B. Gilad and S. Kaish (eds), *Handbook of Behavioral Economics*, Greenwich, CT: JAI Press, pp. 151–88.

Winter, S.G. (1995), 'Four R's of profitability: rents, resources, routines and replication', IIASA Working Paper, WP-95-07, Laxenburg, Austria.

Young, H.P. (1993), 'The evolution of conventions', *Econometrica*, 61, pp. 59–84.

7. The one world and the many theories

Uskali Mäki

---

1. INTRODUCTION

'Pluralism' has become a popular label among those who are not entirely comfortable with what they see as the prevailing situation in economics. As is so typical of many other similar labels, it is not at all clear what is behind it. It is not clear what people mean when they say they advocate pluralism in economics. Not only is it seldom recognized that pluralism proper comes in different kinds and different degrees, it is also easily conflated with the simpler notion of plurality. The following remarks are intended to provide a sketch of two endeavours: first, a partial clarification of the very concept of pluralism; second, a defence of pluralism about theories.

My title hints at a principle – let us call it the 'one world principle' – which I take as imposing a constraint upon the sorts of pluralisms I am willing to espouse. Provided there is only one world – or only one way the world is – pluralism about the world is not acceptable. On the other hand, the actually and potentially obtaining plurality of theories – also referred to in my title – can be justified, hence pluralism about theories is acceptable. This chapter is an attempt to outline a systematic justification for theoretical plurality in economics without succumbing to ontological pluralism.

2. PLURALITIES AND PLURALISMS

When considering the issue of pluralism, the proper place to begin is the more primitive notion of plurality, since the notion of pluralism presupposes that of plurality. We can say that the *plurality of Xs* is a situation where X exists in the plural; there is (where 'is' can take on the meaning of 'is actually', 'is potentially', 'is hopefully') more than one (actual, potential or desired) value for X. Let us look at some of the typical items which may be claimed or required to exist in the plural. In the expression 'plurality of Xs', X may be specified in a number of ways, which gives us pluralities such as the following:

- Ontological plurality – world;
- Veristic plurality – truth;
- Intensional plurality – meaning;
- Theoretical plurality – theory;
- Linguistic plurality – language of formulating theories;
- Epistemological plurality – way of rationally justifying theories or beliefs in them;
- Pragmatic plurality – aim, question, problem;
- Methodological plurality – method, criterion, standard;
- Meta-methodological plurality – methodology;
- Axiological plurality – value;
- Ethical plurality – moral value;
- Ideological plurality – ideology.

The list of pluralities can easily be extended beyond those cited above, but it would be unnecessary for the purposes of our discussion. The important next step is to consider the nature of the distinction between the plurality of *X*s and *pluralism about* *X*. An obvious way of characterizing the difference between the two is to say that pluralism is a theory or principle that justifies or legitimizes or prescribes the plurality of items of some sort. Whenever the plurality of *X*s constitutes an issue, pluralism about *X*s or its denial is an attempt to settle the issue.

A list of pluralisms can be created in the same way as the list of pluralities was constructed above. Thus, we have ontological, veristic, intensional, theoretical, linguistic, epistemological, pragmatic, methodological, meta-methodological and axiological pluralisms about world, truth, meaning, theory, language, knowledge acquisition, problem and goal, method and standard, methodology, value and so on.

A statement about plurality is descriptive in character, while pluralism has a normative connotation. It is one thing to say that a plurality of items obtains or does not obtain in fact, and quite another to argue that it is fine that such a plurality obtains or that such a plurality should obtain.[1]

We have above implied a further distinction between *actual plurality* and *non-actual plurality*. In the former case, the relationship between plurality and pluralism is this: a plurality of *X*s (which actually obtains) is *justified* by pluralism about *X*. For example, one may argue that the actually prevailing multiplicity of approaches in business studies is an applaudable state of affairs. In the latter case, the relationship is as follows: a plurality of *X*s (which does not actually obtain) is *prescribed* by pluralism about *X*. For instance, one may argue that there is little or no plurality of fundamental theories exhibited in mainstream economics journals, and that there should be more of it.

Pluralism involves arguments or reasons for plurality. This adds a further element to the picture: pluralism about X is based on *reasons Y*. The reasons for which a given type of pluralism, and hence plurality, can be defended may be of various kinds, from ontological or epistemological to aesthetic or moral.

Combining the various values of X and Y we then get a number of different pluralisms which either justify actually obtaining pluralities or require actually non-obtaining pluralities for different reasons. Let us gather these elements together in the following definition:

- *Pluralism.* P is an instance of pluralism about X if and only if it is a theory or principle which either justifies an actually obtaining plurality of Xs or prescribes an actually non-obtaining plurality of Xs by appealing to reasons Y.

It is obvious that one may have reasons such that they neither justify an actually obtaining plurality of Xs (because such a plurality does not actually obtain) nor prescribe that such a plurality should obtain (since it cannot obtain). As an example, hard-boiled realists claim to have reasons that preclude ontological and veristic pluralism: a plurality of worlds and truths does not and cannot obtain (to avoid misunderstandings, this idea will be qualified in the next section).

Now that we have come some way to clarifying the basic conceptual setting of the general issue of pluralism, we can specify the particular issue that will concern us in the following. Our X will be theory, and our reasons Y will be mainly ontological and epistemological reasons. In other words, we will be concerned with theoretical pluralism. Whenever a plurality of theories actually obtains, we will ask whether there are good ontological or epistemological reasons that would justify this situation; whenever a plurality of theories does not obtain, we ask whether there are good ontological or epistemological reasons requiring that a plurality of theories should obtain.

3.   ONTOLOGICAL AND SEMANTIC PRELIMINARIES

Before entering the issue of theoretical pluralism it is very important that we understand what is implied by a denial of pluralism about the world and of pluralism about truth. Indeed, our reasons involve the kind of realism that implies the denial of both ontological and veristic pluralism and hence a plurality of worlds and truths.

In a sense, it is trivially true that the world is plural in that it has many facets. The world is constituted by an infinite number of things and their properties, including their behavioural features. Yet it seems possible to say that the world is one in a sense that the many theories we hold do not each create worlds of their own; plurality of theories does not imply plurality of worlds, but rather the many theories are about the one world. This is consistent with saying that the one and only world consists of a huge number of things and properties and processes and potentialities, and also that the world appears in a vast number of ways to an observer or a set of observers viewing it from different perspectives. The one world principle is consistent with a plurality of theories. The denial of ontological pluralism implies that the many facets of the world are discovered rather than created by means of the many theories and perspectives. For example, fix-price theories and flex-price theories do not create fix-price and flex-price worlds, but at most help to illuminate features of the one and only world.[2]

It is also trivially the case that truth is plural in the sense that there is or can be an infinite number of true sentences (or propositions, utterances, beliefs) about the world, each illuminating one aspect or feature of the world and its constituents. However, this does not imply veristic pluralism. To put it in a manner that requires careful qualifications, the denial of veristic pluralism implies that for each question, pragmatically and semantically so circumscribed that it amounts to one unambiguous question, there is only one correct answer. For instance, the denial of veristic pluralism implies that there is only one correct answer to questions such as 'Did Adam Smith write *Foundations of Economic Analysis*?' or 'Do economic agents have perfect information?'

4. THEORIES AS SUBSTITUTES AND COMPLEMENTS

Let us then try to clarify some sorts of theoretical plurality and some reasons that we might have for justifying or recommending the plurality of theories in economics. The plurality of theories actually obtains, but not all economists are happy about its extent and nature. How should the actually obtaining plurality and the desired plurality be characterized? What are the related forms of pluralism and their presuppositions?

We begin with two intuitively simple ideas. The first is the distinction between *nothing but the truth* and *the whole truth*. Economists have a habit of occasionally conflating these two notions, but it is important to keep them separate. The second is the idea that theories can be *substitutes* or *complements* with respect to one another. It is typical of economists to conflate these two cases, too. These two ideas can then be combined in a formulation of two different cases of theoretical plurality. First, a multitude of theories may be based on their being substitutes, being *rival claims to nothing but the truth*. Second, a multitude of theories may be based on their being complements, being *complementary claims to parts of the whole truth.* These simple ideas have to be developed further to see what kinds of reasons there may be for theoretical pluralism.

Let us then note the obvious idea that the apparent claims of a given theory or model are not all equally important or central to the description the theory gives of the world; some claims are more central than others. This idea suggests a simple distinction between two kinds of claims; let us call them the *core claims* of a theory and the *peripheral claims* of a theory. Intuitively, this distinction would seem to be exemplified by claims about gravity as opposed to claims about a vacuum in an account of the behaviour of a falling body; and claims about maximization as opposed to claims about the perfect divisibility of goods in an account of the behaviour of economic agents and markets (granting that such classifications are often very contestable).

The distinction between core claims and peripheral claims can be based on pragmatic or ontological considerations or both: the distinction may be due to a methodological decision to treat certain components of theory differently from others, or it may be due to beliefs concerning the objective constitution of the domain of reality being studied. Let us consider the distinction as ontologically grounded.

We may say that in some cases at least, the core claims and peripheral claims of a theory are supposed to have ontological correlates: the core claims purport to be about the *ontic core,* while the peripheral claims are purportedly about the *ontic periphery* of the domain of the theory. One specific version of the distinction between the ontic core and the ontic periphery is the one between major causes and minor causes that we find in J.S. Mill.

We can now develop the idea of theories being substitutes and complements by giving the following definitions:

- *Strong substitute.* Two or more theories are strong substitutes if and only if they contain rival core claims to nothing but the truth about the ontic core.
- *Weak substitute.* Two or more theories are weak substitutes if and only if they contain rival peripheral claims to nothing but the truth about the ontic periphery.
- *Strong complement.* Two or more theories are strong complements if and only if they contain complementary core claims to parts of the whole truth about the ontic core.
- *Weak complement.* Two or more theories are weak complements if and only if they contain complementary peripheral claims to parts of the whole truth about the ontic periphery.

Keeping to the one world principle, we may now say that there are good *ontological* and *veristic* reasons for a plurality of theories if these theories are strong or weak complements. Such theories do not make conflicting claims about the world; on the contrary, they are supposed to supplement one another. On the other hand, it is less obvious that theoretical plurality can be defended on ontological and veristic grounds if the many theories are strong or weak substitutes. If there is only one way the world is, two or more theories making mutually inconsistent claims about the world cannot all be true at the same time. There is genuine conflict between such theories.

The situation is different in regard to *epistemological* considerations. Given the radical epistemic uncertainty that characterizes economics, there seem to be good epistemological reasons for plurality of theories in all four cases above, including the cases of strong and weak substitutes. Familiar problems related to the availability of relevant evidence and the reliability of testing constitute an example of why the exclusion of rival claims to nothing but the truth involves major risks. There is the further consideration that for similar reasons of epistemic uncertainty it is often difficult to tell theory complements from theory substitutes so as to sort them out for differential treatment from the point of view of pluralism.

5. ABSOLUTE AND RELATIVE PLURALISM

In economics as well as elsewhere, theories seem to be regarded much more often as strong or weak substitutes or as weak complements than as strong complements. A synthesis of strong complements often constitutes a major breakthrough in scientific progress. So does the replacement of a dominant theory by its strong substitute. The replacement of a theory by its weak substitute or weak complement constitutes a less significant episode in the development of a discipline. Indeed, the adjustment of weak complements seems to constitute a major activity in normal research in conventional economics.

These dynamic considerations are important since they are related to differences between kinds of pluralism. One can be a *temporary pluralist* with respect to a specific historical situation without being a *permanent pluralist* irrespective of the historical situation at hand. For example, Thomas Kuhn's theory of the structure of scientific revolutions can be interpreted as involving temporary pluralism about strong substitutes; it involves pluralism about extraordinary research but not about normal research (this has to be taken with the proviso that Kuhn's theory does not easily lend itself to the sort of ontologically inspired account that we have attempted above).

Temporary pluralism is a temporal version of *relative pluralism*, while permanent pluralism is a temporal version of *absolute pluralism.* Someone may endorse absolute pluralism, that is, pluralism irrespective of anything else. Some others, such as myself, hold relative pluralism, that is, pluralism relative to certain conditions. For example, I am willing to accept pluralism relative to a certain epistemic situation in economics; it may be that at some point in time, such as now, the epistemic standing of economic theories is such that we had better tolerate a number of strong substitutes at the same time; it may be that our epistemological and methodological understanding of how to find out the best way of theorizing about the economy falls short of the demands that economists are expected to fulfil. Pluralism may be a wise strategy in such a situation. Let us summarize these notions in the form of the following definitions:

- *Relative pluralism.* P is an instance of relative pluralism if and only if P is pluralism relative to a limited set of conditions.
- *Absolute pluralism.* P is an instance of absolute pluralism if and only if P is pluralism relative to all possible conditions.
- *Temporary pluralism.* P is an instance of temporary pluralism if and only if P is pluralism relative to a limited set of time periods.
- *Permanent pluralism.* P is an instance of permanent pluralism if and only if P is pluralism relative to all times.

6. STRATEGIES WITH RESPECT TO THEORETICAL PLURALITY

The scientific process is characterized by two partly opposing tendencies. On the one hand, scientists, among them economists, do their best to invent new theories and get them accepted by their fellow scientists. This often leads to a tendency towards greater plurality of theories. The reasons for this tendency are several, including the fact that novelty is often valued for its own sake. There are always constraints on theoretical novelty, but the character and strength of such constraints vary from discipline to discipline and from one phase of development to another. An aspect of this is that the nature of novelty which is valued varies similarly. However, there are reasons for the first tendency, which are in some cases related to the second tendency, that of scientists persistently trying to reduce theoretical plurality. Let us briefly consider conditions under which these tendencies obtain.

Obviously, when two or more theories are identified as rival *substitutes,* scientists tend to defend the ones they endorse and, depending on the structure of the field, either to ignore other theories or to try to eliminate them by arguing that they are mistaken. These two approaches to rival theories have consequences for theoretical plurality. *The strategy of negligence* gives support to whatever plurality of theories prevails, while *the strategy of elimination* aims at reducing the number of theories, with or without success.

- *Strategy of negligence.* Practitioners follow the strategy of negligence if and only if they ignore rival theory substitutes, thus supporting the prevailing plurality of theories.
- *Strategy of elimination.* Practitioners follow the strategy of elimination if and only if they try to get rival theory substitutes rejected, thus reducing the plurality of theories.

We may then conjecture that in fields or subfields where the number of theory substitutes is large, practitioners tend to adopt the strategy of negligence, that is, they ignore theories that conflict with those they endorse, *ceteris paribus.* On the other hand, in fields or subfields where the number of theory substitutes is small, practitioners tend to adopt the strategy of elimination, that is, theory substitutes tend to be taken more seriously and attempts tend to be made to eliminate them, *ceteris paribus.* It seems that both cases can be found in economics.

When two or more theories are identified as *complements*, there are again several alternative responses to the situation. The first is to accept the situation as it is and to employ the theories for whatever purpose they seem to serve best, based on the principle of *division of labour.* This strategy tends to retain the plurality of complementary theories. The second strategy is to try to integrate the complementary theories by following the principle of *vector addition* or something similar. The idea is that each complementary theory is taken to identify a separate force or factor that has an impact on the phenomenon under study, and the total effect can be calculated by adding up the separate effects. The third strategy is to pursue integration of the complementary theories by attempting to unify the theories and their subject matters within a more fundamental theoretical framework. This is the principle of *unification.* The unifying theory is taken to be more fundamental in the sense that the objects of the complementary theories are believed to be moments or phases or manifestations of the objects of the more fundamental theory. These two latter strategies involve assigning a subordinate status to some theories. Let us summarize:

- *Strategy of division of labour.* According to the principle of division of labour, practitioners use each theory complement for whatever purpose it seems to serve best, thus supporting the prevailing plurality of theories.
- *Strategy of vector addition.* According to the principle of vector addition, practitioners integrate theory complements by adding up the

components they represent, thus supporting the prevailing plurality of
theories while subordinating them to the total representation.

- *Strategy of unification.* According to the principle of unification, practitioners integrate theory complements by unifying them in terms of a
more fundamental framework, thus reducing the plurality of theories
or assigning a subordinate status to some of them.

It is also notable that the implementation of the strategies of vector addition
and unification, if at all permitted by the attendant difficulties, typically
presupposes revision of component theories.

7.   DEGREES OF PLURALISM

In the foregoing, we have discussed plurality and pluralism as if they were
simple dichotomous notions; either one has them or one hasn't. In fact, it
often seems important to think of them in terms of degree; one may have
more or less of them. The notion of degree of plurality and pluralism appears
to be a useful one. This notion appears in several forms that define different
dimensions or scales on which the degree varies.

To begin, we have already encountered the ontologically based idea of
theories being substitutes or complements. We may now say that there is a
scale on which the degree of pluralism is higher in the case of substitutes than
in the case of complements. In other words, toleration of rival claims to
nothing but the truth is more demanding than toleration of complementary
claims to parts of the whole truth. Furthermore, the strong cases of
substitutionality and compementarity generate higher degrees of pluralism
than the weak cases, because the risks related to the core claims of a theory
are higher than those involved in its peripheral claims. Let us formulate the
idea in the case of these two dimensions:

- *Degree of pluralism 1.* The degree of pluralism about theory is higher
if the two or more theories in question are substitutes than if they are
complements.
- *Degree of pluralism 2.* The degree of pluralism about theory is higher
if the two or more theories in question are strong substitutes or complements than if they are weak substitutes or complements.

There are other dimensions related to the number of theories and the
distribution of their endorsement. First, one may say that the larger the
number of theories, each endorsed by at least one economist, the higher the
degree of plurality and pluralism. At one extreme, were all economists to

endorse one and the same theory, the degree of pluralism would be at its minimum. Note that there is no clearly defined other extreme, such as there being as many theories endorsed as there are economists; this is because each economist may endorse a very large number of theories, to the extent that his or her capacity allows.

Second, one may say that the more even the distribution of endorsement of theories within economics, the higher the degree of plurality and pluralism. At one extreme, all economists except one lonely heretic endorse one theory, while this remaining dissenter alone endorses a different theory. The distribution of endorsement is maximally uneven and the degree of pluralism is at its smallest. At the other extreme, all theories – which are two or more in number – are each endorsed by the same number of economists. The distribution of endorsement is maximally even and the degree of pluralism is at is greatest. Let us summarize:

- *Degree of pluralism 3.* The larger the favoured number of theories endorsed, the higher the degree of pluralism about theory.
- *Degree of pluralism 4.* The greater the favoured evenness of the distribution of endorsement between theories, the higher the degree of pluralism about theory.

With these definitions, it should be obvious that it would be difficult to defend the idea that the higher the degree of pluralism, the better. It may be the case that there is an optimum degree of plurality well below the maximum degree; an adequate form of pluralism has to be able to justify or prescribe this optimum degree. It is likely that there is a limit to a functional number of theories, and that some unevenness of the distribution of endorsement is functional for the advancement of economics.

In any case, I think we are now approaching some of the key issues which explain why the idea of pluralism is nowadays found to be so important by economists who do not identify themselves as mainstream economists. To see this, at least one more step has to be taken. It seems that those who speak in favour of pluralism do not mean to imply that they necessarily prefer the maximum degree of pluralism 3 or the maximum degree of pluralism 4. They are not only concerned about the number of theories endorsed or the evenness of the distribution of endorsement, but also, and emphatically, about the distribution of what may be called the academic power attached to theories. By 'academic power' I mean the amount of relevant resources (relating to publishing, promotion, prestige and so on) controlled by the endorsers of particular theories. The idea of the degree of pluralism can now be linked to the variation in the evenness of the distribution of academic power. We may state the following.

- *Degree of pluralism 5.* The greater the favoured evenness of the distribution of academic power attached to the endorsement of theories, the higher the degree of pluralism about theory.

Again, one may well accept that there are limits to a reasonable degree of pluralism in this sense, and yet insist that the economics profession should advocate a higher degree of pluralism 5 than currently seems to be the case.

8.   CONCLUSION

The foregoing exercise has attempted to serve two purposes. First, it has sought conceptual clarity about some aspects of the issue of pluralism in economics. More specifically, I have suggested that pluralism and plurality have to be kept separate and that the concept of pluralism has to be defined in terms of plurality; pluralism is a theory or statement about plurality. I have suggested distinctions between pluralisms about different things; between absolute and relative (and permanent and temporary) pluralism; and between degrees of pluralism on various dimensions.

The second purpose has been to outline a defence of pluralism about theory in ontological and epistemological terms, constrained by the one world principle. This defence was sketched in terms of theory substitutes and theory complements. The defence was further qualified in terms of relative and absolute pluralism; different strategies that can be followed with respect to theory substitutes and complements; and degrees of pluralism.

My focus has been on pluralism about theory while rejecting pluralism about the world and truth; hence 'the one world and the many theories'. These and other forms of pluralism (such as epistemological and linguistic pluralism) need to be clarified and scrutinized carefully before any justified positions for or against them comes forth in conversations among the Econ.

NOTES

1. However, in the ontological and veristic cases, plurality and pluralism seem to be more closely connected. If one states that there are multiple realities and multiple truths, one commits oneself to a pluralism about reality and truth. On the other hand, if one says that a multitude of theories and methods obtains, this does not yet imply pluralism about theories and methods.
2. For some purposes, it may be useful to employ the notion of thought world or model world, and keep it separate from the real world. Thought worlds are indeed created by means of theories, which means that they exist in a different sense from the real world, which exists unconstituted by acts of theorizing. Of course, those aspects of the real world that are of interest to a social scientist are often subjectively and even theoretically constituted by the

agents of social processes. This, however, is consistent with their being irreducible to the thought worlds of an economist. Importantly, pluralism about thought worlds is consistent with the denial of pluralism about the real world.

8. Methodological pluralism and pluralism of method

Sheila C. Dow

1. INTRODUCTION

Pluralism is the philosophical position that the ultimate reality of the universe consists of a plurality of entities; it is an ontological position. But the concept of pluralism can be applied at a variety of levels: to the (epistemological) understanding of reality (whether its ultimate nature is a plurality or not), to the methods employed to theorize about that understanding of reality, to the methodology which sets the criteria for theory choice, and to the study of methodologies themselves. Pluralism has been advocated at all of these levels in economics discourse. But an understanding of what is entailed by methodological pluralism and pluralism of method has been hampered by lack of reference to epistemological and ontological foundations. In particular, pluralism takes on a different meaning in a closed-system mode of thought (as in mainstream economics) from its meaning in an open-system mode of thought (as in Post Keynesian economics or institutional–evolutionary economics). The former can be thought of as 'pure pluralism', as the dual of a monist position, while the latter involves a more limited, although crucial, pluralism.

It is the purpose of this chapter to attempt to distinguish pluralism at the different levels, and according to different ontological and epistemological positions, and to assess whether the validity of the pluralist position differs between these different levels. It is concluded that a pure pluralist position is untenable at any level, but that a modified methodological pluralism is to be welcomed if grounded in an appropriate ontological and epistemic position, that is, that reality and knowledge of it are understood as open systems.

2. OPEN AND CLOSED SYSTEMS

Much of the following argument rests on the distinction between open and closed systems. Therefore, before considering pluralism as such, we consider first the nature of that distinction. An open system is one whose boundaries are not predetermined. Further, the nature and range of its constituent variables and the structure of their interrelationships are not predetermined. This is not a matter of stochastic variation. In contrast, the boundaries of a closed system are predetermined, as are the full range of constituent variables and the structure of their interrelationships. This does not preclude the possibility of stochastic variation. While closed systems are the province of classical logic, open systems are the province of a broader system of logic – ordinary logic, or human logic, as exemplified by Keynes (1973). While including classical logic as a special case for application under conditions of certainty, ordinary logic can also be applied to conditions of uncertainty, as pertain in open systems.

At the ontological level, the system is a system of real processes and phenomena. An understanding of reality as conforming to an open system may involve notions of human creativity and freedom of choice, for example. A closed-system understanding of reality may involve the notion of a grand plan on the part of the deity, and the absence of free will. Knowledge systems applied to this reality may be open or closed in either case. On the face of it, it might seem that an open-system ontology would entail an open-system epistemology, and similarly for a closed-system ontology. But, even if reality is an open system, it can be argued that knowledge can only be acquired by proceeding as if reality were a closed system. Alternatively, even if reality is a closed system, it can be argued that human knowledge inevitably cannot encompass the full system, so that it must itself conform to an open system.

General equilibrium theorizing is a fine example of a closed-system theoretical structure. Variables are clearly defined with fixed meaning, and the boundaries of the system are well defined according to which variables are endogenous and which exogenous. The aim is to reach agreement on the best representation of the structural relationships between variables, for universal application. This entails conformity of representation through formalism. The appraisal criterion of conformity to the principles of classical logic reflects a closed-system epistemology; where the additional criterion is applied of goodness of fit in econometric testing, a closed-system ontology is evident.

If reality is an open system, then any closed theoretical system can only have partial application. Formal systems are necessarily closed, since it is necessary to give variables fixed meaning, and to specify structural relationships and the exogenous variables. Other methods, however, can themselves be open; verbal analysis in particular allows for shades of meaning.

Once we move away from a closed-system ontology and/or a closed-system epistemology, the question of pluralism – its meaning and role – becomes interesting. If reality is an open system, how do we specify open systems of knowledge, and what role can closed subsystems of knowledge play? If knowledge is open (even if reality is closed), how do we choose the forms of (inevitably partial) knowledge to aim for? In what follows, we attempt to unravel the different possible senses of pluralism, and how they relate to different ontological and epistemological positions.

3.   ONTOLOGICAL PLURALISM

Pluralism at the ontological level involves the belief that reality constitutes a plurality of entities. If this position is to be non-trivial, it involves a rejection of the notion of the unity of nature. In its pure form, ontological pluralism denies the existence of unifying forces in nature; if nature is pluralistic, then there is no scope for general theorizing. In economics, this position is most closely associated with postmodernism; postmodernism emphasizes fragmentation, even of the self (see Amariglio, 1988). Ontological pluralism entails epistemic pluralism (understanding is fragmented). Together these pluralisms deny any scope for theory (see Amariglio, 1990); indeed some postmodernists embrace the term 'nihilism' (see Amariglio and Ruccio, 1995), the term with which Gordon (1991) chooses to characterize pluralism. Similarly, they deny any role for methodology.

Yet the content of postmodernism belies these implications; general statements are made about reality, theories are put forward and methodological statements made. In other words, pure ontological pluralism and its implications are untenable; any theoretical statement requires the belief in some regularity in understanding and/or in nature. The only possibilities then, if discourse is to occur at all, are a modified pluralism (partial regularities), or the belief in universal regularities. Many non-mainstream economists, other than postmodernists, hold a modified pluralist position, based on an organicist ontology (see for example Carabelli's, 1995, account of Keynes's organicism). This position holds that there are regularities in nature which science should aim to identify, but that these regularities are of process rather than events (see Lawson, 1989, 1995); they cannot be isolated from evolutionary or other irregularities. The economy, like knowledge, is therefore best understood as an open system.

Mainstream economics on the other hand has traditionally seen its scope as being defined by universal regularities, which can be separated dualistically from irregularities and are best understood within a closed theoretical system (see Dow, 1990a). Most mainstream economists, notably deductivists, are not explicit about their ontological position. But Lawson (1994) demonstrates that the view of science on which deductivism is based entails what he refers to as a 'Humean' ontology in terms of event regularities.

How far regularities can be perceived, if they exist, is an epistemic issue. We shall see in the next section that epistemic pluralism is not the sole preserve of ontological pluralists.

4. EPISTEMIC PLURALISM

Epistemic pluralism entails a plurality of understandings of reality; there is no known way of establishing what constitutes true knowledge. Logical positivism requires that theory be appraised with reference to an independent set of facts, implying that there is only one way in which (correctly) to know facts. Logical positivism came under serious threat in the 1960s, a period in which the notion that authority had sole access to the truth was fundamentally questioned. In the philosophy of science, Popper's (1959) fallibilism had laid the groundwork, but it was Kuhn (1962) who captured the imagination with his argument that understanding is paradigm-specific; what appears to be contrary evidence may not be perceived as such if it threatens the power of the dominant paradigm.

Out of this change developed a distinctive perspective on understanding; this perspective is evident both in the rhetoric/hermeneutic approach as well as in postmodernism. Both take a pluralist position on understanding. The postmodernist epistemic pluralism follows directly from the postmodern pluralist ontology; even the individual has the potential for a plurality of understanding. The rhetoric/hermeneutic approach is inspired by Rorty's (1979) view that philosophy cannot mirror nature; no position is taken on whether ultimate reality is a plurality or not. (See the exchange between Mäki's, 1988, attempt to tease out an ontology of rhetoric, and McCloskey's, 1988, reply.) Rather, understanding of reality is expressed by means of a plurality of narratives. Thus not only is reality discussed by means of a plurality of narratives, but that reality itself is to be read as a plurality of narratives (see Lavoie, 1990, Introduction, and Brown, 1994). There is no basis for choosing one narrative over another.

The logical positivist belief in a unitary, objective understanding of facts nevertheless persists in much of economics (see Boland, 1991 and Lawson, 1994). The difficulty of devising definitive empirical tests has thrown increasing doubt on the truth value of theory (see Boland, 1989, p. 88), but in general the truth value of the facts themselves is not questioned among mainstream economists. For the increasingly dominant deductivists, the truth value of facts is seen as having relevance only regarding axioms, and these are asserted to be self-evident. A significant exception is the explicitly pluralist epistemic position taken by Weintraub (1989); his position has shifted from being Lakatosian (which as a basis for theory appraisal requires a unitary set of facts) to denying the scope for theory appraisal on the grounds that facts are theory-laden, that is, there is a plurality of understanding of reality.

Epistemologically, there should be a direct parallel between a pluralist understanding (possibly of a pluralist reality) among economic agents and economists alike. This is the case for postmodernists and the rhetoric approach; there is no basis for choosing between understandings among agents or among economists. In contrast, the logical positivist position entails a unitary understanding of facts by agents and a corresponding unitary understanding by economists (though both may be expressed probabilistically). Curiously no such parallel is evident in Weintraub's work; if facts are theory-laden for economists, surely they must also be theory-laden for agents. An acceptance of this point would have profound implications for general equilibrium theorizing. It is the plurality of understanding by economic agents, in the postmodern view, which undermines theorizing in general.

Non-mainstream economists other than employers of postmodernism and the rhetoric approach (PostKeynesians, or institutionalist-evolutionary economists, for example) employ an open-system epistemology that allows for a range of understandings but also for theorizing. Following directly from an organicist ontology, or from the view that human understanding of reality (whether ultimately organicist or not) is necessarily limited, it is argued that we can only understand reality as an open, organic system. Keynes's (1973) philosophy provides an epistemology for open organic systems; since knowledge in general is based on imperfect knowledge, it is inevitable that there will be a range of understandings of reality, among agents as well as economists. But this epistemology differs from pure pluralism in that there are regularities in the knowledge generation process of agents and economists which limit the range of rational beliefs; the choice of belief (among agents and economists) is a matter for rational debate.

We now see how these different epistemologies feed through into positions on method, and then on methodology.

5.   PLURALISM OF METHOD

Pluralism of method is the methodological position that there are no decisive criteria for selecting one best method of analysis (for example, the deductivist method, or the experimental method); economists should therefore employ a plurality of methods. The major influence is Popper (1959), who saw a role for situational logic in the social sciences, given the difficulties with falsificationism; the choice of method should then be problem-dependent (see Caldwell, 1991, who also appears supportive of pluralism of method). This version of pluralism (also known as eclecticism) has been advocated by Hutchison (1988), Boland (1982) and Solow (1988) without any hint of pluralism at the epistemic or ontological levels; all three subscribe to a unitary epistemology and ontology.

But if there is unitary understanding of such regularities as can be perceived (that is, the epistemology and ontology conform to those of logical positivism), then pluralism of method can only be explained in terms of the failure of traditional methodology to produce satisfactory criteria for choosing methods. Practising economists must choose methods by some criteria; on what grounds are these criteria to be selected? In principle, it should be possible to construct a taxonomy of problem types and advocate methods accordingly, given the starting point that economics aims to identify regularities that are presumed to exist. Boland (1989) takes case studies to illustrate the process of method choice. Mayer (1993) advocates a particular set of criteria based on the distinction between pure and applied theory. He advocates internal, formalist criteria for deductive theory and client satisfaction for empirical theory. But without any epistemological explanation for the need for a range of methods, given a unitary ontology and epistemology, a body of thought made up of pure theory and applied theory, with no explicit connection between the two, appears simply incoherent.

It might seem that pluralism of method could be justified by a pluralist epistemology. Since reality may be understood in a variety of ways, and there are no grounds for preferring one understanding over another, there are no grounds for choosing one method of acquiring knowledge over another. The rhetoric/hermeneutic approach takes an agnostic position (different methods arc takcn on thcir own mcrits but thcrc is no advocacy of pluralism, indeed there is a denial of methodology in general). The postmodernist approach might be interpreted as advocating a plurality of methods; one of its most notable features is the denial of general theories. But, as has been suggested above, any postmodern position on method is self-contradictory; the essence of postmodernism is to eschew normative statements, and indeed theory in general.

The advocacy of a range of methods is entailed by the open-system epistemology of approaches, such as that adopted by Post Keynesian economists, or institutional/evolutionary economists. But this is not pluralism of method in the eclecticism sense, although it is commonly misunderstood by others as such. It is entailed by an open-system epistemology that knowledge is acquired by gathering evidence and constructing arguments in order to build up rational belief. These contributions to knowledge are incommensurate in the sense that they do not build up to a single probability statistic, that is, they do not fit into closed-system theorizing. Certainly the choice of a range of methods depends on the nature of the problem and the context. But the choice is guided (and thus limited) by reason, by convention and by vision; it is differences in these that account for different schools of thought, which have in common open-system theorizing (see Dow, 1990b). To distinguish this approach from that of the eclecticists, it must be emphasized that reason, conventions and vision all take on a particular meaning and play an explicit part in open-system epistemology (terms do not have unitary meaning). Closed-system reason is only a subset of open-system reason (see Carabelli, 1988). Conventions are a necessity in building up knowledge in Keynesian logic (see Hodgson, 1988), while in mainstream epistemology they lack logical foundation, as Boland (1982) has tirelessly pointed out. Finally, vision (or ontology) determines how problems are identified and interpreted (see Dow, 1990b). Given an open-system ontology, there is a range of possibilities; given a closed-system, unitary ontology, there is only one.

6. METHODOLOGICAL PLURALISM

Methodological pluralism is a meta-methodological position; it advocates that methodologists study a range of methodologies (by means of rational reconstruction). Critical pluralism involves the criticism of this range of methodologies by means of a range of criteria. This position has been advocated most notably by Caldwell (1982, 1986, 1988). The underlying reasoning is that there is no basis for deciding on one methodology. Rather than devoting fruitless efforts to finding the best methodology, methodologists should devote their efforts to promoting methodological understanding among economists by clarifying the nature of the different possibilities and demonstrating their strengths and weaknesses according to different criteria. (Boland, 1982, 1991, at times also seems to be a methodological pluralist as well as a pluralist of method. Redman, 1991, advocates a critical rationalist version of methodological pluralism.)

Although this positive role for methodology counters the anti-methodology position of the rhetoric/hermeneutic approach, Caldwell (1990) embraces the hermeneutic idea of taking each approach on its own merits to promote a better understanding among practitioners of different approaches. The critical element is additional, however, and represents the fundamental meta-methodological difference from the hermeneutic approach. The rhetoric/hermeneutic approach accepts plurality of understanding and plurality of method as a description of reality, but refuses to make any normative judgement about the nature or extent of those pluralities; postmodernists positively welcome plurality of understanding and method (the more the better, as a reflection of a fundamentally fragmented reality). Caldwell, rather (from his Popperian starting point), appears to regard a wide plurality of methodologies as a regrettable necessity, and looks forward to the outcome of methodological pluralism as being a narrowing down of possibilities (see Caldwell, 1989).

But, as was pointed out in the discussion of Caldwell's (1988) paper (see de Marchi, 1988, pp. 53–6), Caldwell does not spell out the epistemological

foundations of his methodological pluralism (nor its ontological foundations). What is the reason for a range of methodologies in the first place? Is it
in the nature of knowledge (and reality) that it be so, as the open-system
approach suggests? Or is it a temporary limitation on our understanding, as
the eclecticist approach suggests? Or is it pure folly that methodologies and
methodologists persist at all in spite of the fragmentation of knowledge (and
possibly reality), as the rhetoric approach and postmodernists suggest?

Critical methodological pluralism explicitly aims to go beyond description. But as with eclecticist pluralists, the question arises as to the criteria for
criticism. Caldwell advocates particularly criticism in a methodology's own
terms as a way of promoting greater understanding of a particular methodology. Such an effort is clearly preferable to the all too common criticism of
one methodology by the criteria of another (see Caldwell, 1986). But it is
only feasible up to a point. If the justification of methodological pluralism is
epistemic, then, just as facts are theory-laden and theories are methodology-
laden, so must the knowledge of methodologists be coloured by their own
vision of reality and of how knowledge is constructed; epistemic pluralism,
after all, is a recognition that there are different understandings of reality, but
in general any one economist or methodologist only has one understanding. I
can attest from personal experience of trying to present a range of schools of
thought in their own terms (Dow, 1985) that it is not possible to switch fully
satisfactorily in a detached fashion from one ontology-plus-epistemology to
another. But without a pluralist epistemology, what is the justification for
methodological pluralism?

While I share Caldwell's view that trying to understand different methodologies in their own terms is a worthwhile exercise and should serve to
promote more constructive debate among economists, the scope for that
understanding is always conditional on the methodologist's own ontological
and epistemological position. This applies even more strongly to the application of external criteria, which must be chosen according to some further
criteria if the exercise is to have meaning.

Caldwell's statements of methodological pluralism have tremendous appeal in their advocacy of civilized, reasoned, non-self-serving behaviour. But
methodological pluralism, as presented so far, lacks force because of its lack
of epistemic and ontological foundations. In traditional epistemic (that is,
dualist) terms, methodological pluralism can be interpreted as non-methodol-
ogy because it does not establish standards. Understood as the dual of
traditional methodology, methodological pluralism may be understood as
according with the rhetoric approach, which denies methodology any role.
But understood as a means of improving knowledge, where knowledge is
understood as an open system, methodological pluralism is fully justified.
Methodologists cannot escape their own preconceptions any more than any-

one else. But an ontological and epistemic awareness can enhance awareness of these preconceptions, which in turn can enhance awareness among economists at large of their preconceptions.

7.   CONCLUSION

I conclude therefore that methodological pluralism in a pure form, like pluralism of method, pluralist epistemology and pluralist ontology, is untenable as a basis for knowledge. Pure pluralism is taken here to be the dual of the traditional unitary position of mainstream economics. Further, the justification of methodological pluralism or pluralism of method is not at all clear when either is combined with a unitary, closed-system epistemology and/or ontology. On the other hand, the recognition of the inevitability of a range of methodologies and the advocacy of the employment of a particular range of methods is the logical outcome of an open-system epistemology and ontology.

This chapter is offered as an exercise in open-system meta-methodology. It offers an attempt at a rational reconstruction of a range of positions with respect to pluralism, in the full knowledge that these reconstructions may be flawed, not least because of my own preconceptions. But this is how knowledge progresses: offering arguments provides scope for feedback to correct misunderstandings and to direct modifications in thinking. Within an open-system approach there is no contradiction involved in arguing for one's own viewpoint while respecting and being open to the viewpoints of others.

REFERENCES

Amariglio, J.L. (1988), 'The body, economic discourse, and power: an economist's introduction to Foucault', *History of Political Economy*, 20(4), pp. 583–613.
Amariglio, J.L. (1990), 'Economics as a postmodern discourse', in W.J. Samuels (ed.), *Economics as Discourse*, Boston: Kluwer, pp. 15–46.
Amariglio, J.L. and D.F. Ruccio (1995), 'Keynes, postmodernism and uncertainty', in S.C. Dow and J. Hillard (eds), *Keynes, Knowledge and Uncertainty*, Aldershot: Edward Elgar, pp. 334–56.
Boland, L.A. (1982), *The Foundations of Economic Method*, London: Allen & Unwin.
Boland, L.A. (1989), *The Methodology of Economic Model Building: Methodology after Samuelson*, London: Routledge.
Boland, L.A. (1991), 'The theory and practice of economic methodology', *Methodus*, 3(2), pp. 6–17.
Brown, V. (1994), 'The economy as text', in R.E. Backhouse (ed.), *New Directions in Economic Methodology*, London: Routledge, pp. 368–82.
Caldwell, B.J. (1982), *Beyond Positivism: Economic Methodology in the Twentieth Century*, London: Allen & Unwin.

Caldwell, B.J. (1986), 'Towards a broader conception of criticism', *History of Political Economy*, 18, pp. 675–81.

Caldwell, B.J. (1988), 'The case for pluralism', in N. De Marchi (ed.), *The Popperian Legacy in Economics*, Cambridge: Cambridge University Press, pp. 231–44.

Caldwell, B.J. (1989), 'Post-Keynesian methodology: an assessment', *Review of Political Economy*, 1(1), pp. 43–64.

Caldwell, B.J. (1990), 'Does methodology matter? How should it be practised?', *Finnish Economic Papers*, 3(1), pp. 64–71.

Caldwell, B.J. (1991), 'Clarifying Popper', *Journal of Economic Literature*, 29(1), pp. 1–33.

Carabelli, A. (1988), *On Keynes's Method*, London: Macmillan.

Carabelli, A. (1995), 'Uncertainty and measurement in Keynes: probability and organicness', in S.C. Dow and J. Hillard (eds), *Keynes, Knowledge and Uncertainty*, Aldershot: Edward Elgar, pp. 137–60.

de Marchi, N. (ed.) (1988), *The Popperian Legacy in Economics*, Cambridge: Cambridge University Press.

Dow, S.C. (1985), *Macroeconomic Thought: A Methodological Approach*, Oxford: Blackwell.

Dow, S.C. (1990a), 'Beyond dualism', *Cambridge Journal of Economics*, 14(2), pp. 143–58.

Dow, S.C. (1990b), 'Post Keynesianism as political economy: a methodological discussion', *Review of Political Economy*, 2(3), pp. 345–58.

Gordon, S. (1991), *The History and Philosophy of Social Science*, London: Routledge.

Hodgson, G.M. (1988), *Economics and Institutions*, Cambridge: Polity Press.

Hutchison, T.W. (1988), 'The case for falsification', in N. de Marchi (ed.), *The Popperian Legacy in Economics*, Cambridge: Cambridge University Press, pp. 169–81.

Keynes, J.M. (1973), *The Treatise on Probability. Collected Writings*, Vol. VIII, London: Macmillan for the Royal Economic Society.

Kuhn, T.S. (1962), *The Structure of Scientific Revolutions*, Chicago: Chicago University Press.

Lavoie, D. (ed.) (1990), *Economics and Hermeneutics*, London: Routledge.

Lawson, T. (1989), 'Abstractions, tendencies and stylised facts: a realist approach to economic analysis', *Cambridge Journal of Economics*, 13(1), pp. 59–78.

Lawson, T. (1994), 'Why are so many economists opposed to methodology?', *Journal of Economic Methodology*, 1(1), pp. 105–34.

Lawson, T. (1995), 'Economics and expectations', in S.C. Dow and J. Hillard (eds), *Keynes, Knowledge and Uncertainty*, Aldershot: Edward Elgar.

Mäki, U. (1988), 'How to combine rhetoric and realism in the methodology of economics', *Economics and Philosophy*, 4(1), pp. 89–109.

Mayer, T. (1993), *Truth versus Precision in Economics*, Aldershot: Edward Elgar.

McCloskey, D.N. (1988), 'Two replies and a dialogue on the rhetoric of economics: Mäki, Rappoport, Rosenberg', *Economics and Philosophy*, 4(1), pp. 150–66.

Popper, K. (1959), *The Logic of Scientific Discovery*, London: Harper & Row.

Redman, D.A. (1991), *Economics and the Philosophy of Science*, Oxford: Oxford University Press.

Rorty, R. (1979), *Philosophy and the Mirror of Nature*, Princeton: Princeton University Press.

Solow, R.M. (1988), 'Comments from inside economics', in A. Klamer, D. McCloskey and R.M. Solow (eds), *The Consequences of Economic Rhetoric*, Cambridge: Cambridge University Press.

Weintraub, E.R. (1989), 'Methodology doesn't matter, but the history of economic thought might', *Scandinavian Journal of Economics*, 91, pp. 477–93.

PART III

Varieties of Capitalism

9. Institutions and employment performance in different growth regimes

Eileen Appelbaum and Ronald Schettkat*

INTRODUCTION

Although the OECD countries are all capitalist market economies, their institutional settings as well as their economic performance varied substantially in the 1970s and 1980s. Therefore, whether institutions matter is not controversial in economics, but rather the question is which institutional arrangements best support the performance of the economy. Many economists became interested in understanding how institutional differences influence economic performance. However, the industrialized economies varied less with respect to GDP growth than with respect to employment (see Figure 9.1). This suggests that differences in GDP growth rates are not sufficient to explain variations in labour market performance. One of the most obvious candidates for the explanation of differing economic performance in market economies is the wage-bargaining system, which differs remarkably between countries.

Source: Based on OECD statistics.

Figure 9.1   Standard deviations of growth rates of GDP, employment to population ratios, and unemployment rates

Wage-bargaining can take place at several levels. At one extreme, individual companies and employees may negotiate the wage (decentralized bargaining), whereas at the other extreme, national unions and employers' associations may bargain over wages for a whole country (centralized bargaining). Countries can occupy any position on this continuum. Traditionally economists favoured the decentralized model of wage-bargaining because it is best suited to achieving efficient allocation in perfectly competitive markets. But this may not be the case in an imperfect world where asymmetric information, transaction costs, uncertainty, interdependence of actions and so on exist and where employers and unions have market power. In such an imperfect world – which has gained importance in economic theory – even centralized wage-bargaining systems can produce a superior economic performance, as recent theoretical and empirical work suggests. Political scientists have discussed these issues under the label 'corporatism', and more recently economists have taken up this discussion, often under the label 'wage-bargaining and economic performance'.

The general result in this literature is that institutions have a strong influence on labour market performance, but the specific relationship between wage-bargaining institutions and economic performance remains unclear. Some economists take the view that more organized wage-setting increases the ability to compensate for external shocks, and thus reduces the non-accelerating inflation rate of unemployment (NAIRU). This view of a negative linear relationship between the centralization of wage-bargaining and unemployment has been challenged in recent work, which argues that both centralized and decentralized wage-bargaining systems are able to produce favourable employment outcomes through wage restraint, although this is achieved in each case through completely different mechanisms. In a decentralized bargaining system wage restraint is achieved by market pressure, whereas in the centralized system the central wage negotiator internalizes the negative effects of overly high wage increases and thus acts as if the market coordinates wage-setting. Countries with wage-bargaining at an intermediate level, such as branch-level negotiations, suffer from the market power of organized labour, which does not internalize negative feedback effects. These countries, therefore, experience a poorer employment performance.

Usually, the literature discusses the employment and unemployment impacts of the aggregate real wage and does not explicitly deal with the wage structure; nor does it discuss the employment structure of economies with respect to industries. However, the industrialized economies differ enormously concerning the industry composition of employment and wage differentials. Therefore, a second effect of wage-bargaining institutions on wages, namely on wage dispersion, may also be important. The argument is that wage-bargaining institutions affect wage dispersion and, through this mechanism, affect employment growth in activities with below-average rates of productivity growth. In the last two decades or so, the industrial economies have exhibited a negative or at best zero correlation between productivity growth and employment growth by industry (Appelbaum and Schettkat, 1995). This contrasts with the positive correlation, which Salter (1960) and others such as Kaldor (1987) described as characteristic of industrialized economies earlier this century, and which provided the underlying rationale for the Swedish (Rehn and Meidner) model of wage and industrial policy.[1] Under the new circumstances, aggregate employment growth depended on the expansion of employment in lower-productivity growth activities (mainly consumer services). This change in the growth regime coincided with rising unemployment, that is, with disequilibrium in the labour market. In this context, labour market institutions became increasingly important. In the earlier conditions of near-full employment, and with nominal wages and employment rising most strongly in high-productivity growth industries, there was little scope for institutional differences among countries to affect outcomes. As an inverse relationship began to develop between employment growth and productivity growth, however, whether an overall increase in employment could be achieved came to depend on an expansion of industries with lower productivity growth. Institutional differences between countries then became important, as different institutional settings have to have been more or less successful in promoting employment growth in lower productivity growth industries, usually services.

In this chapter we discuss theories of wage-setting in industrialized economies as well as efforts to measure those institutional arrangements that affect wage-setting. We investigate the relationship between wage-setting systems and wage dispersion and employment performance. Our conclusion is that overall employment growth was weakest in the 1980s in those countries that lacked both high wage dispersion and highly developed corporatist institutions. In addition, we argue below that a broader definition of corporatism that includes coordination with government may affect employment growth in publicly provided or subsidized services.

WAGE-BARGAINING SYSTEMS AND ECONOMIC PERFORMANCE: THEORY AND MEASUREMENT

Theoretical Considerations

Wage-bargaining can take place at (a) the firm (establishment) level, (b) the branch level and (c) the national level. In a decentralized bargaining system, unions or even individual workers negotiate the wage with single employers (single-employer or decentralized bargaining). At the branch level, unions and employers' associations negotiate (multi-employer bargaining), while at the national level the peak organizations of unions and employers negotiate (centralized bargaining). In practice, bargaining can occur on more than one level (multi-level bargaining) with the national or the branch-level agreements setting (minimal) standards, which may be modified at lower levels.

Increasing centralization of wage-bargaining can have two different effects: with increasing comprehensiveness, unions gain market power which may be used to push up wages and working standards; at the same time, bigger organizations encompass larger groups, that is, the negative effects of wage-bargaining become endogenous. These two effects thus work in different directions. Mancur Olson's (1982) theory suggests that special interest groups are most damaging when they have gained a certain amount of power but little responsibility. An encompassing organization can exist at different levels but it always requires that the membership over which the organization has effective authority be coterminous with the population that will bear any adverse consequences of action (Crouch, 1992). This has allowed economists (Calmfors and Driffill, 1988) to argue that wage-bargaining at the company level (decentralized) but also at the national level (centralized) leads to favourable macroeconomic outcomes such as low unemployment and inflation rates. Economies with an intermediate level of wage-bargaining, however, suffer from union power, which does not internalize negative effects. These countries are therefore expected to produce less favourable macroeconomic outcomes.

Calmfors and Driffill (1988) argue that both extremes (countries with decentralized and with centralized bargaining systems) achieve positive employment results through wage restraint, although by different means. Company-level unions are constrained by competition in the product market[2] but they can externalize the negative effects of their actions. Company unions thus have limited power but they do not carry the burden of negative effects, that is, they are in a free-rider position with respect to negative effects which do not affect their membership. A centralized union, on the other hand, can expect its policy to influence the macroeconomy, that is, the negative effects of wage-setting will affect the union's members directly. If workers lose their jobs and depend on benefits, these benefits will be financed by members of the union, and hence overly high wage increases will directly affect members' net wages. Similarly, if wage rises induce inflation this will directly affect the real wage of the union's members. Therefore, it is argued that centralized unions (and employers' associations) will take the macroeconomic effects of their action into account because there is simply no outside world to which negative effects can be shifted. A branch-level union, in contrast, has market power but it externalizes the negative effects of its

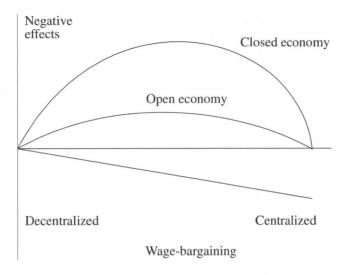

Figure 9.2   Possible relationships between negative effects and wage-bargaining systems

action. This relation between external effects and the centralization of wage-bargaining is illustrated by the hump-shaped curve in Figure 9.2.

So far the theoretical argument has been developed for a closed economy. The impact of increased competition should have flattened the trade-off curve between centralization of the wage-bargaining system and likely negative effects.[3] In the extreme case, when foreign products are perfect substitutes for domestic products, national institutions would become irrelevant and the upper curve in Figure 9.2 would become horizontal. In effect a national industry has no more power over price-setting than a competitive firm.

The hump-shaped relation between centralization of the bargaining system and possible negative effects is under debate for other reasons as well. A linear negative relation is the proposed alternative. Michael Bruno and Jeffrey Sachs, Richard Layard, Stephen Nickell and Richard Jackman, as well as David Soskice, all assume such a linear negative relationship. The more centralized (Soskice uses the term 'coordinated' and Bruno and Sachs use 'corporatist') a bargaining system is, the more it takes account of macroeconomic impacts. This view is supported by the fact that the share of wage costs increases with aggregation. The share of wage costs in output is roughly 20 per cent at the firm level but at the aggregate level it is about 70 per cent (Nickell, 1988). This suggests that the impact of the negative effects of wage-setting falls monotonically with aggregation. In other words, the more encompassing the organizations are, the more they take the negative effects of their action into account. As the degree of corporatism increases, the micro horizon widens to the macro horizon (linear falling curve in Figure 9.2).

Measurement

Many efforts have been made to measure the degree of coordination in wage-bargaining or, more generally, the institutional factors which affect responsiveness of wage-setting to macroeconomic conditions. Union density was used to explain variations in economic performance between countries (see, for example, Blanchflower and Freeman, 1992) but there are also efforts to measure 'corporatism'.[4] Whereas it is relatively straightforward to measure union density,[5] it is more difficult to measure the degree of corporatism. The problems are manifold: (a) no standard definition of corporatism exists; (b) it is often difficult to quantify institutional features; and (c) combining different variables in one indicator causes problems.

Many of the researchers who have developed indices for corporatism have a deep institutional knowledge of some countries, but there remains a substantial subjective component in their classifications. In addition, the definition of corporatism used differs between studies (see Table 9.1 for a brief charac-

Table 9.1   A brief characterization of indices representing wage-bargaining systems

Comprehensiveness index	Coverage and bargaining level (Schettkat, 1995)
Soskice	Covert and overt coordination of unions and employers' associations
Calmfors and Driffill	Centralization of unions and employers' organizations
Bruno and Sachs (Crouch)	Centralization of unions, shop-floor representation, employers' coordination, existence of works councils
Blyth	Level of bargaining, union and employers' cooperation
Schmitter	Organizational centralization and the number of unions
Cameron	Centralization of unions, control capacity of central organization, union membership
Tarantelli	Degree of ideological and political consensus of unions and employers, centralization of bargaining, regulation of industrial conflict
Lehmbruch	Influence of unions in the policy formulation process
Lijphardt and Crepaz	Average of several other indices
Layard, Nickell and Jackman	Unions' plus employers' coordination

terization of the indices). It is therefore not surprising that the various indicators differ substantially and that some countries are classified as highly corporatist by some authors, whereas others classify them as non-corporatist.[6]

Institutions are often regarded as very stable, and most studies on corporatism and economic performance were published in the early and mid-1980s and refer mainly to the 1970s. Since then, however, substantial changes have taken place in some countries. In Sweden, centralized bargaining disappeared in the early 1980s, in the United Kingdom the unions' influence diminished, and New Zealand switched from multi-employer to single-employer bargaining. However, there is no uniform trend to more decentralized bargaining. In some countries wage-bargaining became more centralized and many countries did not change at all (see, for details, OECD, 1994).

The theoretical debate suggests that an index which characterizes wage-bargaining needs to capture the coverage and the level at which wage-bargaining takes place. Even centralized wage-bargaining will have little effect if only a small proportion of workers is covered. Some authors use union density to capture the share of the workforce affected by collective bargaining as an estimate of coverage. High union density leads by definition to high coverage, but as the example of France shows (see Table 9.2), high coverage can be achieved even with low union density through legal extension of collective agreements (for an overview, see Hartog and Theuwes, 1993).[7] The level at which wage-bargaining takes place is still important. If the agreements are extended to the whole economy, bargaining parties might be expected to take macroeconomic effects into account. This will be the case if negotiations take place at the national level, no matter how high the union density rate. If only specific parts of the workforce are organized, collective negotiations may be biased in favour of the organized workers.

Both variables, the bargaining level and the coverage rate, have the advantage that they can 'easily' be measured, that is to say, such an index does not so much rely on subjective classifications as do many other efforts to classify bargaining systems. Bargaining level and coverage are combined in the comprehensiveness index displayed in Table 9.2.[8] The advantage of this index is that it captures the components regarded as most relevant in the theoretical literature and in addition both components can be measured objectively. Most importantly, data for the 1970s and the 1980s are available for both components for most countries. This makes it possible to account for changes in the wage-bargaining systems. Furthermore, the comprehensiveness index shows a high positive correlation with coordination (see Table 9.4).

The most dramatic change to decentralization occurred in the United Kingdom, where unions' influence and coverage declined in conjunction with a shift to single-employer bargaining during the 1980s. These changes have moved the United Kingdom to the less centralized end of the spectrum.

Table 9.2   Bargaining indices, union density and wage differentials

	Comprehensiveness				Calmfors/ Driffill Ranking[a]	Union Density (% of labour force)		Earnings Inequalities[b] D9/D1 D9/D1	
	Values		Ranking[a]						
	1970–80 (1)	1980–90 (2)	1970–80 (3)	1980–90 (4)	1970s (5)	1975 (6)	1985 (7)	1980 (12)	1990 (13)
USA	26	18	1	1	2	22.8	18.0	4.8	5.6
Japan	28	23	2	2	4	34.4	28.9	3.0	3.2
Canada	37	38	3	3	1	34.4	35.9	4.0	4.4
Switzerland	106	106	4	6	3	32.9	28.8		2.7
New Zealand	134	134	5	7	8	50.1	47.3	2.9	3.0
Portugal	140	198	6	16	n.a.	52.4	51.6	3.6	3.5
UK	140	47	7	4	5	48.3	45.5	2.8	3.3
Netherlands	152	142	8	9	10	38.4	28.7	2.5	2.6
Spain	168	136	9	8	n.a.	30.4	16.0	n.a.	n.a.
France	170	184	10	14	6	22.8	16.3	3.3	3.3
Australia	176	80	11	5	7	56.0	56.5	2.8	2.8
Belgium	180	180	12	12	9	55.3	54.3	2.4	2.3
Germany	182	180	13	13	11	36.6	37.4	2.7	2.5
Austria	196	196	14	15	15	56.1	48.6	3.5	3.5
Norway	225	225	15	17	14	52.7	55.7	2.1	2.0
Sweden	249	166	16	11	13	82.1	94.2	2.0	2.0
Finland	285	143	17	10	12	67.4	68.6	2.5	2.5
Correlations									
D9/D1(1980)	–0.71	–0.52	–0.65	–0.45	–0.61	–0.68	–0.58	1.00	
D9/D1(1990)	–0.75	–0.63	–0.72	–0.57	–0.68	–0.65	–0.55	0.98	1.00

Notes:
[a]   Low rankings = low degree of comprehensiveness (centralization).
[b]   From OECD, *Employment Outlook 1996*; earning inequality specifics: USA from *Employment Outlook 1993*, Canada 1981, New Zealand 1984, Portugal, Netherlands 1985, Belgium 1986, Germany 1984, Norway 1979, 1991.

Sources: Data on the comprehensiveness index: Schettkat (1995b); union density: OCED, *Employment Outlook*.

Australia moved from being a middle-ranking country to being a much less coordinated country, mainly because the level of coordination shifted to the company level. Substantial changes also occurred in the Nordic countries, where both Sweden and Finland gave up centralized wage-bargaining, as is clearly shown in the change in the index between the 1970s and the 1980s. Norway, on the other hand, remained an economy with centralized wage-bargaining.

Bargaining Systems and Wages

Aggregate wage flexibility

Wage-bargaining institutions can influence employment and unemployment through two channels: (a) a coordinated wage policy may lead to wage restraint in the overall economy; and (b) centralization may have an impact on wage differentials and the wage structures.

Originally the discussion of corporatism and economic performance was not related to wage structure but rather emphasized the behaviour of the aggregate wage. Flanagan *et al.* (1983), Bruno and Sachs (1985), Calmfors and Driffill (1988) and Soskice (1990) all discuss the impact of wage-bargaining institutions on aggregate wage restraint and on inflation, employment and unemployment. The main argument is that wage restraint is best achieved in corporatist bargaining systems although there is dissent as to whether this is a linear (Bruno and Sachs, 1985; Soskice, 1990; Layard et al., 1991) or a non-linear relationship (Calmfors and Driffill, 1988).[9]

Bruno and Sachs, for example, focused on the ability of economies to absorb external shocks, such as the oil price increases in the early and late 1970s, and argue that corporatist countries are likely to achieve a better economic performance than non-corporatist countries because they are able to follow an accommodatory wage policy: that is, inflationary pressure is lower and thus reduces the NAIRU, which allows for higher employment and lower unemployment. In addition to the degree of corporatism (as measured by the Calmfors–Driffill index) Layard *et al.* (1991) argue that the characteristics of the unemployment insurance system (replacement ratio and benefit duration) are important in explaining variations in the responsiveness of wage-setting to unemployment across countries. Using regression analysis of the responsiveness of wage-setting to unemployment, these authors find a negative linear relation to the centralization index of Calmfors and Driffill.[10]

Wage differentials

Only a few studies of bargaining systems and economic performance take wage dispersion into account (Freeman, 1988; Rowthorn, 1992; Appelbaum and Schettkat, 1993, 1995), although 'equal pay for equal work' is part of almost any union's programme and more comprehensive unions are expected to enforce such a concept on a broader scale than are less comprehensive unions. In the literature, however, it is seen that unions can have a positive and a negative impact on wage differentials. Unions raise the wages of organized workers and thus raise the wage differential (Friedman, 1962), but they may also increase standards and thus reduce wage differentials (Blanchflower and Freeman, 1992). At the firm level, union–non-union wage differentials differ substantially from 0.22 in the United States to 0.07 in

Austria (ibid.), suggesting that unions can have a different effect depending on their type of organization (company unions as in the United States, centralized unions in Austria).

In cross-country comparison,[11] wage differentials decline with increasing union density. Not only the degree of unionization but also wage-bargaining institutions are expected to have an impact on wage differentials. Sweden, for example, was a country ranking high on the comprehensiveness scale and was known for its solidaristic wage policy, which was intended to reduce wage differentials between industries and skill groups (Meidner and Hedbʋrg, 1984; Flanagan, 1987). Sweden's wage differentials are still outstandingly low, although they did increase through the 1980s. The United States, on the other hand, is the leader in wage dispersion and has the least comprehensive wage-bargaining system. Austria has a high value on the comprehensiveness index but at the same time wage differentials there are very high (see Table 9.2). Austria, however, seems to be an outlier, because countries with a high comprehensiveness tend to have low wage differentials. One explanation for the Austria–Sweden difference that has been put forward is the different historical development of the corporatist arrangements in the two countries (Therborn, 1992). In Sweden, corporatist institutions – highlighted by the Saltjöbadan agreement (Meidner and Hedborg, 1984) – developed as a solution to industrial conflicts that were damaging economic performance. In contrast, the Austrian labour movement was more markedly based on consensus after the Second World War (Guger, 1992). In general, however, wage-bargaining systems are associated with wage differentials in a negative linear way: low-ranking countries on the comprehensiveness scale have high wage differentials and high-ranking countries have low wage differentials (see correlation coefficients in the lower panel of Table 9.2).

It may be concluded from these exercises that wage-bargaining institutions seem to be very important for inequality. Less comprehensive bargaining systems and less centralized bargaining systems allow more easily for earnings inequality. These results support Richard Freeman's (1996) call for a policy to strengthen institutions in order to prevent inequality from rising further in the United States. The results, however, will also please those who see institutions as rigidities that prevent economies from creating employment.

UNEMPLOYMENT AND EMPLOYMENT TRENDS

The non-linear relationship of the impact of wage-bargaining institutions on unemployment (hump-shaped) and employment (U-shaped) was discovered in the 1980s (Calmfors and Driffill, 1988; Freeman, 1988; Rowthorn, 1992).

Table 9.3   Regression analysis of labour market performance on wage-bargaining systems

Dependent Variable	Independent Variables			Summary Statistics		
	Constant	Comp R70-U	CD-U	R^2	F	N
Level						
Unemployment rate						
1970–73	2.89	–0.18		0.06	0.86	15
	[1.05]	[0.18]				
	3.32		–0.28	0.15	2.3	15
	[1.25]		[0.21]			
1985–89	2.02	1.00		0.41	9.11	15
	[1.58]	[0.33]				
	3.13		0.74	0.23	3.78	15
	[1.81]		[0.38]			
Employment to population ratio						
1970–73	71.31	–0.92		0.12	1.75	15
	[3.35]	[0.70]				
	69.69		–0.54	0.04	0.55	15
	[5.35]		[0.73]			
1985–89	77.65	–2.53		0.42	9.33	15
	[3.97]	[0.83]				
	74.67		1.84	0.22	3.67	15
	[4.60]		[0.96]			
Change						
Unemployment rate						
70/80	–0.87	1.18		0.67	26.67	15
	[1.09]	[0.23]				
	–0.19		1.02	0.5	13.11	15
	[1.34]		[0.28]			
Employment to population ratio						
70/80	6.34	–1.61		0.38	8.1	15
	[2.71]	[0.57]				
	5		1.3	0.25	4.3	15
	[3]		[0.63]			

Notes:
1. CompR70-U = ranking of countries according to the comprehensiveness index of the 1970s (see Table 9.2) in U-shaped form: the lowest values were assigned to the highest and lowest ranking countries; the highest values were assigned to countries in the middle.
2. CD-U = ranking of countries according to the Calmfors–Driffill index, in U-shaped form.
3. Level refers to average of the rates for the indicated period.
4. Changes are computed as follows: 70/80 = average for the period 1958–89 minus 1970–73. The linear version of the indices was never significant.
5. The real values of the comprehensiveness index (Comp) produced slightly different results, but rankings are displayed for comparison with the Calmfors–Driffill index.
6. In brackets: heteroscedastic consistent standard errors.

Calmfors and Driffill proposed a theoretical explanation for these non-linear relations in which extremes of the wage-bargaining institution scheme do well because they create aggregate wage restraint (see discussion above). However, Rowthorn, using the Calmfors–Driffill index, discovered that these relationships hold for the 1980s but cannot be found for the early 1970s when almost all industrialized countries experienced full employment.

In Table 9.3 we display regression analysis for unemployment rates and employment to population ratios (employment rates) on the comprehensive-ness index and on the Calmfors and Driffill index. In line with Rowthorn's results (based on the Calmfors–Driffill index), we do not find empirical evidence for a non-linear relation between the wage-bargaining system (with either index) and employment to population ratios or unemployment rates for the early 1970s. If anything, there is a negative, linear relationship between the unemployment rate and the index. This changes in the 1980s, when the hump-shaped (U-shaped) relation for unemployment (employment) emerges. This is most clearly seen if changes in the rates rather than levels are used (lower panel of Table 9.3). In other words, the relationship between wage-bargaining systems and unemployment (employment) seems to have changed substantially from the early 1970s to the 1980s.[12]

Why is it, then, that the hump-shaped relation can be found in the 1980s, but that it is not apparent during the full-employment period of the early 1970s?[13] Although institutions may have changed substantially, it is unlikely that the structures in the economy created by these institutions have changed as rapidly.[14] In view of the fact that most employment growth has occurred in service industries and that some services are suffering from the 'cost disease' (Baumol, 1967), some institutional settings may have made expansion easier than others. But it remains a puzzle why the two extremes, the decentralized and the centralized bargaining systems, achieved similar results. An explana-tion may be sought in differences between public and private sector growth. Employment in services with low productivity growth rates may be traded in private markets if wages have sufficient downward flexibility. This may over-come the negative demand effect of rising relative prices in these services. Thus, in countries with less centralized wage-bargaining systems, which usually have higher wage dispersion, employment expansion may have taken place in privately provided consumer services.[15] But economies with compre-hensive bargaining systems and low wage differentials also experienced high employment growth mainly in industries which provide services to consum-ers as well (Scharpf, 1990), but here employment and service provision is publicly organized (financed or directly provided). Public provision (de-marketization: Glyn, 1992) overcomes the negative effect of rising relative prices for consumer services and thus allows for employment expansion in these industries without high wage differentials. These considerations are

Table 9.4   Coordination and comprehensiveness

Coordination (Layard *et al.*)	Comprehensiveness (1970–80)		
	Low	Medium	High
Low	USA	UK	
	Canada	New Zealand	
Medium	Japan	Australia	Belgium
	Switzerland	Spain	
		Netherlands	
		France	
High			Germany
			Austria
			Finland
			Sweden

Coordination (Layard *et al.*)	Comprehensiveness (1980–90)		
	Low	Medium	High
Low	USA		
	Canada		
	UK		
	New Zealand		
Medium	Japan	Australia	France
	Switzerland	Spain	Belgium
		Netherlands	
High		Sweden	Germany
			Austria
			Finland

Notes:
1. Coordination according to Layard *et al.* (1991, pp. 52–3, Table 6) computed as employers' coordination (1 to 3) plus union's coordination (1 to 3); low = 1 and 2; medium = 3 and 4; high = 5 and 6.
2. Comprehensiveness as computed in Table 9.2; actual values for the indicated period divided by the average of 1970–80 (both periods); low = 0.8; medium = 0.8–1.2; high = 1.2.

supported by the positive linear relationship between the indices representing wage-bargaining systems and the ratio of public employment to population, and the negative relationship to the ratio of private service employment to population, respectively (see Figure 9.3).[16]

These trends in private service employment and public employment seem to be the major differences in the stylized employment development in coun-

Varieties of capitalism

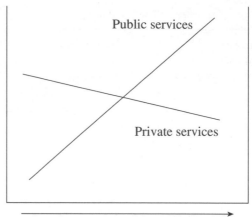

Centralization of the wage-bargaining system

Notes:
Private services: community, social, personal, recreational.
Public services: public administration, government sector according to national accounts.
CD = rankings according to Calmfors and Driffill (1988).
Regressions:

average growth rate of private services = $1.5 - 0.08$ CD; $R^2 = 0.37$, $F(1,8) = 4.8$
[9]   [0.03]

average growth rate of public services = $-0.25 + 0.23$ CD; $R^2 = 0.48$, $F(1,8) = 7.6$
[0.42] [0.08]

Heteroscedastic consistent standard errors in brackets.

*Figure 9.3   Behind the U-shape: stylized relations between private and
            public service employment growth and the wage-bargaining
            system*

tries with centralized and decentralized wage-bargaining systems. High wage
dispersion allowed for an increase in private service employment even in jobs
which do not have high productivity growth, but this means of employment
creation was not available in the countries with centralized bargaining systems. Here public employment expansion was the solution to the employment
problem; that is to say, it was less the integration of different interest groups
in the bargaining system itself (corporatism in the narrow sense) than the
interaction with government (corporatism in the broadest sense) that underlay
the favourable employment trends.

CONCLUDING SUMMARY

In this chapter we discussed the impact of wage-bargaining institutions on labour market performance as measured by the employment-to-population ratio and the unemployment rate. We found a U-shaped (hump-shaped) relation between the degree of centralization of the wage-bargaining system and the employment-to-population ratio (unemployment rate) in the 1980s but not in the early 1970s. The widely discussed non-linear relationship between centralization of the wage-bargaining system and labour market performance was mainly the result of developments which occurred during the 1970s and 1980s. Unemployment rose little – although from different levels – in economies at the decentralized end but also at the centralized end, whereas the middle experienced substantial increases in unemployment and low growth rates of employment.

Michael Bruno's and Jeffrey Sachs's argument that inflationary pressure is reduced by aggregate wage restraint and thus that the NAIRU declines with the degree of corporatism in a linear way may hold for the 1960s and early 1970s. But inflation was not a major problem in the 1980s, economic growth was much lower and unemployment was in general higher than in earlier periods. In the 1980s, wage differentiation was probably more important for employment growth in the private sector than aggregate wage restraint, which is almost automatically achieved by high unemployment. The underlying employment trends are very different in countries with decentralized bargaining and those with centralized bargaining systems, although both increased employment in services in the 1980s. It is private, market-oriented employment that expanded in countries with less centralized bargaining systems while in countries with centralized bargaining systems it was mainly public employment which expanded and which raised tax rates. Countries with an intermediate degree of centralization in the wage-bargaining system, however, did not experience the employment growth of the extremes but tried to hold unemployment down by a reduction of labour supply (through early retirement, for example). But high transfers are costly as well, and consequently tax rates rose here also, but without the advantage of additional production, consumption and employment.

NOTES

*   Earlier versions of this chapter gained substantially from critique and comments by Wendy Carlin, Andrew Glyn, Richard Jackman, Guenther Schmid and David Soskice. We are grateful for research assistance by Susanne Fuchs, Alice Wurche, Keinan Tang and Yan Yuan.
1.   The designers of the solidaristic wage policy (Gösta Rehn and Rudolf Meidner, see

Meidner and Hedborg, 1984) argued that it generates a shift to more productive activities and hence a stronger rise in aggregate productivity growth compared with the market outcome. This policy works perfectly well as long as employment in high-productivity growth industries grows, which was characteristic of industrial development (Salter, 1960). By setting wage increases in every industry at a level equal to productivity growth in the median industry, space is created for relative price reductions in industries with above-average productivity growth rates, where wages rise less than productivity. This allows for market expansion and employment expansion in these industries. At the lower end, however, wages rise more than productivity and relative prices increase, which causes contraction of markets and employment in these industries. The policy runs into trouble, however, if employment in high-productivity growth industries ceases to expand. Then the positive employment impact in high-productivity growth industries does not occur and at the same time jobs in low-productivity growth industries disappear.

2. If a union and an individual employer bargain over the wage, the trade-off between wage increases and employment strongly depends on the price elasticity of demand for the firm's product. Most firms are confronted with competitors who provide products that serve as substitutes. At the extreme, in an atomistic, perfectly competitive market, firms face a completely price-elastic demand so that cost and subsequent price rises will reduce the demand for the specific firm to zero. Therefore, in perfectly competitive markets the trade-off between wage increases and employment at the firm level is quite clear and will be recognized by company unions in wage-bargaining.

3. Danthine and Hunt (1994) discuss this effect for economic integration, such as the integration of the European Union.

4. In some work corporatism refers to the wage-bargaining system only, whereas in others it is used to characterize the concerted action of organized labour, capital and government. Lehmbruch (1984) identifies three standard definitions of corporatism:

    1. the development and strengthening of centralized organizations with an exclusive right of representation;
    2. the privileged access of centralized organizations to government; and
    3. social partnership between labour and capital to regulate conflict between both groups and coordination with government.

    The first definition is the one most in line with debates in economics on wage-bargaining. The third definition is the most comprehensive and includes governments, and it underlies the classification of some political scientists.

5. For measurement problems of union density, see, for example, Visser (1991).

6. Soskice (1990) criticized the Calmfors and Driffill index on the grounds that wage policy can be coordinated without being formally centralized and without a central union. Rowthorn (1992) also argues that coordination of wage-bargaining does not necessarily depend on formal structures but the unions may coordinate wage-bargaining outside of formal structures, as is the case with covert coordination for example in Germany, where the metalworkers' union set the benchmark for wage increases in other industries (see Meyer, 1990; OECD, 1994).

    Soskice claims that it is wage coordination by employers that makes Japan a coordinated economy. In the Soskice index, therefore, Japan is classified as an economy with coordinated wage-setting although it has a formally decentralized bargaining system. Some Japanese firms are closely connected in corporate groups (*keiretsu*, Aoki, 1988), mainly in the manufacturing sector where large export-oriented firms dominate. However, the six major corporate groups (*keiretsu*) in total cover only 4.8 per cent of all employees (ibid., p. 121). According to Layard *et al.* (1991, p. 52) employers' coordination of wage policy in Japan is middle ranking (see also the Layard/Nickell/Jackman index in ibid., Tables 3.2 and 3.3).

7. As France in the summer of 1995 shows, even unions that organize only a fraction of the labour force may have substantial power.

8. The comprehensiveness index is obtained as the product of the coverage rate and the bargaining level (1, 2, 3). Countries with a high coverage and centralized bargaining show a high score, whereas those at the other extreme (that is, low coverage and decentralized bargaining) have a low score.
9. Freeman (1988) actually critizes Calmfors and Driffill because they regress unemployment and employment performance on their centralization index but the effect is transmitted via wages, which are not modelled.
10. This result is confirmed by the comprehensiveness index. It raises the responsiveness of wage-setting to unemployment in its linear form but fails to do so in its U-shaped form (Schettkat, 1995b).
11. Of course, wage differentials are difficult to compare between countries because gross and net wages may differ substantially as do the services the public sector provides.
12. It is not true, however, that countries with low increases in unemployment rates achieved this through reduced labour force participation. On the contrary, labour supply and unemployment performed better in countries at the extremes of the bargaining system than in the intermediate countries.
13. The sensititivity of the aggregate wage-setting process to unemployment supports a positive linear relationship with the comprehensiveness of the wage-bargaining system (see Layard *et al.*, 1991; Schettkat, 1995b).
14. Although wage-bargaining institutions changed over time, wage differentials did not change substantially when countries moved to less centralized bargaining. Decentralization seems to be connected to rising wage differentials, but this is a slow process and the bargaining structure of the 1970s still explains international differences in wage differentials in the 1980s quite well (Schettkat, 1995b).
15. It must be kept in mind that while international comparative analysis is able to account for institutional variety, at the same time the number of available variables is very small, which limits the possibilities for analysis.
16. The distinction between private sector service employment and public sector employment is, of course, only a rough approximation for the theoretical arguments made for the expansion of the two sectors.

REFERENCES

Aoki, M. (1988), *Information, Incentives, and Bargaining in the Japanese Economy*, Cambridge: Cambridge University Press.

Appelbaum, E. and Schettkat, R. (1993), *Employment Developments in Industrialized Economies*, Discussion Paper I–101, Berlin: Wissenschaftszentrum Berlin.

Appelbaum, E. and R. Schettkat (1995), 'Employment and productivity in industrialized countries', *International Labour Review*, 134(4–5), pp. 605–23.

Baumol, W. (1967), 'Macroeconomics of unbalanced growth: the anatomy of the urban crisis', *American Economic Review*, 57, pp. 415–26.

Blanchflower, D.G. and R. Freeman (1992), 'Unionism in the United States and other advanced countries', *Industrial Relations*, 31(1), pp. 307–23.

Blyth, C.A. (1987), *Interaction between Collective Bargaining and Government Policies in Selected Member Countries*, Paris: OECD.

Bruno, M. and Sachs, J. (1985), *Economics of Worldwide Stagflation*, Cambridge, MA: Harvard University Press.

Calmfors, L. and J. Driffill (1988), 'Bargaining structure, corporatism and macroeconomic performance', *Economic Policy*, 6, April, pp. 14–61.

Cameron, D.R. (1984), 'Social democracy, corporatism, labour quiescence and the representation of economic interest in advanced capitalist society', in J.H.

Goldthorpe (ed.), *Order and Conflict in Contemporary Capitalism*, Oxford: Oxford University Press, pp. 147–76.

Crouch, C. (1992), 'Trade unions in the exposed sector: their influences on neo-corporatist behaviour', in R. Brunetta and C. Dell'Aringa (eds), *Labour Relations and Economic Performance*, London: Macmillan, pp. 105–39.

Danthine, J.-P. and J. Hunt (1994), 'Wage bargaining structure, employment and economic integration', *Economic Journal*, 104, pp. 528–41.

Flanagan, R. (1987), 'Efficiency and equality in Swedish labor markets', in B. Bosworth and A. Rivlin (eds), *The Swedish Economy*, Washington, DC: Brookings Institution, pp. 125–84.

Flanagan, R.J., D. Soskice and L. Ulman (1983), *Unionism, Economic Stabilization, and Income Policies: European Experience*. Washington, DC: Brookings Institution.

Franz, W. (1995), 'Die Lohnfindung in Deutschland in einer internationalen Perspektive: Ist das deutsche System ein Auslaufmodell?', Diskussionspapier 24–1995, Konstanz, Germany: Centre for International Labour Economics, Universität Konstanz.

Freeman, R. (1988), 'Labour market institutions and economic performance', *Economic Policy*, 6, pp. 63–80.

Freeman, R. (1996), 'The new inequality and what we might do about it', Harvard University, Cambridge, MA, ms.

Friedman, M. (1962), *Price Theory: A Provisional Text*, Chicago: Aldine Press.

Glyn, A. (1992), 'Corporatism, patterns of employment, and access to consumption', in L. Calmfors (ed.), *Wage Formation and Macroeconomic Policy in Nordic Countries*, Oxford: Oxford University Press, pp. 132–77.

Guger, A. (1992), 'Corporatism: success or failure? Austrian experiences', in J. Pekkarinen, M. Pohjola and R.E. Rowthorne (eds), *Social Corporatism: A Superior Economic System*, Oxford: Clarendon Press, pp. 338–77.

Hartog, J. and J. Theeuwes (1993), *Labour Market Contracts and Institutions: A Cross-national Comparison*, Amsterdam: North-Holland.

Kaldor, N. (1987), *Causes of the Slow Rate of Economic Growth of the UK*, Cambridge: Cambridge University Press.

Layard, R., S. Nickell and R. Jackman (1991), *Unemployment. Macroeconomic Performance and the Labour Market*, Oxford: Oxford University Press.

Lehmbruch, G. (1984), 'Concertation and the structure of corporatist networks', in J.H. Goldthorpe (ed.), *Order and Conflict in Contemporary Capitalism*, Oxford: Oxford University Press, pp. 60–80.

Lijphart, A. and M.L. Crepaz (1991), 'Corporatism and consensus democracy in eighteen countries: conceptual and empirical linkages', *British Journal of Political Science*, 21, pp. 235–56.

Meidner, R. and Hedborg, A. (1984), *Modell Schweden. Erfahrungen einer Wohlfahrtsgesellschaft*, Frankfurt am Main and New York: Campus.

Meyer, W. (1990), *Bestimmungsfaktoren der Tariflohnbewegung. Eine empirische, mikroökonomische Untersuchung für die Bundesrepublik*, Frankfurt am Main and New York: Campus.

Nickell, S. (1988), 'Discussion of Calmfors/Driffill', *Economic Policy*, 52, pp. 55–60.

OECD (1994), 'Collective bargaining: levels and coverage', *Employment Outlook 1994*, Paris: OECD.

OECD (1996), *Employment Outlook 1996*, Paris: OECD.

Olson, M. (1982), *The Rise and Decline of Nations: Economic Growth, Stagflation, and Social Rigidities*, New Haven, CT, and London: Yale University Press.

Rowthorn, R.E. (1992), 'Centralisation, employment and wage dispersion', *Economic Journal*, 102, May, pp. 506–23.

Salter, W. (1960), *Productivity and Technical Change*, Cambridge: Cambridge University Press.

Scharpf, F.W. (1990), 'Structures of post-industrial society, or, does mass unemployment disappear in the service and information economy?', in E. Appelbaum, and R. Schettkat (eds), *Labor Market Adjustments to Structural Change and Technological Progress*, New York, Westport, CT, and London: Praeger, pp. 17–35.

Schettkat, R. (1995a), 'The macroperformance of the German labor market', in F. Buttler, W. Franz, R. Schettkat and D. Soskice (eds), *Institutional Frameworks and Labour Market Performance: Comparative Views on the German and US Economies*, London and New York: Routledge, pp. 316–42.

Schettkat, R. (1995b), 'Behind the U-shape: wage bargaining systems and economic performance', paper prepared for OECD, Paris.

Soskice, D. (1990), 'Wage determination: the changing role of institutions in advanced industrialized countries', *Oxford Review of Economic Policy*, 6(4), pp. 36–61.

Tarantelli, E. (1986), 'The regulation of inflation and unemployment', *Industrial Relations*, 25(1), pp. 1–15.

Therborn, G. (1992), 'Lessons from "corporatist theorization"', in J. Pekkarinen, M. Pohjola and R.E. Rowthorne (eds), *Social Corporatism: A Superior Economic System*, Oxford: Clarendon Press, pp. 24 43.

Visser, J. (1991), 'On union density', in OECD, *Employment Outlook*, pp. 97–134.

10. Emergence of path-dependent mixed economies in Central Europe

Bernard Chavance and Eric Magnin

1. CAPITALISM AND THE MIXED ECONOMY

The notion of the 'mixed economy' has been the target of wide criticism. In the 1980s, the negative Hayekian assessment of interventionist policies in general and of mixed economy tendencies was revived, as part of the general questioning of the 'Keynesian' consensus that had dominated for years. When the post-socialist transformation began in Eastern Europe there was a strong free-market orientation by new governments (often with the active participation of economists who had been until the late 1980s proponents of a radical reform of the socialist economy). International influence too pushed in this direction – especially the IMF, whose leaders strongly and repeatedly asserted that a mixed economy model should be avoided in order to guide the 'transition'. The shift of focus from a reform of socialism to a 'transition to a market economy' had in some countries, such as Poland, either been tacitly accepted in public opinion in the late 1980s, or took place during the big political change of 1989–90. The rejection of the 'mixed economy' was at that time part of the struggle of new pro-market forces against neocommunist or social-democratic tendencies in these societies (both trends often being confused in political debates).

The opposition in principle by economic liberalism to the notion of the mixed economy has obscured the real nature and variety of types of capitalism, and the specific problems of systemic change in the post-socialist world. The concept of a 'market economy' understood as a kind of pure or simple system reducible to a single universal coordination mode is misleading. Capitalist systems, in their historical and national diversity, have all been characterized by a high degree of institutional and organizational variety, and by a complex repertoire of coordination modes or governance forms (Boyer, 1992; Hollingsworth et al., 1994; Zysman, 1994). Such diversity can be understood both as a result and as a cause of the system's dynamics. In place of a monocausal, pure system, we find in the family of capitalist systems combined or mixed economies in which various forms are present and different principles are at work. This is one of many reasons why important theoreticians such as Marx, Keynes or Schumpeter contrasted 'capitalism' in different ways with the model of a 'market economy' – with its weak or oversimplified institutional content and its static equilibrium implications. Post-socialist transformation has produced complex developments in the economy that cannot be reduced either to marketization and privatization as general trends, or to simple obstacles and delays in this direction. Specific and evolving configurations of post-socialist economies are characterized by their composite, combined or mixed features. Such heterogeneity does not boil down to the simple 'transitory' nature of economies moving from one alleged pure system to another. It depends on the historical and path-dependent character of systemic change and on the complex nature of capitalism in general.[1] In this chapter we try to analyse the emergence of various specific post-socialist mixed economies, with reference to the Czech, Hungarian and Polish cases, concentrating particularly on ownership and coordination aspects of systemic change.

2. PATH-DEPENDENCE IN ECONOMIC TRANSFORMATION

The concept of path-dependence refers to evolutionary features of system trajectories characterized by out-of-equilibrium self-organization. Among the different possible patterns of long-term behaviour, one is somehow selected through the cumulation of various events or disturbances that have occurred in the previous evolution of the system. The expression 'history matters' is a frequent way of summarizing the concept. Applied to the problem of systemic change in post-socialist economies, a path-dependence approach focuses on the duality of heritage and creation.

Different levels of analysis should be distinguished when discussing path-dependence in post-socialist countries. First, the general level of the family of systems that went from socialism to post-socialist transformation; second, the individual level of given countries in the family. An intermediary level may be considered, namely subgroups of individual countries with similar paths within the family (for example, reformed economies in the late socialist period). Time scales should be differentiated too. In a long-term perspective on path-dependence, it is necessary to push the analysis back to pre-socialist times; in a middle-term perspective, the evolution since socialism (or late socialism) should be focused upon; in a short-term one, the trajectory observed since the big change (1989) will be the main concern.

At the time of the former socialist countries embarking upon post-socialist transformation, they had followed diverse paths of change since the early

Table 10.1   Forces of identity and difference in post socialist countries

---

Factors of similarity

- Post-socialist common features (systemic family path-dependence)
- Institutional mimetism towards the West, desire to join the European Union
- Influence of international organizations (IMF) and of their conditions
- Globalization trends

Factors of dissimilarity

- Diversity in initial conditions resulting from the past evolution of socialist economies
- National specific paths, after 1989 (unique political, social and economic conditions and events: individual path-dependence)
- Variety of institutional external influences (for example, Anglo-Saxon vs West European, or German vs British or French)
- Idiosyncratic institutional bricolage, spontaneous adaptation and transformation of imitated institutions according to nationally specific societal contexts

---

common imitation or imposition of the Soviet-type model. In the conventional approach that dominated the first years of change, such diversity in initial conditions was underestimated. Moreover, the notion of a future convergence towards a single model – a standard view of a 'market economy' of the West European flavour – was dominant. In the following years, a variety of national paths could be observed where some common trends coexisted with divergent tendencies (see Table 10.1). It is too early to reach conclusions about the similarity or the divergence of future stabilized systems in Central Europe. Only comparative analysis of historical paths, as opposed to wishful thinking about convergence, will provide a clue to such a complex question, but strong national specificities are likely to remain or to expand in the middle term.[2]

The last decade of socialist systems in Central Europe saw the emergence of a 'socialist mixed economy'. The term was coined by institutional sociologists (Nee and Stark, 1989) discussing mainly the Hungarian and Chinese cases, but it can be extended to the Polish case in that period. The role of the developing private sector in these countries was stressed, as was the move away from the organizational homogeneity of the traditional socialist economies. By contrast, Czechoslovakia, where the reform attempts of 1968 had been radically suppressed, was still close to this traditional model when the regime collapsed in 1989.

The radical systemic transformation was initiated by an unexpected and somewhat new historical form of political change, which was neither a reform nor a revolution but a 'refolution' (Garton-Ash), a 'regime change' (Kiss) or a 'gentle demise' (Hausner). This change, although almost simultaneous, took different forms in accordance with national socio-political conditions. While in Czechoslovakia there was a 'capitulation' by the communist leaders, a 'negotiated demise' was observed in the two other countries, a 'compromise' in Poland and an 'electoral competition' in Hungary. Stark (1992) has insisted upon the influence of these different 'extrication paths' on the variety of later national evolutions and of privatization strategies. In the post-socialist period, common trends and national specificities appeared, both among state or government strategies and in the spontaneous evolution of different economies and societies. Klaus (1994) has argued, in a neo-Hayekian spirit, that the systemic change should be seen as a 'delicate mixture of intentions and spontaneity'. Such a mixture is actually typical of the evolution of modern economic systems in general; it is not only a temporary feature of specifically post-socialist conditions – even though the particular content of the mixture is, to be sure, dictated by such conditions.

Following the 'structural adjustment' philosophy of international organizations, all governments of the region proclaimed stabilization and institutional change, especially privatization, as the most important and immediate means of reaching the target model of a market economy based on private ownership. Differences in initial conditions and in policy orientations resulted in various paths: in Poland 'shock therapy' was applied early, but political conditions constantly delayed the mass privatization envisaged, and the actual change in ownership of the previous state sector was rather slow. In Czechoslovakia shock therapy was adopted but after a longer preparation and under better initial conditions than in Poland. Mass 'voucher' privatization was organized successfully, starting in 1992. Hungary adopted from the beginning a more gradual approach to stabilization and privatization, opting for conventional (Western) methods. In the three countries 'small privatization' of small state or 'cooperative' enterprises, notably in the retail trade, proceeded quite fast and successfully, while an impressive development of newly created private firms, generally small, was seen especially in the service sector. Another common feature was the almost immediate disruption of the vertical dependence of firms linked to previous 'bureaucratic coordination' (Kornai, 1992), either in its direct (Czechoslovakia) or indirect form (Hungary, Poland). An unexpected development affected all three countries (similar to others undergoing transition): the post-socialist 'great depression' (Chavance, 1994b) or 'transformational recession' (Kornai, 1994), with important path-dependent effects such as a growth of arrears (interenterprise debts, bad loans of banks, delays in tax payments), a fiscal crisis of the state, and a slow or rather defensive restructuring of the productive system linked to the collapse of investment. Some peculiarities in the development of hybrid forms of ownership discussed below are linked to adaptation to the consequences of the depression (Stark, 1994).

In all countries a wide array of continuities became manifest in the process of global systemic mutation. A 'self-reorganization' of the economic system is at work, where rearrangements or recombinations of inherited organizational or institutional forms are combined with the genuine creation of new forms.[3] Among the latter, some bear close resemblance to their Western capitalist counterparts, but others have peculiar post-socialist features.

3.   AN ORIGINAL COMBINATION OF OWNERSHIP FORMS

The 'transition' process in Eastern Europe is marked by the transformation of the national mixed configurations of ownership forms under the reformed socialist system into new, complex transitional configurations. The mixed reformed socialist ownership regimes of the 1980s are themselves the outcome of the traditional Soviet-type system evolution. The transformation of property relations is a complex process characterized by the spontaneous creation of a newly private sector, the privatization of state enterprises by various methods implemented by the state, and the interaction between institutional (systemic and national) legacies and state strategies in an uncertain environment leading to the emergence of new organizational forms.

The post-socialist combined economy is characterized by an original diversity of capital ownership forms and owner–manager relations: a continuum of forms, ranging from private forms to public ones (see Table 10.2). Moreover, no clear correlation appears in the first years between ownership forms and the hardening of budget constraints. Finally, many enterprises are themselves of a composite nature; for example, they may combine within a single organizational form employee ownership, managerial ownership, bank participation, foreign participation and public ownership. The common institutional legacy of Central European countries makes this new configuration typical of transforming economies, as can be observed in various fields: the persistence of some socialist economy-type behaviours (more or less soft budgetary constraints, risk aversion, 'good contacts' with the state, state resources pumping, cheating), the presence of intertwined or blurred ownership forms, and the importance of public ownership (although decreasing) and of employee ownership in some countries. From the table, two salient features can be noted.

On the one hand, small- and medium-sized private enterprises (SMEs)[4] have mushroomed in all countries in a similar way since 1989. On the other hand, peculiar interwoven ownership forms are emerging in Central European countries in the first half of the 1990s.

3.1 The Proliferation of Diversified Small- and Medium-sized Private Enterprises

The impressive increase in the number of private SMEs in all Central European countries is accompanied by a proliferation of company forms: limited liability companies, joint ventures, joint stock companies, individual business units, partnerships, illegal entities and so on (Earle *et al.*, 1994). The diversity of organizational forms is another feature of the small private sector development and the rise in the number of economic actors. Many factors are at work, related to: the separation or otherwise of ownership from management, the size of firms, sector (services, industry, agriculture), capital intensity, the links with large domestic state-owned enterprises (SOEs) – subcontracting firms for example – the presence of foreign investors (joint venture or 100 per cent subsidiary).

The similarity of the expansion of private SMEs in transitional countries is the result of three groups of factors. First, it was caused by the same combination of various privatization methods implemented in most countries: small-scale privatization programmes, management/employee buy-outs, sale of all or part of the capital to a foreign or a domestic investor. The creation of new small- and medium-sized private firms through privatization sometimes involves the break-up of larger units; in other cases only a transformation of ownership occurs.

Second, it can be explained by the 'conversion' of small private businesses, legal or semi-legal units of the former second economy, and the few legal forms of the reformed socialist system, into legal (or illegal) entities on the model of the Western capitalist mixed economies. Economists expected that the transformation process would result in the 'whitening' of the 'black' economy. On the contrary, the hidden economy has been growing since 1989, but its nature has changed. In the socialist economy, people entered the black economy in order to compensate for the failures of the system and to add a little to the kitty. In the transitional economy, people go underground to avoid paying tax and to win the price competition against 'honest, tax-paying' businessmen.

In Hungary, the development of the small-scale private sector began in 1982, with the government entitlement to set up quasi-private businesses. The most important of the newly permitted business forms was the so-called Enterprise Contract Work Association (VGMK), which made it possible to

Table 10.2 Emerging configuration of ownership forms

Ownership Forms/ Capital Management and Budget Constraint	Ownership Separated from Management	Ownership not Separated from Management
Newly created private ownership		
• Hard budget constraint	Foreign companies' subsidiaries (strong management control)	SMEs with low tax evasion (honest taxpayers) and difficult credit access
• ± Soft budget constraint	Foreign companies' subsidiaries benefiting from tax preferences	SMEs with high tax evasion (grey actors, half-entrepreneurs, multiple ventures) or good relations with the financial sector
Illegal private ownership		
• ± Soft budget constraint	Underground businesses working for an outside owner	Growing second economy (small individual businesses)
Legal private ownership without any economic activities	• 'Dummy firms' (figurehead in the privatization process)	• 'Shell companies' (small units created only to obtain tax or credit preferences) • 'Phantom firms' (false business ventures created for swindling)
Employees' privatized ownership	Employee buy-outs Employee Stock Ownership Plans scheme	Cooperatives
Private ownership stemming from the privatization process	Large profitable enterprises sold through public tender, straight auctions, invitation to tender, direct sales (mainly joint ventures)	SMEs from the 'small-scale' privatization programme
• Hard budget constraint	Of which quasi-private enterprises (Polish conglomerates)	SMEs bought by managers (with low tax evasion)

- ± Soft budget constraint

  Joint ventures entering governmental bargaining in search of state protection (tax preferences, access to preferential credits, privileged competitive positions)

  SMEs from the 'hidden' form of 'spontaneous privatization', i.e. set up as suppliers or customers of a large SOE to strip it of part of its assets

Emerging interwoven privatized ownership

  Institutional quasi-public cross-ownership

- ± Hard budget constraint

  Large SOEs after corporatization in Hungary. Important role of banks. Multiple owners. Weak management control

  Private cross-ownership between small- and medium-limited liability companies in Hungary, with a majority stake of the capital held by the manager, other stocks being distributed among various shareholders (mid-level managers, professional staff, quasi-public holding)

- Soft budget constraint

  Attenuated interwoven ownership

  Large SOEs under mass privatization in Poland. Multiple private owners (various investment funds (NIFs), employees) and state. Complex governance structure.

  Institutional quasi-private cross-ownership

  Large SOEs after denationalization through the 'voucher privatization' in the Czech Republic. Dominant role of banks. Multiple owners. Weak management control

Public ownership (state permanently holding controlling shares, or temporarily before privatization in the short term)

  Non-profitable companies surviving for social reasons in regions dependent on a single economic activity (e.g. mining, iron and steel production)

- ± Soft budget constraint

  ± Profitable large SOEs (diversified situations, weak management control)

- ± Hard budget constraint

  Banks (renationalization as a result of debt consolidation)

Note: Kornai's concept of soft budget constraint includes here a fiscal side (tax rate bargaining but also tax evasion) and a credit side (credit access, subsidies). The expression 'more or less (±) soft' refers to more or less important softenings on the credit and fiscal sides.

form a contract relationship between groups of employees in a state enterprise and allowed the enterprise itself to work independently within the firm
in its spare time. The other important form was the Economic Contract Work
Association (GMK), which was essentially a private business that could be
formed outside the state enterprise. Other business forms that could be established included industrial and service cooperative groups (VGMK in the
cooperative sector), small cooperatives and civil law associations (associations of private professional people who could use the assets of a large SOE
under a leasing arrangement or be hired by an enterprise under a contractual
agreement) (Neumann, 1993). The development of this sector served as a
basis for the subsequent development of the small private sector in Hungary
(with small limited liability companies entangled in the 'corporate satellite'
organizational form mentioned below) and provided the first entrepreneurial
knowledge, not born, however, under market conditions.[5]

The diversity of private organizational forms broadened from the early
1980s onwards in Poland too, and the Polish private sector experienced a
period of rapid expansion. Direct investment was encouraged through small-
scale 'Polonia' firms, theoretically owned by Poles living abroad. After a
period of rapid expansion during 1982–84, the growth of the 'Polonia' firms
slowed down. Private individuals were also authorized to lease shops, restau-
rants and kiosks and to manage them privately from the 1970s onwards. After
1987, leasing spread to other activities.[6] Economic Working Groups, which
were contractual arrangements between workers and the management of a
state enterprise, similar in principle to the Hungarian VGMKs, were also
permitted but did not expand much. The existence of small private or quasi-
private enterprises in the reformed socialist system may explain why
entrepreneurship in Poland has taken off more quickly than in, say, the Czech
Republic. However, in the Czech Republic, the limited existence of private
activities before 1989 resulted in a dramatic growth in the number of small
entrepreneurs in the first years of the transition process.

The third factor explaining the similar expansion of SMEs is the spontaneous creation of national (legal or illegal) SMEs or of foreign group subsidiaries.
It should be noted that some of the newly created small private enterprises do
not represent the same thing as their Western counterparts (Szabo, 1994).
Some businesses are 'forced individual enterprises' founded in order to avoid
unemployment; their aim is survival, not profit. Other registered business
ventures are 'spare-time enterprises', that is, the entrepreneur is a full-time
employee in another enterprise and works overtime for his business. It should
be remembered that many people had a second job in the socialist reformed
economy. Another version is the 'multiple business venture', namely the
creation of several small enterprises, which are only partly active, essentially
in order to limit the tax burden. Newly privatized SMEs may in fact also

behave in a non-entrepreneurial way for systemic legacy reasons such as the lack of market culture.

It is not possible to determine precisely the relative importance of privatization and of newly created private businesses in the development of the private sector. SMEs represent a numerical majority, but the above remarks incline us to qualify their importance in terms of economic activity measures in spite of the official share of the private sector in GDP (see Table 10.3). The small private sector output is in fact concentrated in the retail trade, construction and agriculture, that is, low capital-intensive activities. Its share in industry – though increasing – is generally much lower.

3.2 The Emergence of Interwoven Ownership

In the countries of Central Europe, various forms of interwoven ownership are emerging in the first years of the transition process as a consequence of the transformation of the former state sector (privatization and changes in organizational forms). Interwoven ownership has three main characteristics: a multiplicity of heterogeneous owners, a fuzzy border between public and private forms with the development of hybrid types, and cross-ownership ties involving banks in industrial property. In the three countries under study, while emergence paths were different, interwoven ownership has been developing (with the partial exception of Poland as far as the cross-ownership aspect is concerned: see Table 10.4). But it can be found in most post-socialist economies.[7] It represents a significant share of national assets and economic activity (see Table 10.3).

The emergence of an interwoven ownership form in Hungary is linked to the 'spontaneous privatization' process which started in 1988, in the last two years of the former reformed socialist system, as a result of new pieces of legislation facilitating property transformation. In some cases, a large state enterprise contributes some of its assets in kind, which are pooled together with other capital from foreign investors in new companies, and the remaining part of the state enterprise continues to operate. But the basic form of 'spontaneous privatization' is the 'transformation' of a large state enterprise into a group of new companies (most often limited liability companies), set up on the basis of each of its factories, plants and even administrative departments, which then distribute the assets of the public firm among themselves. The former public enterprise centre (a joint stock company) keeps the controlling shares of the new companies (called 'corporate satellites' by Stark). In these public holding companies, foreign investors, state-owned organizations such as banks and other enterprises, joint stock or limited liability companies, mainly business partners (suppliers and customers), also participate in share ownership. Thus, it is not privatization in the strict sense of the

Table 10.3   Estimates of the relative importance of ownership forms

Ownership Forms	Hungary	Poland	Czech Republic
Official share of the private sector (% of GDP, mid-1995)	60%	60%	70%
Large- and medium-sized SOEs	2200 units in 1990	8450 units in 1990	3500 units in 1991
Small registered private enterprises			
• Individual	700 000 (1994) (20% of the labour force)	1.7 million (end 1993) (12% of the labour force)	> 1.1 million entrepreneurs (22% of the labour force)
• Legal personalities	64 000 in September 1993. 40% of small units could be 'false entrepreneurs' (shell, dummy, phantom firms, half and multiple entrepreneurs)	n.a.	n.a. Estimates of registered half-time entrepreneurs range from 60–80% of the total; 33% could be inactive
Illegal private ownership. Second economy (% of GDP) (various estimates)	30% (1993)	20% (1994)	10–15% (1994)
Employee privatized ownership	n.a.	700 workers' buy-outs by October 1993 (220 000 employees), 15% of shares of enterprises involved in mass privatization	0.9% of shares of firms involved in voucher privatization (first wave)
Cooperatives (1992)	>8000 units	17 000 units	5879 units

Private ownership stemming from the privatization process			
• Small-scale privatization	10 300 units	30 000 to 80 000 according to sources	26 000 units
• Joint ventures	21 500 operational units (1993)	16 000 registered units	5000 registered projects
• Trade sales (medium- and large-sized enterprises)	114 (1992), 6 initial public offerings	119 (in mid-1994) of which 99 sold to a domestic foreign core investor and 17 public offerings	n.a.
Interwoven ownership	40% of all state enterprises and 10% of their assets before mid-1990	6 big conglomerates	Voucher privatization (two waves): 1619 enterprises (30% of state enterprises in terms of employment and production)
	40% of the 220 largest companies in 1994	512 enterprises involved in the mass privatization programme	
Public ownership	50% of assets still in state hands in mid-1995, of which 140 companies in which the state will remain majority owner	6000 firms still in state hands in early 1994 (60% of industrial output)	40% of the initial portfolio of the National Property Fund still in state hands in April 1995

Note: These data are compiled from various sources: UNO, OECD, *The Economist National Statistical Offices*, Bouin (1995), EBRD (1995), Gabor (1994), Stark (1996). They must be treated cautiously. The aim of the table :s to provide a rough estimate of the relative importance of ownership forms in the first half of the 1990s.

Table 10.4 National privatization trajectories

Ownership Forms and Dynamic Features	Hungary	Poland	Czech Republic
Interwoven ownership	Institutional quasi-public cross-ownership	Attenuated interwoven ownership	Institutional quasi-private cross-ownership
	Spontaneous privatization initiated from 1988 onwards	Multiple owners, private and public partners, not yet developed cross-ownership ties	Voucher privatization. Began in 1992
	± Hard budget constraint	Diversity of ownership transformation processes with uncertain consequences, which might involve a marginal development of cross-ownership ties:	± Soft budget constraint
	Important role of banks: debt equity swap 'Corporate satellites': legacy of the conglomerates dissolved in the early 1980s: more relative independence between units (loose network relations) Shareholders: state property agency, banks, cross-ownership between domestic enterprises (suppliers, customers), foreign companies, local authorities, employees, managers. Weak management control	• debt-equity swaps between banks and industrial companies, • expansion of conglomerates, • mass privatization programme	Dominating role of banks: founders of investment privatization funds (IPFs). Holdings: legacy of the industrial associations (VHJs): strong technical and financial links (tight network relations) Shareholders: citizens, Fund of National Property, cross-ownership between banks via IPFs, domestic enterprises (suppliers, customers), foreign companies, local authorities, employers, managers. Weak management control

Employees' privatized ownership	Limited participation by employees (preferential shares)	SME bought after leasing of the firm's assets by its workers, workers' buy-outs	Weak participations of employees
	Employee stock ownership plan and preferential credits: uncertain results	Legacy of the Workers' Councils. 15% of shares reserved for firms' workers in the mass privatization programme	Pre-war legacy of cooperatives
'Creative destruction'	Effective bankruptcy law but overburdened courts	Privatization by liquidation under the law on SOEs	Limited number of bankruptcies
Lock-in?	State–bank–industry links Marginalization of the small private sector	Pronounced dualism between large public enterprises and small private businesses	State–bank–industry links

word (hence our expression 'quasi-public') even if some private investors buy shares in the new companies (mainly SOE managers, who can also establish their own private firms and integrate them in the holding as suppliers or customers). The fastest growing new property form in the first years of the transition process is 'a limited liability company owned by private persons, by private ventures, and by other limited liability companies owned by joint stock companies, banks, and large public enterprises owned by the state' (Stark, 1996, p. 1007) (see Figure 10.1). The changing economic and political environment at the end of the 1980s directly triggered the transformation of SOEs. Firms were about to become insolvent and needed additional capital because of a restrictive economic policy, including the cut-back of budgetary subsidies (UNO, 1994). After 1989, the post-socialist 'great depression' made the insolvency problem more acute. In the case of enterprises in a difficult

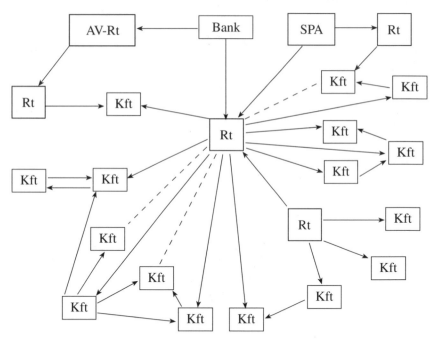

AV-Rt = state holding corporation
SPA = state property agency
Rt = shareholding company
Kft = limited liability

Source: Stark (1996).

Figure 10.1   A Hungarian metamorphic network

financial situation, corporatization (the transformation of an enterprise into a corporate company with a legal personality) offered the possibility of a debt-to-equity swap with banks or other creditors (state, local authority, suppliers). Quasi-public holdings are then linked to each other by ownership ties (what Stark calls a 'recombinet', see Figure 10.1), often via their numerous limited liability companies. Thus in Hungary, property relations in the middle of the 1990s are complex and interwoven between public (for the major part) and private organizations. The hardening of the budget constraint was the precondition for spontaneous 'privatization'.

In the Czech Republic, the emergence of an interwoven ownership form is the unexpected result of the voucher mass privatization organized by the government from 1991 onwards. During the first wave of privatization, 72 per cent of all available voucher points for citizens were collected by the investment privatization funds (IPFs) spontaneously created in the process. The 'average Czech firm' is then controlled by a group of IPFs (see Figure 10.2). The largest IPFs are controlled by major banks (via investment companies), which were also privatized within the voucher scheme; the state remaining however their biggest shareholder with about 40 per cent of shares. Moreover, the state – through the National Property Fund – holds majority participations in many companies on a permanent or temporary basis. Thus after the first wave, the major commercial banks, controlled by the state, are the co-owners of many Czech companies through their IPFs; they mutually hold some shares in other banks' capital, and in some cases banks indirectly own their own shares. For example, the Czech Investicni Banka owns 17 per cent of its own shares and many shares of other banks (Mladek, 1993). In the second wave, funds collected fewer points and the latter were more dispersed than in

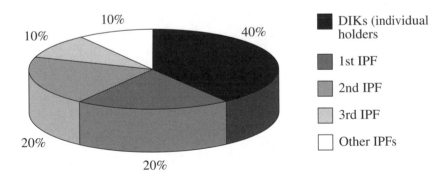

Source: Bouin (1995).

Figure 10.2   The typical structure of a Czech enterprise's capital after distribution through the voucher method

the first wave, but the general framework of property relations at the end of the first wave was not challenged.

Thus in the Czech Republic, a highly interwoven set of property relations between banks, enterprises, the state and IPFs (on behalf of citizens) can be

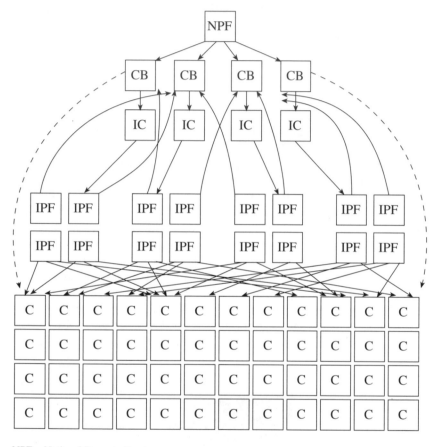

NPF = National Property Fund
CB = commercial bank
IC = investment company
IPF = investment privatization fund
C = company
————— Ownership control
– – – – Credits

Source: Mertlik (1995).

Figure 10.3 Ownership structure of the Czech economy after mass privatization

observed in the first half of the 1990s (see Figure 10.3). The close relations between state banks and industry seem to be slowing down the hardening of the SOEs' budgetary constraint.

In Poland, the transformation of property relations requires a more qualified assessment. Indeed until 1996 only a small part of the SOE sector had been truly privatized. Liquidation under the Privatization Law has been the main method of privatization. The most common technique has been the leasing of the liquidated firm's assets by its workers. However, an attenuated interwoven ownership is emerging, characterized by a multiplicity of owners and a mixture of public and private partners, but without complex cross-ownership relations. While it seems difficult to draw any conclusion for the time being, three simultaneous but separate processes seem to open the possibility of some crossed configuration by different routes. First, the mass privatization programme set up in 1991, but implemented only since 1994, which concerns about 512 enterprises, involves the participation of new actors, the national investment funds (NIFs), established by the state. Sixty per cent of the shares of enterprises included in the programme will be distributed to the NIFs, while the state will keep 25 per cent and workers will receive 15 per cent free of charge. Each of the 15 NIFs is to hold 33 per cent of the capital of nearly 30 firms and about 2 per cent of the stocks in the remaining firms. Citizens will be able to exchange their property certificates for one tradeable share in each of the 15 NIFs in 1997. After the programme's implementation, the enterprises concerned will have an initial distribution of their capital of 33 per cent for the main NIF, 2 per cent for each of the 14 other NIFs, 25 per cent for the state and 15 per cent for their employees (Nivet, 1994; Slay, 1995). Second, the development of debt–equity swaps within the framework of the Law on financial Restructuring of Enterprises and Banks (March 1993) is likely to increase the share of industrial equity holdings in the banks' portfolios, in spite of the initial reluctance of banks to invest in industrial firms. Third, the transformation of most former socialist state foreign trade organizations into big conglomerates contributes to an attenuated interwoven configuration of property rights. These represented in 1995 a third of the value of the Polish stock market.

They used their large foreign currency receipts earned in the first transformation period to buy not only the companies they had represented abroad but also banks and other firms far from their core businesses. Moreover, the state owns a large stake in several conglomerates along with domestic and foreign investors. Bad debts and scarce finance facilitate this process, as well as the breaking up of big monopolies by the government which created firms that were too weak to survive, that became prey to foreign and domestic investors. Elektrim, a former state trading monopoly for electrical goods, was Poland's biggest domestic investor in 1993. At the end of 1993, it had stakes in 87 companies, including banks, put up for sale by the privatization ministry (*The Economist*, 1995b). The state owns 16 per cent of Elektrim's equity but two-thirds of the voting shares. Universal holds large stakes in 50 companies and Mostostal has bought shares in financial companies.

Thus in Poland, a multiple ownership configuration and a diversity of organizational forms (quasi-private conglomerates, public holdings as in the mining industry, private holdings (NIFs)) emerged in the first half of the 1990s, while opening the door to a lesser extent to crossed ownership links.

4.   THE EMERGING REPERTOIRE OF COORDINATION MODES

The classical problem of the coordination of the division of labour in capitalism has been approached in various ways. An extreme position sees the market as the single existing or desirable coordination mode. Other theories refer to dual models: state and market, or markets and hierarchies (firms). Recent views stress the importance of other types of coordination modes in economic and social life, such as networks (Thompson *et al.*, 1991). Considering coordination at a general level, and including the coordination of both the social and technical division of labour, a complex – but still simplified – scheme of coordination modes can be proposed by considering the articulation of state, networks, hierarchies and markets.[8] A distinction has been introduced in relation to the traditional socialist system between the mega-hierarchy or general control hierarchy above the enterprise and the micro-hierarchy within the enterprise (see the discussion of the concept of hierarchy in transaction cost economics in Chavance, (1995). The three categories of traditional socialist system, reformed socialist system and post-socialist transforming economy are used as ideal-types based on stylized historical facts.

In the proposed evolutionary approach, the complexity of the coordination set-up is stressed in order to show the importance of previous endogenous changes in the socialist period, and to localize essential qualitative changes in the 'mix' of various modes in the post-socialist phase. While in the ownership sphere we witnessed a growing diversity of forms, in the coordination sphere we mainly see a transformation of different modes and changes in their articulation and interaction.

The standard view of 'marketization' of the economy is too reductionist. Let us define markets abstractly by the mediation of monetary exchange between production and consumption, as a result of both immediate independence and general interdependence of producers and consumers, depending on the division of labour. On this view the determination of prices and quantities, and the question of market power, depend on different *forms* of markets. Consequently, post-socialist transformation should not be understood as simple *marketization* following the abolition of central planning, but as a process of radical change in market forms, along with modified relations between markets and other coordination modes (state, networks and micro-hierarchies (firms)).

Table 10.5 illustrates both the breaks and the continuities in the field of coordination modes before and after the collapse of socialist regimes. The most important changes are the abolition of the Communist Party and of its coordinating function through its links with the state hierarchy, the shift to state macromanagement, the high diversification of the corporate types and of their internal arrangements, and the transformations concerning markets. The latter include modifications of the institutional set-up in which markets are embedded (legal provisions and codes, including property rights, role of the transforming or emerging banking and financial system, and so on), transformation in the behaviour of different agents, and changes in the market's processes and forms (modes of determination of prices and quantities, switch from seller's to buyer's markets, forms of competition).

The relative spheres of coordination modes are transformed. 'Destatization' and 'depaternalization' are at work through a contraction of the state's fields of intervention, notably at the micro level and in the sphere of foreign trade. 'Marketization' is under way not in the sense of changes to price formation mechanisms or in the types of competition – which depend, as observed, on radical modifications in market forms – but in the sense that markets extend their scope to new products and services such as, for instance, education, health and culture, and some new markets emerge gradually (for example, financial markets, housing markets). The so-called 'labour market' is not created *ex nihilo* either, but undergoes deep changes in the mechanisms determining the employment level and structure and level of wages. The hierarchical constraint in enterprises is generally hardened by the mentioned changes in state and market coordination.

In reformed socialist economies, such as Hungary or Poland in the 1980s, the mix of coordination modes had moved from the traditional system to evolve in the direction of the future post-socialist configuration. The weakening of microregulation, increased polycentrism in the state administration and the partial activation of money in the state sector had stimulated changes in various markets, but in a context of increased macroeconomic (and sometimes social) tensions. Nevertheless, the importance of the break after 1989 should not be underestimated. In the (almost) non-reformed Czechoslovakia, no transition through a reform period took place, so the elements of continuity in coordination were less important. They are not totally absent though, as can be seen in late socialist emergence of macroeconomic policy (notably monetary policy; Klaus, 1990), and in the importance of industrial networks in the post-socialist period.

Table 10.5 A changing mix of coordination modes

	Traditional Socialist System	Reformed Socialist System	Post-socialist Transformational Economy
State	• Party-state direct microregulation based on mega-hierarchical web (petty tutelage and coordination through priorities plus bargaining within centralized planning)	• Limited disentangling of state and party hierarchies. Abolition or effective weakening of direct microregulation and of mega-hierarchy. Attempts at indirect planning, fragmented vertical bargaining with enterprises, shifting to monetary factors (as opposed to physical targets)	• Abolition of party and related hierarchies, abolition of mega-hierarchy leading to early coordination disruption on this level. Emergence of state indirect macromanagement, intensive legislative work and institutional transformation policies. Tendency to 'state desertion' in some spheres but maintained involvement in others; legitimacy and credibility problems. Fuzzy border between public and private spheres
Networks	• Stable forward and backward linkages between enterprises in the first and second economies. Clientelist and clan-like relations in the second economy	• Reproduction and sometimes activation of sectoral or regional networks, in the first or second economy	• Reproduction of some ancient networks; emergence of a few networks inherited from the abolished mega-hierarchy; creation of new networks through ownership transformation (as in cross-ownership ties or in relations between enterprises and banks or investment funds)
Microhierarchies (enterprises)	• One-man management. Hard hierarchical constraint, mitigated by workers' pressure helped by macro labour shortage	• Weakened hierarchical constraint (introduction of self-management forms; weak activation of unions; or limited introduction of quasi-private contracting within large enterprises)	• Development of great variety of forms of microhierarchies, according to ownership changes, transformation of unions, multiplication of new domestic or foreign enterprises, reorganization of corporate arrangements. Dominant tendency to hardening of the hierarchical constraint

Market for consumption goods	• Choice of consumers mainly constrained by quantities (shortages) • Dominance of sellers' markets. Active money. Prices fixed by hierarchy	• Choice of consumers constrained by quantities or by prices according to the type of goods or services • A variety of sellers' and buyers' markets. Active money. Prices fixed by price administration, with some bargaining	• Choice of consumers mainly constrained by prices • Dominance of buyers' markets. Active money. Flexible prices for most goods and services
Markets for production goods	• Vertical mediation in horizontal relations between enterprises (centralized material supply). Passive money • Prices fixed by mega-hierarchy	• Partial de-mediation of horizontal links between enterprises (extension of 'wholesale trade' with dominance of sellers' markets). Passive money weakly activated • Prices fixed by price administration, with some bargaining	• Total de-mediation of horizontal links • Dominance of buyers' markets. Active money. Flexible prices for most goods
'Labour market'	• Relatively free labour mobility helped by macro labour shortage. No formal bargaining (but informal pressure from below) for wages, mainly regulated by mega-hierarchy	• Relatively free labour mobility helped by macro labour shortage. Increasing space for informal pressure for higher wages at the enterprise level • Segmentation between first and second economy	• Switch from labour shortage to mass unemployment, with some continuation of labour hoarding. State gradual retirement from wage regulation (except for minimum wage policy). Introduction of weak wage bargaining at the enterprise and at the national level (tripartite commissions) • Segmentation between small and large enterprises, between public sector, legal private and illegal private sectors

189

4.1   Coordination and Ownership

The link between ownership forms and coordination mechanisms, suggested by von Mises from 1920 onwards, has been stressed in a neo-Misesian perspective by Kornai (1990, 1992), who has asserted a strong 'affinity' between private ownership and market coordination on the one hand, and state ownership and bureaucratic coordination on the other, with other combinations such as state ownership plus market coordination ('market socialism') displaying a weak affinity. While there appears to be wide consensus on this topic, it can be observed that such a reasonable but very general view is not based on a rigorously developed theoretical argument. If the negative systemic consequences of dominant public ownership can be inferred from many historical experiences, it remains the case that various economic theories have not yet given a satisfactory answer to the question of 'why private ownership is important' (Grosfeld, 1993). The Misesian approach, the theory of property rights or the theory of corporate control are confronted with difficulties when dealing with managerial forms of capitalism, and with the great variety of relations between ownership and management of capital observed in economic history – as well as with their coordination and dynamic efficiency consequences (Lazonick, 1992). An institutional and evolutionary comparative analysis at an intermediate level of abstraction of the various patterns in the links between capital ownership/management and coordination modes in the history of Western capitalism, of socialist and of post-socialist economics, remains to be done.

In the post-socialist mixed economies, where the 'blurring of frontiers' is a widespread tendency,[9] no clear affinity between ownership and coordination changes can be asserted until now. While some clarification can be expected as time goes by (Korsun and Murrell, 1995), it remains difficult to find unequivocal relations between developments in the ownership and coordination spheres in a middle-term perspective. Destatization and marketization in the above sense have developed much quicker than privatization. In reformed socialist economies such as Poland and Hungary in the 1980s, or China in the 1980s and 1990s, changes in the coordination mix were significant while changes in the formal ownership structure were mainly confined to the private or 'collective' spheres outside the state sector. The primary importance of the clarification of property rights in view of the shift to a 'market economy', stressed by the theory of property rights as opposed for instance to the extension of competition, is questioned by the experience of post-socialist Central Europe and reformed socialist China. This should not lead to the conclusion that privatization could be neglected in the shift to a modern form of capitalism, but it should lead to a qualification of the widespread idea of the first years of transformation that it was the solution for most problems.

Some 'affinity' can nevertheless be observed in some fields. For instance, the emergence of interwoven forms of ownership points to the role of new network modes of coordination, or of the 'hybrid forms' that are neither market nor hierarchy, stressed in recent versions of transaction cost economics.

5.   THE UNCERTAIN CONSEQUENCES OF THE POST-SOCIALIST COMPOSITE ECONOMY

5.1   Possible Lock-in

The ownership transformations in the three Central European countries in the first half of the 1990s have presented one remarkable feature. On the one hand, a similar process leads to similar effects in most countries, that is, the proliferation of small- and medium-sized private enterprises; on the other hand, different processes result in a quite similar outcome, namely the emergence of new, complex, interwoven ownership forms. This non-linear evolution is the result of complex interactions between different levels – national (different national legacies) and family-systemic – of path-dependence effects and various state-organized privatization strategies, in a rather uncertain environment where unexpected events spontaneously occur. These interactions trigger the emergence of new hybrid forms within the range of possibilities determined by a common systemic legacy. The lack of fresh capital at the beginning of the transformation process and the decapitalization of public firms during the 'transformational recession' is one of the features which may explain the importance of the role of the banks in the privatization processes. But the diversity of interwoven ownership forms is related to different national trajectories: a process of corporatization begun in the late 1980s in Hungary, an original mass privatization programme implemented in 1992 in the Czech Republic, the development of industrial giants and debt–equity swaps in Poland and maybe the result of the Polish version of the mass privatization programme.

Institutional and organizational transformation trajectories in Eastern Europe may become locked into inferior paths of development (Arthur, 1989, 1990; Hodgson, 1994) or, conversely, atypical capitalist forms may become institutionalized and then may prove to be somehow efficient.[10]

One question facing transition countries now is whether small private enterprises will be able to grow and evolve into medium and large-sized enterprises. SMEs stemming from large SOEs (subcontracting firms) tend to face growth difficulties owing to narrow specialization related to enterprise needs. But scarce finance is the most serious problem. Tight credit access and self-financing out of gross savings may be a major barrier to SME growth, especially in capital-intensive industrial activities.

Moreover, we have noted that some of the small private enterprises, supposedly the best guarantee of a shift to the market economy, are not really market actors, but hybrid actors sometimes still pervaded by the socialist heritage. Some of them will become real market actors, others will disappear, but certain survivors may tend to direct private sector evolution towards inferior development paths. Scarce finance and hybrid actors may lead to a marginalization of the small private sector in Hungary (Gabor, 1994).

In Poland, conflicting interests between the political actors, management and workers' collective have considerably slowed down the privatization process and led the Polish authorities in the first years to place much of the policy emphasis on the growth of the new private sector. More than in any other Central European country, a dualism can be observed in Poland between large state-owned firms, some of which have been corporatized but not yet privatized and which are in an uncertain situation under the formal control of the state treasury, and a dynamic and prolific small private sector. However, the share of the private sector in total investment has been relatively less dynamic, and the gross profitability ratio seems to have been lower in the private than in the state sector for most branches of the economy (UNO, 1994).[11]

5.2   Ownership and Control

The Czech trajectory seems to be now locked in by the role of banks, which exert important control on the country's economy. Some problems may result from the links observed between the state, banks and industrial enterprises, the 'permissive' banking attitude, the artificial survival of non-profitable enterprises, collusion risks, and the limited entry of new firms and exit of outdated ones (Grosfeld, 1994). An unexpected conflict may arise between a bank's will to initiate the bankruptcy of firms and the interests of its investment fund which has shares in these firms (Svejnar, 1994), or between different IPFs holding shares in the same enterprise but with different strategies and interests (Mertlik, 1995). The intertwined property relations make managers' control by shareholders rather uneasy. Similar risks could be conjectured in the emerging Hungarian institutional framework.

It should be noted, however, that standard theories of corporate governance stressing the importance of direct or indirect control of owners (shareholders) on managers, mainly based on the US case, have limited explanatory power when applied to the history of European latecomers such as France, Germany or Italy (Tamborini and Targetti, 1995), or to other national capitalist institutions such as those in the Japanese or Asian economics (Schaede, 1994).

Managerial capitalism or the 'corporate economy' (Marris, 1987) is more frequent in the contemporary world than 'proprietary capitalism' – a model inherited from the nineteenth century, which has remained a hidden reference in more sophisticated theories of agency or of corporate governance (Lazonick, 1991; Nuti, 1995).

In other words, if some disturbing consequences arise in the relations between owners and managers of capital, they will result from the specific conditions of these transforming economies, rather than from their distance from the questionable normative model of efficient corporate governance. One source of concern might be the weak initial capacities and competencies of banks on the one hand, and of 'inherited' managers on the other hand. Co-learning will remain crucial in this respect.

In recent years, the relation between ownership changes and enterprise behaviour has appeared quite indeterminate – except in the positive case of foreign involvement. While a diversification of managerial attitudes had been observed, for instance, in Poland in the 1980s within the then prevalent state-owned sector (Beksiak, 1989), the variety of behavioural responses to the new context has not been clearly connected with privatization. Active restructuring can be observed in a number of still public enterprises, while the behaviour of many privatized (or formally privatized) ones has undergone little change. Firms 'afloat' or 'adrift' (Brada et al., 1994) can be found in various property rights configurations. In a period of weak systemic coherence and of institutional uncertainty, enterprise-specific factors such as the personality of managers confronted with many new constraints or the form of coalitions built within or around the firm, can be decisive, along with increased competitive pressures.

5.3   Future Selection and Evolution Processes

Systemic change is by nature a complex process as elements, subsystems, the whole system and its environment are all changing at the same time (England, 1994). Moreover, institutions are both the objects of change and the agents of change. The co-learning of agents and co-evolution of organizations and institutions takes place in a context of weak systemic coherence with partial rigidities and emerging irreversibilities. Given such a complexity of systemic change, the beneficial or detrimental macro-social effects of such crystallized tendencies cannot be predicted in advance.

The transformation of ownership in transition countries is an evolutionary process. The implementation of privatization programmes does not put an end to the process. On the contrary, a post-privatization redistribution of property is likely to result, reinforcing the ownership structure (lock-in), or leading to new post-socialist, path-dependent configurations. Such a process is already under way in the Czech Republic, where IPFs are reselling their corporate shares to other owners anxious to increase their equity stake (other IPFs, beneficiaries of restitution, foreign investors) or privatized (quasi-private) companies are buying back restituted plants, reselling others (sometimes to clear debts) and so on (Mertlik, 1995). In Poland, given the size of the conglomerates, a slimming reorganization of property is likely to occur.

Evolutionary authors have underlined that macroeconomic growth requires not only microeconomic diversity and instability, but also processes of harmonization, regulation, standardization and routinization 'to avoid chaotic instability and to reap the benefits of scale economies' (Freeman, 1994). Post-socialist transformation is associated with a great increase in the degree of organizational and institutional diversity. A large number of new small enterprises coexist dynamically with a more restricted number of large firms undergoing various types of adaptation, innovation or survival strategies.[12] Some of the big old firms are fragmented or gradually reduced in scale, while some small or medium ones grow or try to expand. This change in the enterprise population takes place in the context of a rapidly evolving institutional and legal environment, and in a period of initial economic depression with large shifts in the structure of global demand (and rather quick opening up to foreign competition). When the population structure (in terms of enterprises, scale, legal types, ownership forms) stabilizes or comes to evolve more gradually, the problem of 'harmonization, regulation and routinization' will inevitably come to the fore. The increase in diversity is also an increase in complexity. Which type of stabilized order will emerge, with which growth properties, remains to be seen. A dynamic and competitive economy, although possible, cannot be expected as an automatic product of 'transition'.

Selection processes taking place in Central Europe are not unambiguous either. They have taken place mainly through differential growth and decay of enterprises and industries rather than by bankruptcies proper. The number of bankruptcies is still limited, even if the situation varies among countries. In the Czech Republic, the number of bankruptcies is very low (the government suspended the law in 1992 for a year) and has essentially affected private enterprises. In 1993, 2000 bankruptcy requests were filed and only 60 effectively pronounced. In Hungary, the new Bankruptcy Law of 1 January 1992 resulted in debtors and creditors reaching agreements, including state-owned commercial banks and other state or central institutions (tax office, customs, social security). Up to August 1993, some 5000 bankruptcies and more than 15 000 liquidation requests were filed, but only 4300 bankruptcies and 4000 liquidation proceedings were actually started (UNO, 1994). In Poland, privatization under the law on SOEs (real bankruptcy and the subsequent sale of assets) led to the actual liquidation of 1171 firms by mid-1994 (OECD, 1994). The balance sheet of the destructive and creative aspects of the ongoing change remains unclear in a middle-term perspective. Moreover, even in a stabilized, Western capitalist, competitive context, it is dubious whether the selection process simply favours the 'fittest' enterprises (Hodgson, 1993).

More generally, selective processes of internal and external competition have not abolished country-specific enduring features in institutional arrangements and organizational forms, as the history of capitalist economies shows. Path-dependence is linked with 'locality of learning, opaqueness of environment, embeddedness of organizations within particular institutional contexts', which explains the persistence of national forms of corporate and industrial organization 'even when ex post they lead to different competitive performance' (Dosi, 1994). This remark can easily be extended to the present and the future of post-socialist national economies.

6. POST-SOCIALIST FORMS OF CAPITALISM

In place of a (difficult but) simplistic 'transition to a market economy', we see in Central Europe the emergence of various path-dependent mixed economies. The common features of these post-socialist mixed economies in the 1990s, beyond the very high number of small enterprises, are interwoven ownership forms and a composite coordination set-up.

Capital ownership in medium and large enterprises is characterized by a great multiplicity of owners, including the state – still present to a greater or lesser extent – by specific mixtures of public and private forms including numerous hybrids[13] and by complex cross-ownership ties between enterprises, various institutional investors and banks. The relations between ownership and management of capital are very diversified, and although they are likely to be modified in a middle-term perspective, a common characteristic remains the relative power of managers *vis-à-vis* frequently dispersed, inexperienced, absentee or dependent owners. These economies can thus be defined as a type of managerial capitalism, or a peculiar corporate economy.

The coordination set-up includes different modes or governance types, as in advanced capitalist economies in general, but the nature of the mix has strong post-socialist characteristics. The content of each mode has undergone important changes, and the articulation of various modes has consequently changed. Markets have shifted from the dominance of sellers to the dominance of buyers, and competition forms are coming closer to the imperfect, Western types (Kornai, 1995). State intervention has shrunk considerably and has shifted to macromanagement and management of institutional change. It is marked by limited initial competencies in the new context, reduced legitimacy and often budgetary crisis, but the presence and importance of the state remain great, because of a still extensive public sector, the state's role in privatization and institution-building processes, and more generally because of the scale of societal tasks and problems. Economic networks, sometimes inherited from the socialist period, sometimes new, play a significant role in coordination, often related to developing cross-ownership ties. Corporate hierarchies in large enterprises are reorganized following competitive pressure and imitation of Western models, with authority being strengthened in general but remnants of paternalist or 'corporatist' relations not disappearing altogether.

The banking sector, which in most cases seems to be evolving towards a model of universal banking, appears crucial in the future evolution of these economies, but it is still concentrated, unsophisticated, with limited competencies, sometimes potentially fragile. The representation of interests, especially for wage earners, is still poorly organized following the crisis of the trade unions in the different countries. More generally, the structure of civil society is evolving only slowly.

While an evolutionary approach stressing path-dependence gives some clues as to the emerging shape of post-socialist capitalisms and the formation of systemic irreversibilities, the middle- and long-term dynamic perspectives of these economies remain partially uncertain and relatively open.

NOTES

1. The contemporary transformation of advanced capitalist economies has been characterized as a shift from one mixed economy regime to another mixed constellation. 'In fact, the last two decades have exhibited a chaotic and rather myopic transition out of one mixed economy regime, which the regulation approach calls Fordist, Beveridgian and Keynesian. This label characterizes respectively the capital-labour compromise, the welfare system deriving from a citizen-state compromise inherited from the great depression of the inter-war years, and finally the counter-cyclical use of monetary and fiscal instruments to smooth economic fluctuations. The rather likely outcome will be another configuration of mixed economies. Tentatively, these regimes have been labelled Toyotist for Japan, Uddevalist for Sweden, or nostalgic and Fordist for US and France. If true, such a diagnosis strongly contradicts any institutional convergence, be it among the Western world, or for East European countries' (Boyer, 1991).
2. Discussing the shift from autocratic to democratic regimes in a comparative perspective, P. Schmitter and T. Lynn Karl (1994) observe that 'national differences in consolidation are likely to be greater than national differences in transition'. As for the debate on convergence in the West, see Boyer (1993), Hollingsworth *et al.* (1994), Zysman (1995).
3. Stark (1994), in his remarkable work on the emerging new forms of property and corporate structures in the former state sector, has insisted on 'recombination' in organizational innovation, as 'reconfiguration and rearrangements of existing institutional elements'. The term 'recombination' may carry some ambiguity in so far as it seems to understate the role of new institutions or organizational forms that are not reducible to rearrangements. Recombined and brand new forms emerge from both intentional and spontaneous processes. Transformative systemic 'bricolage' (Stark, 1994) is thus at work.
4. Most new small- and medium-sized enterprises are small businesses (up to 20 employees),

among which a high number of individual enterprises can be observed. Medium-sized enterprises essentially stem from the break-up of large units.

5. The OECD assesses that prosperous small private enterprises had generally been founded before 1989 (OECD, 1993b).

6. In early 1989, for example, the state-owned electronics firm Omig in Warsaw was entirely leased to its manager (Patterson, 1993).

7. Interwoven ownership is a striking feature of recent evolution in Russia, following mass voucher privatization, but also in China, as a result of the ongoing corporatization of large state enterprises: the capital of an enterprise is usually distributed initially among various other state enterprises (leading to cross-ownership ties), local or regional government, the management, less often the employees, while a part of the capital may be simultaneously sold for participation by foreign investors. The Chinese authorities, wishing to avoid a perverse relationship between indebted enterprises and banks, have explicitly forbidden bank participation in industrial (public) ownership. Let us remark here that China has entered the post-socialist transformation too, but by a different route than Eastern Europe. While in the latter the institutional base of the socialist system was broken down by the dismantling of its first political pillar, the one-party regime, in the former it has been gradually eroded by the extension of the 'non-state' sector, modifying the second pillar, the dominance of state ownership (since the beginning of the 1990s the non-state sector has overtaken the state sector in industrial production, while agriculture has been decollectivized since the beginning of the 1980s). China can now be considered as an example of the 'post-socialist mixed economy', with diverse intertwined, fuzzy and hybrid ownership forms and a composite evolving coordination set-up. We believe that extending the comparative analysis to this important experience would strengthen the case for this notion.

8. Some authors would rather insist on the interpenetration of different modes (Bradach and Eccles, 1989). Even though this is an important topic for post-socialist transformation as well, for the sake of simplicity we have only dealt with the *articulation* of various modes.

9. Stark (1996) writes about a 'triple boundary blurring': between property forms (public/private), between organizational boundaries and between justificatory principles.

10. It is amusing to find in *The Economist* (1995a), in which the concept of mixed economy has so often been criticized in the first years of post-socialism and where peremptory assertions can often be read about the necessary convergence of 'market economies' towards an idealized Anglo-Saxon model, the apt observation that 'to speak about "mutant" capitalism is to imply that "proper" capitalism must always take a constant form. Yet the share-based capitalism of America and Britain clearly differs from the bank-based capitalism of most of Western Europe. The "mutant" corporate structures emerging in Eastern Europe borrow elements from each of these models and mix in novelties of their own. It would be a funny sort of evolution in which at least some of the mutations did not turn out to be thoroughly robust'.

11. This information is to be treated with caution because small private firms tend to overstate their costs and understate their profits in order to avoid tax payments.

12. The danger of a detrimental segmentation of firms exists in Central Europe: once formed, many private firms do not expand, so that 'a shrinking large firm sector combined with an insider-dominated, small-firm sector could leave many in long-term unemployment' (Busse, 1994).

13. Sticking to the questionable division between the private and the public sector, it can be observed that the former has become important everywhere, with a proportion of nearly half of national production. It is imbricated with the public sector (Hungary), or in a dualistic relation with it (Poland), or has itself a dualistic structure (large privatized enterprises/small greenfield or privatized ones – Czech Republic).

REFERENCES

Andreff, W. (ed.) (1995), *Le Secteur Public à l'Est: Restructuration Industrielle et Financière*. Paris: L'Harmattan.

Arthur, W.B. (1989), 'Competing technologies, increasing returns, and lock-in by historical events', *Economic Journal*, 99(1), pp. 116–31.

Arthur, W.B. (1990), 'Positive feedbacks in the economy', *Scientific American*, 262(2), pp. 80–85.

Beksiak, J. (1989), 'Role and functioning of the enterprise in Poland', in *Economic Reform in the European Centrally Planned Economies*. New York: Economic Commission for Europe (UN).

Bouin, O. (1995), 'Privatisation et transformation economique en Europe Centrale et Orientale: l'exemple de la république Tchèque', PhD dissertation, EHESS, Mag.

Boyer, R. (1991), 'Markets within alternative coordinating mechanisms', mimeo, Paris: CEPREMAP.

Boyer, R. (1992), 'Markets: history, theory and policy', paper presented to the EAEPE Conference, Paris, November.

Boyer, R. (1993), 'The convergence hypothesis revisited: globalization but still the century of nations?', Paper presented to the conference 'Domestic Institutions, Trade and Pressures for National Convergence', Bellagio, February.

Brada J., I. Singh and A. Török (1994), 'Firms afloat and firms adrift: Hungarian industry and the economic transition', *Eastern European Economics*, 32(1), pp. 3–101.

Bradach, J. and R. Eccles (1989), 'Price, authority and trust: from ideal types to plural forms', *Annual Review of Sociology*, 15, pp. 97–118.

Busse, M. (1994), 'Restructuring and recovery of output in Russia', IIASA, Working Paper, Laxenburg, September.

Chavance, B. (1994a), *La Fin des Systèmes Socialistes. Crise, Réforme et Transformation*, Paris: L'Harmattan.

Chavance, B. (1994b), 'Transition et dépression', in Chavance (1994a).

Chavance, B. (1995), 'Hierarchical forms and coordination problems in socialist economies', *Industrial and Corporate Change*, 4(1), pp. 271–91.

Dosi, G. (1994), 'Microfoundations of macroeconomic competitiveness', in G. Hodgson, W. Samuels and M. Tool (eds), *The Elgar Companion to Institutional and Evolutionary Economics*, Vol. 2, Aldershot: Edward Elgar, pp. 72–78.

Earle, J.S., R. Frydman, A. Rapaczynski and J. Turkewitz (eds) (1994), *Small Privatization: The Transformation of Retail Trade and Consumer Services in the Czech Republic, Hungary and Poland*, Budapest: Central European University Press.

EBRD (1995), *Transition Report 1995*, London: EBRD.

England, R. (1994), *Evolutionary Concepts in Contemporary Economics*, Ann Arbor: University of Michigan Press.

Freeman, C. (1994), 'The economics of technical change', *Cambridge Journal of Economics*, 18(5), pp. 31–65.

Gabor, R.I. (1994), 'Small entrepreneurship in Hungary: ailing or prospering?' *Acta Oeconomica*, 46(3, 4), pp. 333–46.

Grosfeld, I. (1993) 'J. Kornai: the socialist system, book review', *Economics of Transition*, 1(2), pp. 227–81.

Grosfeld, I. (1994), 'Financial systems in transition: is there a case for a bank based system?', Discussion Paper No. 1062, London: CEPR, November.

Hodgson, G. (1993), *Economics and Evolution: Bringing Life Back into Economics*, Cambridge: Polity.

Hodgson, G. (1994), 'Lock-in and chreodic development', in G. Hodgson, W. Samuels and M. Tool (eds), *The Elgar Companion to Institutional and Evolutionary Economics*, Vol. 2, Aldershot: Edward Elgar, pp. 15–19.

Hollingsworth, J., R. Schmitter and W. Streeck (eds) (1994), *Governing Capitalist Economies: Performance and Control of Economic Sectors*, New York and Oxford: Oxford University Press.

Klaus, V. (1990), 'Monetary policy in Czechoslovakia in the 1970s and 1980s and the nature and problems of the current economic reform', *Communist Economies*, 2(1), pp. 61–71.

Klaus, V. (1994), 'Systemic change: the delicate mixture of intentions and spontaneity', address to the Mont Pélerin General Meeting, Cannes, 26 September.

Kornai, J. (1990), 'The affinity between ownership forms and coordination mechanisms: the common experience of reform in socialist countries', *Journal of Economic Perspectives*, 4(3), pp. 131–47.

Kornai, J. (1992), *The Socialist System: The Political Economy of Communism*, Oxford: Clarendon Press.

Kornai, J. (1994), 'Transformational recession: the main causes', *Journal of Comparative Economics*, 19(1), pp. 39–63.

Kornai, J. (1995), 'Eliminating the shortage economy: a general analysis and examination of the developments in Hungary', *Economics of Transition*, 3(1, 2), pp. 13–37, 149–68.

Korsun, G. and R. Murrell (1995), 'History versus policy: how much does enterprise governance change affect mass privatization', IRIS Working Paper No. 147, College Park, MD, University of Maryland, June.

Lazonick, W. (1991), *Business Organizations and the Myth of the Market Economy*, Cambridge: Cambridge University Press.

Lazonick, W. (1992), 'Controlling the market for corporate control: the historical significance of managerial capitalism', *Industrial and Corporate Change*, 1(3), pp. 445–8.

Marris, R. (1987), 'Corporate economy', in *The New Palgrave Dictionary of Economics*, Vol. 1, London: Macmillan.

Mertlik, R. (1995), 'Legal and organizational restructuring of Czech enterprises', paper presented to the conference, 'Enterprise Restructuring at Different Stages of Ownership Transformation: The Czech Republic and Poland', MSH, Paris, 3–4 July.

Mladek, J. (1993), 'Czech privatization process: time for corporate governance', Paper presented to the conference, 'Output Decline in Eastern Europe: Prospects for Recovery?', IIASA, Laxenburg, Austria, 18–20 November.

Nee, V. and D. Stark (eds) (1989), *Remaking the Economic Institutions of Socialism: China and Eastern Europe*, Stanford, CA: Stanford University Press.

Neumann, L. (1993), 'Decentralization and privatization in Hungary: towards supplier networks', in G. Grabher (ed.), *The Embedded Firm: On the Socioeconomics of Industrial Networks*, London and New York: Routledge, pp. 179–201.

Nivet, J.F. (1994), 'La privatisation en Pologne: d'une approche plurielle aux difficultés de la privatisation de masse', *Economie et Statistique*, 279–80, pp. 121–33.

Nuti, D.M. (1995), 'Corporate governance et actionnariat des salariés', *Economie Internationale*, 62, pp. 13–34 (2 trimestre).

OECD (1993b), *Trends and Policies in Privatization*, CEET, Paris: OECD.

OECD (1994), *Pologne*, Etudes Economiques de l'OCDE, CCET, Paris: OECD.

Patterson, R. (ed.) (1993), *Capitalist Goals, Socialist Past: The Rise of the Private Sector in Command Economies*, Boulder: Westview Press.

Schaede, U. (1994), 'Understanding corporate governance in Japan: do classical concepts apply?', *Industrial and Corporate Change*, 3(2), pp. 285–323.

Schmitter, P and T. Lynn Karl (1994), 'The conceptual travels of transitologists and consolidologists: how far east should they attempt to go?', *Slavic Review*, 53(1), pp. 63–82.

Slay, B. (1995), 'Mass privatization (in Poland): better late than never?', *Transition*, OMRI 1(14), pp. 16–22 (11 August).

Stark, D. (1992), 'Path dependence and privatization strategies in East Central Europe', *East European Politics and Societies*, 6(1), pp. 17–51.

Stark, D. (1994), 'Not by design: recombinant property in East European capitalism', Document de Travail, IRSES, MSH, Paris.

Stark, D. (1996), 'Recombinant property in East European capitalism', *American Journal of Sociology*, 101(4), pp. 993–1027.

Svejnar, J. (1994),'Obstacles to restructuration post privatization', in P. Aghion and N. Stern (eds), *Obstacles to Enterprise Restructuring in Transition*, London: EBRD, Working Paper No. 16, December.

Szabo, K. (1994), 'From the privatization to the marketization: schizophrenic actors in the transitory economies', Paper presented to the third EACES conference, Budapest, 8–10 September.

Tamborini, R. and R. Targetti (1995), 'Privatisation, intermédiation financière et système bancaire dans les economies en transition', in Andreff (1995), pp. 155–76.

The Economist (1995a), 'Eastern Europe capitalism: who's boss now?', 20 May.

The Economist (1995b), 'Polish companies: the accidental conglomerates', 5 August.

Thompson, G., J. Frances, R. Levacio and J. Mitchell (1991), *Markets, Hierarchies and Networks: The Coordination of Social Life*, London: Sage Publications.

UNO (1994), *Economic Survey of Europe in 1993–94*, New York: ECE, United Nations.

Zysman, J. (1994), 'How institutions create historically rooted trajectories of growth', *Industrial and Corporate Change*, 3(1), pp. 243–83.

Zysman, J. (1995), 'National roots of a "global" economy', *Revue d'Economie Industrielle*, 71, pp. 107–21 (1 trimestre).

11. Varieties of capitalism and varieties of economic theory

Geoffrey M. Hodgson*

The twentieth century was dominated by the ideological polarization between capitalism and socialism. Strikingly, what has emerged out of the collapse of the Eastern Bloc in 1989–91 is the view that we are now at 'the end of history' (Fukuyama, 1992). It is widely held that liberal-democratic capitalism is the normal or ideal state of affairs: once established and refined it cannot be surpassed.

I challenge this view here – but not by arguing for the feasibility or superiority of a socialist or any other alternative to capitalism. Essentially, pronouncements of the 'end of history' ignore the tremendous variety of forms of capitalism itself. In addition, a theoretical blindness to the immense variety within the modern system is curiously engendered by influential economic theorists from both right and left. In particular, although both Karl Marx and Friedrich Hayek have contributed an enormous amount to our understanding of how capitalist systems function, they both sustain a view of a singular and purified capitalism.

Furthermore, there is no unique or optimal combination of subsystems and institutions within capitalism that will necessarily triumph over other combinations. Although not all capitalisms are equal in performance, the advantages or efficiencies of one type of capitalism over another are typically dependent on their historical path and context and thereby none can be said to be ultimately superior to all the others.

The views of the American institutional economists, particularly Thorstein Veblen, provide an important counter to the differing approaches of Marx, Hayek and other authors on these questions. This chapter is about the theoretical and conceptual tools required to perceive and understand the actually existing variety of different forms of capitalism.

THE UNIVERSALITY OF NEOCLASSICAL ECONOMICS

Instead of the characteristic features of a given economic system, the starting point of neoclassical economics is the ahistorical, abstract individual.[1] The features and institutions that characterize a given economy do not form part of its core analysis. In starting from allegedly universal and ahistorical concepts, neoclassical economics fails to become rooted in any specific socio-economic system. Its very generality becomes a barrier to a deeper understanding of capitalism or other systems. Instead of attempting to confront a particular economy, or *real* object, it becomes confined to a remotely abstract and artificial *idea* of an economy.

Lionel Robbins (1932) encapsulated this approach with his famous but ahistorical definition of economics as the 'science of choice'. The economic problem becomes one of the allocation of scarce means in the pursuit of given ends. Individuals are assumed to have fixed and given utility functions and they exchange resources with each other to maximize their own utility. It is alleged that a wide range of social and economic phenomena can be analysed in these terms.

The door is thus opened to what is described by its practitioners as 'economic imperialism': the invasion of other social sciences with the choice-theoretic methods of neoclassical economics, informed by the presumed universality of such ideas as scarcity, competition and rational self-interest.[2] Yet scarcity and competition are not so universal as the economic imperialists presume.[3]

The Hidden, Ideological Specifics

In a direct attack on neoclassical economics, Marshall Sahlins (1972) shows that tribal economies differ from capitalism in that they do not generate ever-increasing wants. Tribal, hunter-gatherer societies in tropical regions are faced with such an abundance of food and other necessities that resources are, for practical purposes, unlimited. Thus, against the neoclassical view, it is possible for there to be vast resources and scarce wants.

Robbins (1932, pp. 12–16) explicitly related the concept of scarcity to the notion of a resource that is 'limited'. However, several important items in socio-economic systems are not 'scarce' in this Robbinsian sense. The problem with his concept of scarcity is also exhibited with respect to the issue of information and knowledge. Information is a peculiar commodity because if it is sold it can still be retained by the seller. Neither skills nor knowledge are given or limited, because of the phenomenon of 'learning by doing'. As Albert Hirschman (1985, p. 16) points out, 'Use of a resource such as a skill has the immediate effect of improving the skill, of enlarging (rather than depleting) its availability'. Especially in the growing and knowledge-intensive economies of modern capitalism, the Robbinsian 'law' of scarcity is thus broken. Even if neoclassical economics abandons its universalist claims and applies itself to a more limited set of types of economic system, it still ill-fits the modern age.[4]

The concept of the utility-maximizing individual in a world of scarcity that is seemingly typified in a capitalist society is frequently extended without warranty by neoclassical economics to all forms of socio-economic system. Although neoclassical economics often claims to be universal, by stressing individualism, scarcity and competition, its analysis reflects dominant ideological conceptions found in Europe and America in the modern age.

However, ideology does not necessarily correspond with reality. It is inaccurate to suggest that neoclassical economics strictly represents a capitalist or market economy (Hodgson, 1992a). It is admitted – even by leading exponents – that neoclassical economic theory does not satisfactorily encompass money, markets or firms![5] Neoclassical economics is not only strictly inaccurate but also insufficiently specific. The irony is that by attempting to erect a universal analysis of socio-economic behaviour, neoclassical economics ends up basing itself on a specific set of concepts seemingly associated with an individualistic and competitive market economy. That which is meant to be universal turns out in the end to be specific. Yet the specificity is not that of the real features of any actually existing capitalism.

The Limits of Contract and Exchange

Importantly, neoclassical economics addresses all social relations as if they were subject to contracts and exchange. Accordingly, neoclassical theorist Gary Becker (1976a) has developed a theoretical model of the family that treats the household as if it were itself a market and contract-based institution, essentially indistinguishable from a capitalist firm. Yet modern cultural norms make a very strong differentiation between, on the one hand, domestic and sexual activities obtained by money payment, and, on the other, those obtained by non-commercial means. Neoclassical theory is generally blind to these moral, cultural and institutional distinctions. There is no conceptual dividing line between the family and the marketplace. Accordingly, neoclassical economics is unable to conceptualize the specific institutional features of the household and the special human relations within that sphere.

This conceptual blindness is a serious handicap. Apart from failing to recognize the difference between commercial and non-commercial institutions and practices within capitalism, the question of the intrinsic limits to markets and contracts is thereby not addressed. This has devastating consequences both for the analysis of different types of capitalism and for the recognition of the limits to capitalism itself.

Notably, the modern family is still not completely invaded by commercial relations, and cultural norms are still sensitive to this fact. In fact, there are practical and more general limits to the extension of market and contractual relations within capitalism. Indeed, an overextension of market and purely contractarian relations would threaten to break up cultural and other bonds that are necessary for the functioning of the system as a whole. As Joseph Schumpeter (1976, pp. 423–4) argues, 'no social system can work which is based exclusively upon a network of free contracts between (legally) equal contracting parties and in which everyone is supposed to be guided by nothing except his own (short-run) utilitarian ends'.

Consideration of the uncertainty governing the employee–employer relationship in the capitalist firm leads Alan Fox (1974) to argue convincingly that an element of supra-contractual trust is essential to industrial relations, and that a purely contractual system is not feasible.[6] The whole point about trust is that it is undermined by the cost calculus. As Arrow (1974, p. 23) candidly remarks: 'Trust is an important lubricant of the social system. ... If you have to buy it, you already have some doubts about what you've bought'. On reflection, trust is not best explained as a phenomenon resulting simply from the rational calculation of costs and benefits by given individuals: something else is involved. Accordingly, trust cannot be modelled with the universal contractarian framework of utility-maximization and exchange upon which neoclassical economics is based. Such an approach, which misses the specific cultural features and social relations involved in the generation and protection of trust, will be unable to understand some essential and specific features of any capitalist system.

In fact, the distinction between commercial and non-commercial relations within any capitalist society is both indelible and central to the nature of capitalism. Significantly, the precise boundaries of the demarcation profoundly affect the nature of the specific variety of capitalist system.

Actor and Structure

Neoclassical economics places great emphasis on individuality and choice. However, it is not only arguable that free choice is in fact denied, but also that neoclassical theory makes the individual a prisoner of his or her immanent and often invariable preferences and beliefs (Loasby, 1976, p. 5).

In modern neoclassical economics the individual, in all her richness and complexity, is simply reduced to a well-behaved preference function that obeys textbook axioms. The possible origins of this preference function in the human psyche or the social world are left unexplained. As argued at length elsewhere (Hodgson, 1988), this conception of the individual regards the person as detachable from the rich cultural world and the web of institutions upon which we depend. Instead, the individual is regarded as a self-contained contractarian atom. Institutions, in so far as they exist, are treated as the product of individual interactions and not as the moulders of individual purposes and preferences.

FRIEDRICH HAYEK AND THE INEVITABILITY OF MARKETS

With the Austrian School of economists an ahistorical conception of the individual with 'purposes and individual knowledge' is the point of departure. There are obvious differences of policy outlook between Marx and Hayek. However, we are less concerned here about policy conclusions and more with Hayek's theoretical framework and his explicit or implicit conception of capitalism. On these points some remarkable convergences with Marx will later be noted.

In some passages, Hayek (1982, Vol. 3, p. 162) treats the market as the general context in which competition takes place: a forum in which individual property owners collide. Criticizing Hayek on this point, Viktor Vanberg (1986, p. 75) points out that the market 'is always a system of social interaction characterized by a specific *institutional framework*, that is, by a *set of rules* defining certain restrictions on the behavior of market participants'. Whether these rules are formal or informal the result is that there is no such thing as the 'true, unhampered market', operating in an institutional vacuum. 'This raises the issue of what rules can be considered "appropriate" in the sense of allowing for a beneficial working of the market mechanism' (ibid., p. 97).

Notably, the market itself is a *social institution*, governed by sets of rules defining restrictions on some, and legitimating other, behaviours. Furthermore, the market is necessarily embedded in other social institutions such as the state, and is promoted or even in some cases created by conscious design.[7] Accordingly, it is reasonable to pay significant attention to the possibility of the emergence of different kinds of markets, with varied structures and constituent rules. Yet Jim Tomlinson (1990, p. 121) finds that Hayek, along with most other economists including neoclassicals and Marxists, treats the market as an abstract principle, independent of its institutional and cultural integument. In reality, however, markets are highly varied phenomena.

The Problem of Necessary Impurities

Clearly, higher levels of competitive selection must involve the selection of different types of institution, including varieties of both market and non-market forms. To work at such higher levels, institutional competition must involve different types of ownership structure and resource allocation mechanisms, all coexisting in a mixed economy. This is quite contrary to Hayek's preferred policy stance. Hayek follows the views of his teacher, von Mises (1949, p. 259), in proposing not only that a mixture of socialism with capitalism is impossible, but that capitalism prospered best in a 'pure' form. However, while Hayek and von Mises provided strong arguments as to why a socialist economic system planned entirely from the centre is not feasible (Hayek, 1935), they fail to demonstrate satisfactorily why a mixed economy is either unfeasible or disadvantageous.

Hayek and his co-thinkers have inspired policies to extend 'free markets' and 'roll back the state'. The view is that such policies are necessary both for economic efficiency and personal liberty. It is assumed that the extension of commercial contracts and individual property rights is both possible and desirable, and even necessary if civilization is to survive.

However, far from heralding an era of individual liberty, governments committed to these or similar ideas have often taken an authoritarian tone, such as that in Britain in the 1980s under the premiership of Margaret Thatcher. As Karl Polanyi (1944) argues in his classic study of the Industrial Revolution in Britain, the initial extension of the market was very much an act of the state. Subsequently there was strong pressure from all quarters to restrict the market through legislation to limit the working day, ensure public health, institute social insurance and regulate trade. Not only to provide social cohesion but also to ensure the smooth working of the market itself, the state had to protect, regulate, subsidize, standardize and intervene. Thus the extension of markets did not mean the diminution of the powers of the state, but instead led to increasing intrusion and regulation by central government. Accordingly, even in Victorian Britain, the introduction of free markets, far from doing away with the need for control, regulation and intervention, enormously increased their range. This was true *a fortiori* in France and Germany, where markets were typically more closely regulated.

Polanyi argues that the creation and maintenance of private property rights and functioning market institutions require the sustained intervention of the state to eject economic forms and institutions that are antagonistic to the private market system. Paradoxically, therefore, 'free-market' policies can lead to a substantial centralization of economic and political power. Hayekian policies in practice actually threaten both economic and political pluralism and grant extended powers to the central state. Extreme individualism paradoxically takes on a totalitarian quality. Social forms and ideologies other than free-market individualism and private property are driven out.

It should again be emphasized that the unqualified goal of the 'free' market ignores the fact that trade and markets rely on other antiquated and often rigid institutions and other traditional features of social culture. As we shall see below, and despite their policy differences, both Marx and Hayek ignore the necessary 'impurities' in a market system.

There are many examples of essential but non-commercial spheres of activity within capitalism. One such example is the family, but this topic is awkwardly side-stepped in Hayek's writings. As Tomlinson (1990, p. 131) points out, families 'are extremely problematic in their implications for liberty in Hayek's sense'. Hayek ignores the question of what kind of liberty is provided for children within this institution, as well as the implications for liberalism of a lifelong marriage contract between partners. To address this issue, Hayekians may well have to abandon either extreme liberalism, or a conservative commitment to family values, or both.

Admittedly, the market continues to play an indispensable role in the modern era, but it is deceptive to suggest that it is the primary arena of social interaction for most agents. Even in contemporary economies, much more daily activity is internal to organizations and outside the market (Simon, 1991).

Actor and Structure

Hayek does not believe in the inevitability of capitalism, socialism or any other type of economic system. In part this is because he emphasizes the essential creativity and potential novelty of human action. Yet in emphasizing the indeterminacy of human action the task of explaining what lies behind it is abandoned. While Marx assumes that individuals are driven by their class position and interest, Hayek is reluctant to attempt to explain individual human actions. Both specific human motivations and systemic outcomes are indeterminate in his theory.

The polar opposite position would be to suggest that structures and institutions entirely determine human behaviour. Elsewhere it has been argued that some intermediate position is possible (Giddens, 1984; Hodgson, 1988). There are external influences moulding the purposes and actions of individuals, but action is not entirely determined by them. The environment is influential but it does not completely determine either what the individual aims to do or what he or she may achieve. The individual is ridden by habits of thought but not bereft of choice.

Both neoclassical and Austrian theorists start from universal assumptions about socio-economic systems and human behaviour. For Hayek the trans-historical elements of theoretical analysis are individuals and rules. There are markets but generally their specific nature is regarded as unproblematic and their prior existence is often assumed. Because of the extreme generality of his perspective, and despite the sophistication of his systemic view, he cannot enrich his theory with the specificities either of capitalism or of any particular type of capitalism. All Hayek can do is to recommend the best constitutional arrangement that is compatible with the bland generalities of markets, private property and individual liberty. On the abundant, actual or potential variety of forms of capitalism – and of human cultures and behaviours within capitalism – he has nothing of significance to say.

KARL MARX AND THE TRIUMPH OF CAPITALISM

Mainstream economists take the analytical starting point of the ahistorical, abstract individual. Marx's approach is different. As revealed in a letter to Pavel Annenkov, written in 1846, Marx expounds the methodological rule that *'economic categories* are but *abstractions* of … real relations, that they are truths only in so far as those relations continue to exist'. This contrasts 'with bourgeois economists who regard those economic categories as eternal laws and not as historical laws which are laws only for a given historical development, a specific development of the productive forces' (Marx and Engels, 1982, p. 100).

In Marx's view, ahistorical categories such as 'utility', 'choice' and 'scarcity' cannot capture the essential features of a specific economic system. His recognition of the processes of historical development and revolutionary transformation of human society leads him to the choice of sets of specific concepts that capture the essences of particular, transient systems. Marx claims that the core categories in *Capital* are abstract expressions of real social relations found within the capitalist mode of production. Such categories are held to be operational as long as these social relations exist.

Marx's aim is to analyse the type of economy emerging in Britain and Europe in the nineteenth century. Thus in the Preface to the first edition of *Capital* he makes it clear that his objective is to examine not economies in general, nor even socialism, but 'the capitalist mode of production'. It is the 'ultimate aim' of that work 'to reveal the economic law of motion of modern society' (Marx, 1976, pp. 90, 92).

Marx does not start with a general and ahistorical 'economic problem'. Instead, Marx's economic analysis starts from what he regards as the essential social relations of the capitalist mode of production. This is clear from the key words in the titles of the opening chapters of *Capital*: commodities, exchange, money, capital and labour power. Marx did not aim to write a text on economics that would be applicable to all economic systems. No such work, in his view, is possible. He argues that it is necessary to focus on a particular economic system and the particular relations and laws that governed its operation and evolution.

Contrary to empiricism, Marx accepts the need for a prior conceptual framework in order to understand the world. Generally, in their analysis of socio-economic systems, social scientists are obliged to rely on 'ideal types'. Ideal types are abstract descriptions of phenomena that indicate the general features upon which a theorist will focus for purposes of explanation (Weber, 1968). A process of abstraction must occur where the essential structures and features of the system are identified. The crucial question, of course, is which ideal type is to be selected in the analysis of a given phenomenon.

Marx considers several possible types of socio-economic system, such as feudalism and classical antiquity in the past and the possibility of communism in the future. In specifying such different economic systems, Marx sees the need to develop specific analyses of the structure and dynamic of each one.

Clearly the definition of each type of economic system is crucial. The capitalist mode of production is regarded by Marx as a socio-economic system in which most production takes place in capitalist firms. Commodities are defined by Marx as goods or services that are typically exchanged on the market. The products of capitalist firms are commodities. Marx (1981, p. 1019) clearly identifies a 'characteristic trait' of the capitalist mode of production system as follows:

> It produces its products as commodities. The fact that it produces commodities does not in itself distinguish it from other modes of production; but that the dominant and determining character of its product is the commodity certainly does so. This means, first of all, that ... labour generally appears as wage-labour ... [and] the relationship of capital to wage-labour determines the whole character of the mode of production.

In short, for Marx, capitalism is generalized commodity production.[8] It is generalized in a double sense: first, because under capitalism most goods and services are produced for sale on the market, that is, they are commodities; second, because under capitalism one item is importantly a commodity: labour power. In other words, an important feature of capitalism is the existence of a labour market in which labour is hired by an employer.

The general relations that define the capitalist system are seen to validate the primary deployment of core concepts such as the commodity, exchange, money, capital and labour power. For instance, the use of the concept of the commodity is validated by the generality of the commodity form under capitalism itself. The upshot of this methodological procedure is that Marxian economics is distinguished radically from classical, neoclassical and Austrian economics.

The Hidden, Ahistorical Universals

However, there are major problems with this approach. First, while the historically specific analytical system seems to validate the key analytical concepts in the above manner, it does not validate its own meta-theoretical apparatus. Close examination of *Capital* indicates that at crucial stages in his argument Marx himself has to fall back on transcendental, ahistorical concepts. Most obviously, the concept of capitalism invokes the ahistorical concept of the mode of production. Further, in the very first chapter Marx invokes the ahistorical concept of use-value in his discussion of commodities and exchange. It is recognized that specific use-values may be socially and historically conditioned but the very concept of use-value, unlike the concept of a commodity, is not.

Similarly, the analysis of the production process in Chapter 7 of Volume 1 relies on a conceptual distinction between, on the one hand, labour in general – that is, the idea of labour as an activity that permeates all kinds of economic system – and, on the other, the organization and processes of production that are specific to capitalism. Likewise, the distinction between labour and labour power is conceptually quite general although the specific phenomenon of the hiring of labour power by an employer is far from universal. There are many other examples, including the twin concepts of forces and relations of production and Marx's general and quite universal theory that socio-economic change is promoted when the developing forces of production come up against and break down allegedly antiquated productive relations.

Indeed, the very generality and universality of the concept of labour in Marx's analysis helps him to sustain a supra-historical picture of labour as the lifeblood of all economic systems. This leads to the perceptive observation of Marco Lippi (1979) that despite the claimed historical specificity of Marx's analysis of 'value' in *Capital* it rests essentially on an ahistorical and 'naturalistic' concept of labour. Similarly, Elias Khalil (1990) shows that Marx's transhistorical concept of social labour amounts to asserting that the actions of agents can be *ex ante* calculated according to a global rationality. The assumption of global rationality is itself a reflection of the specific Western intellectual culture of the nineteenth century and ironically is prominent in neoclassical economic theory as well. This assumption links Marx's theoretical analysis of capitalism with his faith in the supposedly rational order of socialism.[9]

Marx is not being criticized here for appealing to universal and ahistorical categories. On reflection such an invocation is unavoidable. Any attempt to establish historically specific categories must itself rely on a transcendent imperative. There seems to be no way of avoiding this. However, Marx gives insufficient attention to this problem and provides only a limited discussion of the meta-theoretical issues involved. Furthermore, he falls back on a set of questionable categories and places unwarranted weight on his particular and rationalistic concept of social labour.

Again irony: but with double strength. Neoclassical economists attempt to construct a universal framework of socio-economic analysis but end up viewing the universe through the distorting lenses of a specific type of economic system. The universality of their allegedly universal principles is thus questioned. Marx, on the other hand, knowingly reacts from this kind of approach and attempts to site his analysis of specific systems on specific concepts appropriate to that system. Yet contrary to his own arguments he ends up relying on concepts and theories that are in fact universal. Neoclassical economics aspires to universality but ends up being specific; Marxism aspires to specificity but ends up relying on the general.

The Problem of Necessary Impurities

Further difficulties arise if the dominant system depends upon other subsystems or impurities. When analysing the capitalist system Marx assumes away all the non-capitalist elements in that system. This is not merely an initial, simplifying, assumption. They are assumed away at the outset, never to be reincorporated at a later stage of the analysis. This is because he believes that commodity exchange and the hiring of labour power in a capitalist firm will become increasingly widespread, displacing all other forms of economic coordination and productive organization. Thus in the *Communist Manifesto*, Marx and Engels proclaim:

> The bourgeoisie ... has put an end to all feudal, patriarchal, idyllic relations ... and has left remaining no other nexus between man and man than naked self-interest, than callous 'cash payment'. ... The bourgeoisie has torn away from the family its sentimental veil, and has reduced the family relation to a mere money relation. (Marx, 1973, p. 70)

Certainty of the all-consuming power of capitalist markets is Marx's justification for ignoring impurities within the capitalist system. These are regarded as doomed and extraneous hangovers of the feudal past. Just as capitalism and commodity exchange are assumed to become all-powerful, the theoretical system is built on these structures and relations alone.

Yet it has been noted above that some of the crucial subsystems within capitalism are unlikely ever to become organized on a strictly capitalist basis. Again consider the family. Contrary to Marx, there are practical and theoretical limitations to the operation of the market within that sphere. If the rearing of children was carried out on a capitalist basis then they would be strictly owned as property by the owners of the household 'firm' and eventually sold like slaves on the market. Yet anti-slavery laws within capitalism prevent the possession and sale of one person by another. Hence within capitalism the household can never typically be internally organized on the basis of markets, individual ownership and profit. Ironically, in both neoclassical and Marxian economics the characteristic features of the family disappear from view. Just as the neoclassical economists treat all human activities as if they took the form of contracted exchange, Marx wrongly assumes that the entire capitalist system can be understood solely on the basis of commodity exchange and the exploitation of hired labour power.[10]

As argued above, there are general limits to the extension of market and contractual relations within capitalism. The spread of market and contractarian relations can threaten to break up cultural and other bonds that are necessary for the functioning of the system as a whole. In particular, as Polanyi and Schumpeter have emphasized, the state is partly responsible for the bonding of society and the prevention of its dissolution into atomistic units by the corroding action of market relations.

The 'impurity principle' is proposed as a general idea applicable to all economic systems. The idea is that every socio-economic system must rely on at least one structurally dissimilar subsystem to function. There must always be a coexistent plurality of modes of production, so that the social formation as a whole has the requisite structural variety to cope with change. Thus if one type of structure is to prevail (for example, central planning), other structures (for example, markets, private firms) are necessary to enable the system as a whole to work effectively. As Michel Albert (1993, p. 101) writes succinctly: 'Just as there can be no socialist society in which all goods and services are free, so can there be no capitalist society in which all goods and services may be bought and sold'. In particular, neither planning nor markets can become all-embracing systems of socio-economic regulation. In general, it is not feasible for one mode of production to become so comprehensive that it drives out all the others. Every system relies on its 'impurities'.[11]

Although it cannot be formally proved, part of the justification for this principle can be derived from an analysis of past socio-economic formations in history. Capitalism today depends on the 'impurities' of the family, household production and the state. The slave mode of production of classical times depended on the military organization of the state as well as trade and an external market. Likewise, feudalism relied on both regulated markets and a powerful church. Finally, without extensive legal or illegal markets, the Soviet-type system of central planning would have ceased to function long before 1989. In each of the four major modes of production after Christ (slavery, feudalism, capitalism and Soviet-type societies) at least one 'impurity', that is, a non-dominant economic structure, has played a functional role in the reproduction of the system as a whole. What is involved is more than an empirical observation that different structures and systems have coexisted through history. What is involved is an assertion that some of these economic structures were *necessary* for the socio-economic system to function over time. As shown elsewhere (Hodgson, 1984, pp. 106–9; 1988, pp. 257, 303–4), additional and related arguments for the impurity principle can be derived from systems theory.

However, while the impurity principle contends that different kinds of subsystem are necessary for the system as a whole to function, it does not specify the particular kind of subsystem nor the precise boundaries between each subsystem and the system as a whole. Indeed, a variety of types of system and subsystem can feasibly be combined.[12] Furthermore, the boundaries between subsystem and dominant system are likely to be highly variable. Significantly, the nature of the combination and the precise boundaries of the demarcation profoundly affect the nature of the specific variety of capitalist system. A corollary of the impurity principle is the contention that an immense variety of forms of any given socio-economic system can exist.

Actor and Structure

Another acute problem in Marx's perspective is that human motivations are not explained in any detail: they are assumed to spring in broad and mysterious terms from the relations and forces of the system. As Marx (1981, pp. 1019–20) puts it: 'The principal agents of this mode of production itself, the capitalist and the wage-labourer, are as such *simply* embodiments and personifications of capital and wage-labour – specific social characters that the social production process stamps on individuals, products of these specific social relations of production' (emphasis added).

Accordingly, when discussing the mechanisms of change, Marx is extremely vague. There is reference to 'productive forces', as if technology itself is a driving force. True, it is assumed that workers will typically struggle for bigger wages and shorter hours, and capitalists for enhanced profits. But these are little else than the principles of maximization also common to neoclassical theory. What is missing is an explanation of the historical origin of such calculative behaviour and the mode of its cultural transmission. Marx assumes that values and motives are simply functional to the pursuit of class and economic interests.

Thus Marx believed that the class position of the workers as employed labourers, coupled with the tendency of capitalism itself to bring workers together in larger and larger firms and cities, would lead to the eventual combination and revolt of the working class against the capitalist system. Yet well over a hundred years after Marx's death there still has not been a single successful socialist revolution in any advanced capitalist country. Marx's faith that class positions and relations themselves are sufficient to impel action has to be questioned.

This issue is addressed by Michael Burawoy (1979). His detailed study of production workers in the United States shows that hierarchy and authority on the shop floor are themselves unlikely to lead to the production of socialist ideology or revolt. Shop floor culture and practices are not a likely transmission belt from wage labour to socialist revolution.

INSTITUTIONALISM AND VARIETIES OF CAPITALISM

We now turn to the alternative framework of the 'old' institutional economics. While it is argued that this intellectual tradition has the means to overcome some of the aforementioned problems, the institutionalist solution is underdeveloped.

Veblen's Critique of Marx

Veblen highlights the analytical gap in Marx's analysis between actor and structure. Although sympathetic to much of Marx's analysis of capitalism, he notes that it fails to connect the actor with the specific structure and to explain thereby human motivation and action. Forest Hill (1958, p. 139) elaborates Veblen's critique of Marx as follows:

> In Veblen's opinion, Marx uncritically adopted natural rights and natural law preconceptions and a hedonistic psychology of rational self-interest. On these bases Marx elaborated his labor theory of value, with labor as the source and measure of value, and the corollary doctrines of labor's right to its full product, of surplus value, and exploitation of labor. He attributed rational self-interest not only to individuals but to entire classes, thereby explaining their asserted solidarity and motivation in class struggle. Veblen rejected the concept of rational class interest and the labor theory of value, along with its corollaries and natural rights basis.

Marx saw his scientific analysis of capitalism in *Capital* as a potentially revolutionary instrument in helping the working class both to analyse and end its own exploitation. However, Veblen rejected Marx's view that if working people reflected rationally upon their situation they would be impelled to criticize and revolt against the capitalist system. The questionable assumption of potential rational transparency is crucial here, and connects with Marx's teleology. As Stephen Edgell and Jules Townshend (1993, p. 728) elaborate:

> Marx's portrayal of humankind as potentially rational also resolves the puzzle as to why Marx could simultaneously entertain the idea of an historical telos, with its deterministic implications, and uphold the voluntaristic and reflexive notions of

praxis or practical activity. He assumes that workers – through rational thought, through reflecting on their experience of capitalism, and notably through their increasing immiseration and growing collective strength, will inevitably want and be able to overthrow it.

Essentially, the process of rational reflection is seen to drive the working class to the same 'inevitable' outcome. Even if we stress a more open-ended and less deterministic account of capitalist development than the one in the famous 'Preface' to the *Contribution to the Critique of Political Economy*, 'we are still left with a highly teleological theory of capitalism, with its downfall being the inevitable result of its inner contradictions' (Edgell and Townshend, 1993, p. 729).

Veblen rejected the continuously calculating, marginally adjusting agent of neoclassical theory to emphasize inertia and habit instead. Institutions are defined by Veblen (1919, p. 239) as 'settled habits of thought common to the generality of men'. They are seen as both outgrowths and reinforcers of the routinized thought processes that are shared by a number of persons in a given society. Institutions thereby help sustain habits of action and thought: 'The situation of today shapes the institutions of tomorrow through a selective, coercive process, by acting upon men's habitual view of things, and so altering or fortifying a point of view or a mental attitude handed down from the past' (Veblen, 1899, pp. 190–91). Importantly, Veblen also emphasizes the importance of novelty and human creativity and distances himself from cultural or institutional determinism. Furthermore, it is recognized that institutions are not simply constraints (Commons, 1934, p. 73).

The importance of institutions in shaping thought and action is implied in Veblen's attack on Marx's 'materialist conception of history'. This, according to Veblen (1919, p. 314),

> … has very little to say regarding the efficient force, the channels or the methods by which the economic situation is conceived to have its effect upon institutions. What answer the early Marxists gave to this question, of how the economic situation shapes institutions, was to the effect that causal connection lies through the selfish, calculating class interest. But, while class interest may count for much in the outcome, this answer is plainly not a competent one, since, for one thing, institutions by no means change with the alacrity which the sole efficiency of reasoned class interest would require.

Veblen suggests that the mere class position of an individual as a wage labourer or a capitalist tells us very little about the specific conceptions or habits of thought of the individuals involved. Even if the worker's interests would be served by joining a trade union, or voting for a political party that proclaims common ownership of the means of production, there is no necessary reason why the worker's position as an employee would necessarily impel him or her necessarily to take such actions. Individual interests, whatever they are, do not necessarily lead to accordant individual actions. Hence Veblen criticizes Marx's implicit rationalism in the following terms:

> it must be held that men's reasoning is largely controlled by other than logical, intellectual forces; that the conclusion reached by public or class opinion is as much, or more, a matter of sentiment than of logical inference; and that the sentiment which animates men, singly or collectively, is as much, or more, an outcome of habit and native propensity as of calculated material interest. There is, for instance, no warrant ... for asserting *a priori* that the class interest of the working class will bring them to take a stand against the propertied class. (Veblen, 1919, p. 441)

In other words, the assumption of a class interest and rational calculation tells us nothing about the habits, concepts and frameworks of thought which are used to appraise reality, nor about the mode of calculation used to perceive a supposed optimum.

Contrary to Marx, human agents will not gravitate to a single view of the truth simply on the basis of empirical evidence and rational reflection. As Veblen (1919, p. 442) pointed out, the members of the working class could perceive their own salvation just as much in terms of patriotism or nationalism as in socialist revolution. The class position of an agent – exploiter or exploited – does not imply that that person will be impelled towards any particular view of reality or any particular pattern of action. Contrary to Marx, a given social structure or class system does not imply a tendency towards particular patterns of behaviour. This, as Abram Harris (1932, p. 743) has rightly noted, 'is the weakest link in his chain of reasoning'.

Such arguments have a wide relevance and apply to other calculative or rationalistic conceptions of action. Accordingly, there is also here an implicit attack on the optimizing rationality of neoclassical economics. The attack is especially apposite when upon a central idea of the 'rational expectations hypothesis', that through mere data-gathering, agents will become aware of the basic underlying structure and mechanisms of the economy. This hypothesis likewise neglects the conceptual framing involved in the perception of data and the theory-bound character of all observation.

In general, even if objectives are given, neither class interest nor rational reflection upon circumstances will typically lead to a single outcome in terms of either perceptions or actions. For instance, although the capitalists' interests may be best served by striving for ever greater profits, this tells us little about precise corporate strategy, the mode of management or the precise structure of the firm. In the case of the capitalist the Marxian response to this argument is familiar: capitalist competition will *force* capitalists to follow the more successful route to profit and the accumulation of capital. Lucky or shrewd capitalists will follow this imperative and the others will become marginalized or bankrupt. Thereby the strategy, structure and goals of the firm are uniquely determined by competition. Uncannily, a very similar argument is advanced by the far-from-Marxist Milton Friedman (1953) in a famous paper, where he argues that competitive 'natural selection' is bound to ensure that most if not all surviving firms are profit-maximizing.[13]

In response, Tomlinson (1982) points out that profit cannot act as a simple regulator of the growth or decline of firms. Even if firms are trying to maximize their profits this does not imply a single strategy as to how this maximization is to be achieved. 'Firms like generals have *strategies*, a term which itself implies room for manoeuvre, room for diverse calculations, diverse practices to be brought to bear on the objective' (p. 34). More concretely, case studies reveal a varied repertoire of strategic responses by firms. Note the study by Richard Whittington (1989) of the varied strategic behaviour of firms enduring a common recession, and the remarks about firm discretionary behaviour made by Richard Nelson (1991).

Veblen's theory of cumulative causation is both his answer to the Marxian argument that only strategic response is possible and his rebuff to the neoclassical concept of equilibrium. He sees both the circumstances and temperament of individuals as part of the cumulative processes of change: 'The economic life history of the individual is a cumulative process of adaptation of means to ends that cumulatively change as the process goes on, both the agent and his environment being at any point the outcome of the last process' (Veblen, 1919, pp. 74–5). Directly or indirectly influenced by Veblen, the notion of cumulative causation is developed by Allyn Young (1928), Gunnar Myrdal (1957), K. William Kapp (1976), Nicholas Kaldor (1985) and others. It relates to the modern idea that technologies and economic systems can get 'locked in' – and sometimes as a result of initial accidents – to relatively constrained paths of development (Arthur, 1989). Hence there is 'path dependence' rather than convergence to a given equilibrium. History matters.

Veblen's concept of cumulative causation is an antidote to both neoclassical and Marxian economic theory. Contrary to the equilibrium analysis of neoclassical economics, Veblen sees the economic system not as a 'self-balancing mechanism' but as a 'cumulatively unfolding process'. As Myrdal and Kaldor argue at length, the processes of cumulative causation suggest that regional and national development is generally divergent rather than convergent. This contradicts the typical emphasis within neoclassical economic theory on processes of compensating feedback and mutual adjustment via the price mechanism leading to greater uniformity and convergence.

Contrary to much Marxist and neoclassical thinking, Veblen argues that multiple futures are possible. Equilibrating forces do not always pull the economy back onto a single track. This exposes a severe weakness in Marx's conception of history. Veblen argues against the idea of finality or consummation in economic development. Variety and cumulative causation mean that history has 'no final term' (Veblen, 1919, p. 37). In Marxism the final term is communism or the classless society, but Veblen rejects the teleological concept of a final goal. This means a rejection of the ideas of the 'inevitability' of socialism and of a 'natural' outcome or end-point in capitalist evolution. There is no natural path, or law, governing economic development. Accordingly, and in rejecting any inevitability in capitalist development, Veblen accepts the possibility of varieties of capitalism and different paths of capitalist evolution.

Specificity and Universality

It has been noted that both neoclassical and Marxian economics get trapped in obverse types of problems when it comes to assumptions about specificity or universality in economic analysis. Neoclassical economics is built on allegedly universal assumptions but these are not, in fact, universally applicable; they reflect the specific ideology of a particular moment of capitalist development. The analytical starting point of Marxian economics is the specific features and relations of the capitalist mode of production but the analysis ends up relying on concepts and theories that are in fact universal. Neoclassical economics aspires to universality but ends up being specific; Marxism aspires to specificity but ends up relying on concepts that are ubiquitous.

Two broad conclusions follow. The first is that the theoretical analysis of a specific economic system cannot rely entirely on concepts drawn exclusively from that system. This is because the very organization and extraction of these concepts must rely on other categories of wider applicability. To talk of capitalism we must refer to other economic systems; if we speak of economic systems we are using that transhistorical concept; and so on. While historical and institutional specificity is important, we are obliged to rely to some degree on the universal.

The second conclusion is that the entire analysis of any given system cannot and should not be based on universal concepts alone. The first levels of abstraction must be quite general, but if those universalist layers are extended too far – as in the case of neoclassical theory – then the danger is that we end up with conceptions that are unable to come to grips with reality. The scope of analysis of the first levels of abstraction should be highly confined.

The above discussion suggests that universal concepts have to be grounded in some way. This is a problem that Marx ignored. A framework at a very high level of generality is provided by systems theory (Bertalanffy, 1971; Emery, 1981; Miller, 1978), particularly as developed and applied to economics by Janos Kornai (1971) and to sociology by Niklas Luhmann (1984). Notably, however, recent systems thinking has moved to encompass evolution as a unifying principle (Laszlo, 1987).

For Veblen the transhistorical analytical framework is evolution. The idea of evolution spans both the biotic and the socio-economic spheres and grounds social theory in some general metaphors and principles. This does not mean that biology has to be slavishly imitated in the social sciences (Hodgson, 1993b). Instead, an appeal to a variety of non-reductionist naturalism provides the transhistorical framework for social science.

In Veblen's (1899, 1919) writings the objects of evolutionary selection are institutions. The institution is a universal concept because institutions of various kinds are present in all human societies. However, specific institutions are historically grounded and are manifest in particular localities and periods of socio-economic development: they are delimited in time and space. The concept of the institution thus provides a link between the general and the specific. Institutions require theorization at both these levels.

The concept of evolution provides a ground plan for the general foundations. Inspired in particular by Darwin and Peirce, Veblen saw the importance and ontological priority of both variation and continuity (Hodgson, 1992b, 1993b). First, there must be sustained variation among institutions, and the sources and mechanisms of renewal of such variation must be considered, be they causal, random or purposive. Veblen considered such sources, including his principle of 'idle curiosity' (Dyer, 1986). Second, there must be some principle of continuity by which institutions endure and some principle of heredity by which succeeding institutions resemble their precedents or ancestors. The self-reinforcing and 'conservative' (Veblen, 1899, p. 191) features of habits and institutions are relevant here, as are the ideas of imitation and 'emulation' (ibid., p. 23). Note that these two 'evolutionary' principles are very general and much broader than the specific mechanisms of evolution outlined by Darwin. The issues here are at root ontological, concerning the sources of novelty and the mechanisms of persistence, and do not themselves involve adherence to any specific evolutionary theory taken from biology or elsewhere.

Institutions as Units of Analysis

Abstraction involves identifying what is central and essential to an entity, and ignoring the superficial. More fundamentally, the identification of features, relations and structures depends upon acts of taxonomy and classification, involving the assignment of sameness and difference. Classification, by bringing together entities in discrete groups, must refer to common qualities. For classification to be enduring, it must be assumed that the common qualities themselves must be invariant. As Philip Mirowski (1989) points out, a kind of 'conservation principle' is required. However: 'No posited invariance holds without exceptions and qualifications. We live in a world of broken symmetries and partial invariances' (ibid., p. 397).

The problem is to develop meaningful and operational principles of invariance on which analysis can be founded. As suggested above, the institutionalist tradition has a tentative answer to this problem, locating invariances in the (imperfect) self-reinforcing mechanisms of (partially) stable social institutions. Institutions have a stable and inert quality, and tend to sustain and thus 'pass on' their important characteristics through time. Institutions are both outgrowths and reinforcers of the routinized thought processes that are shared by a number of persons in a given society.

The power and durability of institutions and routines are manifest in a number of ways. In particular, with the benefit of modern developments in anthropology and psychology it can be seen that institutions play an essential role in providing a cognitive framework for interpreting sense-data and in providing intellectual habits or routines for transforming information into useful knowledge (Hodgson, 1988). The cultural and cognitive functions of institutions have been investigated by anthropologists such as Mary Douglas (1987). Reference to the cognitive functions of institutions and routines is important in understanding their relative stability and capacity to replicate. Indeed, the strong, mutually reinforcing interaction between social institutions and individual cognition provides some significant stability in socio-economic systems, partly by buffering and constraining the diverse and variable actions of many agents. Institutions become cumulatively 'locked in' to relatively stable and constrained paths of development.

Hence the institution is 'a socially constructed invariant' (Mirowski, 1987, p. 1034n.), and institutions can be taken as the units and entities of analysis. This contrasts with the idea of the individual as the irreducible unit of analysis in neoclassical economics, and applies to both microeconomics and macroeconomics. The approach based on institutional specifics rather than ahistorical universals is characteristic of institutional economics, and has parallels in some of the works of the Marxian and Post Keynesian schools.

Notably, institutions fill the key conceptual gap that we have identified in neoclassical, Austrian and Marxian theories. Institutions simultaneously constitute and are constituted by human action. Institutions are both 'subjective' ideas in the heads of agents and 'objective' structures faced by them. The concept of institutions connects the microeconomic world of individual action, of habit and choice, with the macroeconomic sphere of seemingly detached and impersonal structures. Actor and structure are thus connected in a circle of mutual interaction and interdependence.

These remarks are general and ahistorical. Taking an 'evolutionary' or naturalist grounding, the gap at this high level of generality can be filled by institutional economics. It is not suggested that this theoretical work is complete – indeed we have little more to work on than a number of key institutionalist passages – simply that institutionalism offers a most favourable basis for further theoretical development with its core concept of an institution and its deployment of the evolutionary metaphor.

Notably, the very concept of an institution points from the sphere of general principles to the study of the specific. Although some general principles regarding institutions can and have to be established, these tell us very little about the nature and dynamics of specific institutions. Institutional economists have thus rightly argued that it is essential to focus on specific institutions and to understand their nature and dynamics.

There are clearly two temptations to be avoided here. One is to erect an ahistorical theory: 'theory without data'. The other is to eschew theory and system-building for data-gathering: 'data without theory'. But it must be emphasized that this is not a matter of finding a golden mean between such extremes. They are both false navigational poles. It cannot be a question of the appropriate mixture of the two basic ingredients of theory and empirics because data cannot be considered or appraised independently of a theory. All attempts to gather data are informed unavoidably by a set of classificatory concepts and implicit or explicit theories. As well as the importance of concrete data, the primacy of theory has to be emphasized.

CONCLUSION

Clearly, institutional economics needs to be developed further to deal with the important issues raised here. This requires methodological work and conceptual analysis to supplement the foundational work of Veblen and other early institutionalists. An important supplementary idea discussed here is the impurity principle.

Variety and the Impurity Principle

It has been argued above that every socio-economic system must rely on at least one structurally dissimilar subsystem to function. As we have seen, neoclassical economists, Hayek and Marx both fail to recognize this point, although it is accepted by a number of other writers. Incorporating no conceptual distinction between commercial and non-commercial activity, neoclassical economics applies the same choice-theoretic framework to all kinds of social institutions and is thus blind to the demarcation between contract-based and other social relations. Hayekian economics, by contrast, recognizes the significance of property and contract and is able to differentiate them from other social relations, but believes unrealistically – and with a strange silence on the question of the family – in the possibility and even necessity of a vast extension of commercial contracts and individual property rights. Finally, although Marx recognizes the coexistence of capitalist with non-capitalist social structures in any capitalist society, he shares with Hayek the view that commodity and market relations could grow to the eventual exclusion of all non-capitalist features.

Neither neoclassical, Hayekian nor Marxian economics recognizes the functional *necessity* of non-capitalist structures and relations within capitalism. The critique implied in the impurity principle thus applies to Marx, Hayek and the neoclassical economists with substantial force. The impurity principle clearly dovetails with the ontological emphasis on variety in institutional economics. If every system relies on structurally dissimilar impurities then some degree of variety will always be with us.

It is necessary to adopt a system of analysis that recognizes both different modes of production and the fact that no single mode can triumph overall. All socio-economic systems are inevitably a combination of multiple types of subsystems or modes of production. Unlike neoclassical economics, the theoretical system of Marx is sufficiently sophisticated to recognize some key differences between one type of mode of production and another. However, the failure to recognize the functional necessity of a combination of different modes of production with a single socio-economic system has to be rectified.

The corollary of the impurity principle should be stressed here. By accepting the possible variety of combinations of subsystems with given systems, it is recognized that an immense variety of forms of any given socio-economic system can feasibly exist. The denial of the impurity principle would involve the denial of such a potential variety of combinations.

It is strange that two authors who have provided us with the deepest understanding of the workings of modern capitalism, Marx and Hayek, have little to say about specific economic policies. Marx advocates the broad but undetailed policy of central planning and public ownership. Hayek's policy stance is diametrically opposed to that of Marx but is hardly less bland: we are offered the generalities of more market competition and extended private ownership. Hayek, like Marx and his followers, has very little to say in detailed, policy terms. The common blindness to varieties of capitalism disables their theoretical systems in policy terms.

Varieties of Actually Existing Capitalism

No longer blind to the potential variety of systemic combinations, we may accept that an immense variety of forms of any given economic system can feasibly exist. Consideration of the contrast between Anglo-American and Japanese capitalism is fruitful, involving different boundaries between commercial and pecuniary relations on the one hand and relations of trust and loyalty on the other. The key to the difference lies in history. Capitalism in Britain and America emerged from a remote feudal past. In contrast, the inception of capitalism in Japan was recent, and quasi-feudal codes of loyalty and chivalry are still paramount.

In a classic and seminal study, Ronald Dore (1973) compares British and Japanese industrial relations. Chalmers Johnson (1982) examines the evolution of a distinctive type of industrial policy in Japan. Michio Morishima (1982) sees the origins of the Japanese economic 'miracle' in distinctive cultural traits formed through the interaction of religious, social and technological ideas and practices. Maureen McKelvey (1993) surveys the different kinds of Japanese institutions supporting technological innovation. Marco Orrù (1993) compares different forms of institutional cooperation in Japanese and German capitalism. Kyoko Sheridan (1993) argues that Japan is not on a convergence route to Western-type capitalism but is sustained on a different track by a distinctive type of politico-economic formation. Charles Hampden-Turner and Alfons Trompenaars (1993) survey the enormous diversity of cultures within modern capitalist countries. Richard Whitley (1994, 1999) provides a detailed examination of the distinctive forms of corporate structure and firm–market relations now found in East Asia and elsewhere. David Williams (1994) turns Fukuyama's view of an 'end of history' in the shape of American capitalism on its head: in his view Japan is not only a quite distinctive type of capitalist formation but also offers a far greater challenge to Western theories and values than the fallen systems of Eastern Europe have ever represented. Economic analysis cannot afford to remain blind to the immense and persistent variety of forms within modern capitalism.

As suggested in Table 11.1, institutions fill the key conceptual gap that we have identified in neoclassical, Hayekian and Marxian theories. Institutions simultaneously constitute and are constituted by human action: actor and structure are thus connected. Institutional economics thus provides a fruitful approach to the formulation of relevant and operational economic policies. Much of this work may appear descriptive, but there is no reason why it should not be guided by the deepest theoretical and methodological insights. Instead of empty formalism, there is the possibility that economics may thus be capable of providing inspiration and sagacious guidance for those in government, finance and business.

Table 11.1 *Varieties of analysis and varieties of capitalism*

	Neoclassical Economics	Austrian Economics	Marxian Economics	Institutional Economics
General Unit of Analysis	Given individuals	Given individuals	Socially formed and socially related individuals	Institutions
Capital-specific Unit of Analysis	—	—	Maximizing individuals	Institutions in capitalist systems
General Analytical Concepts	Utility, scarcity, choice, equilibrium	Individual purposeful behaviour, scarcity, choice	Labour, labour process, forces of production, relations of production, mode of production	Habit, emulation, labour, creativity, cumulative causation, economic relations and systems
Capital-specific Concepts	—	—	Commodities, exchange, money, capital	Transactions, money, capital
General Micro-motive Forces	Utility or profit maximization	Purposeful individuals	Socially conditioned individuals	Habit, emulation, curiosity
Capital-specific Micro-motive Forces	—	—	Capital accumulation, profit maximization and worker resistance	Specific cultural and institutional manifestations of capital accumulation, trade union activity, etc.
General Micro–macro Link	—	—	—	Institutions
General Macro-motive Forces	—	—	Forces of production	Technological change, institutional inertia
Typical Analytical Outcome	Unique general equilibrium, macroeconomic convergence	Spontaneous order	Typical or common path of historical and capitalist development, leading to communism	Cumulatively divergent historical and capitalist developments with no asymptotic state

NOTES

*   The author is very grateful to Charles Hampden-Turner, Björn Johnson, Matthew Jones, Janet Knoedler, Klaus Nielsen, Ernesto Screpanti, Ian Steedman, Lazlo Vajda and others for critical and helpful comments. The material in this essay is expanded considerably in Hodgson (1999).

1. Neoclassical economics may be conveniently defined as an approach which (1) assumes rational, maximizing behaviour by agents with given and stable preference functions, (2) focuses on attained, or movements towards, equilibrium states, and (3) excludes chronic information problems. Notably, some recent developments in modern mainstream economic theory come close to the boundaries of this definition.

2. Prominent 'economic imperialists' include Becker (1976b) and Hirshleifer (1977). See the critiques in Nicolaides (1988) and Udéhn (1992). For a discussion of the place of universal propositions in economics see Hodgson (2001).

3. See, for example, Kropotkin (1902/1972), Mead (1937) and Reinheimer (1913).

4. For such statements see, for instance, Arrow (1986), Hahn (1988) and Machlup (1967).

5. For a deconstruction of the concept of scarcity see Hodgson (2001).

6. This is denied by the transaction cost approach developed by Williamson (1975). For a critique of Williamson and evidence that trust is important see Berger *et al.* (1995).

7. See Commons (1934, p. 713) and Hodgson (1988, Ch. 8).

8. Note, however, that Marx does not explicitly use this three-word definition of capitalism and some Marxist and other economists have expressed a distaste for it. Yet these three words do connote the key issues of property rights, markets, employment relations and thereby class divisions within capitalism.

9. There is a clear link here between Marx's theoretical concept of social labour and his utopian vision of a planned economy. In the *Communist Manifesto* Marx and Engels foresee and welcome the time when 'all production has been concentrated in the hands of a vast association of the whole nation' (Marx, 1973, p. 87). Accordingly, Marx misleadingly assumes that diversity and variety in the organizational and regulatory structures of production can be dispensed with in favour of a single, all-engrossing organization at the macroeconomic level.

10. With the rise of modern feminism in the 1970s, some Marxian theorists attempted to analyse the family as a distinctive entity. Yet the dominant theoretical approach was to subsume this institution within the parameters of the 'labour theory of value' and the guiding prerogatives of the capitalist order, just as neoclassical economists treat the family simply as another contract-based institution within capitalism.

11. The impurity principle is discussed extensively in Hodgson (1984, pp. 85–109, 220–8) and summarized in Hodgson (1988, pp. 167–71, 254–62).

12. For this reason the impurity principle is not subject to the charge of functionalism, as Dow (1991) has contended. Functionalism is typically defined as the notion that the contribution of an entity to the maintenance of a system is sufficient to explain the existence of that entity. However, the impurity principle does not purport to explain why any one given mode of production or subsystem exists.

13. Friedman's theoretical argument is criticized by Winter (1964) and Hodgson (1994).

REFERENCES

Albert, Michel (1993), *Capitalism against Capitalism*, London: Whurr.

Arrow, Kenneth J. (1974), *The Limits of Organization*, New York: Norton.

Arrow, Kenneth J. (1986), 'Rationality of self and others in an economic system', *Journal of Business*, 59, October, pp. S385–99.

Arthur, W. Brian (1989), 'Competing technologies, increasing returns, and lock-in by historical events', *Economic Journal*, 99(1), March, pp. 116–31.

Becker, Gary S. (1976a), *The Economic Approach to Human Behavior*, Chicago: University of Chicago Press.

Becker, Gary S. (1976b), 'Altruism, egoism, and genetic fitness: economics and sociobiology', *Journal of Economic Literature*, 14(2), December, pp. 817–26.

Berger, Hans, Niels G. Noorderhaven and Bart Nooteboom (1995), 'Determinants of supplier dependence: an empirical study', in John Groenewegen, Christos Pitelis and Sven-Erik Sjöstrand (eds), *On Economic Institutions: Theory and Applications*, Aldershot: Edward Elgar, pp. 195–212.

Bertalanffy, Ludwig von (1971), *General Systems Theory: Foundation Development Applications*, London: Allen Lane.

Burawoy, Michael (1979), *Manufacturing Consent*, Chicago: University of Chicago Press.

Commons, John R. (1934), *Institutional Economics – Its Place in Political Economy*, New York: Macmillan.

Dore, Ronald (1973), *British Factory, Japanese Factory: The Origins of National Diversity in Industrial Relations*, London: George Allen & Unwin.

Douglas, Mary (1987), *How Institutions Think*, London and Syracuse: Routledge and Kegan Paul and Syracuse University Press.

Dow, Gregory K. (1991), 'Review of G. Hodgson, Economics and Institutions', *Journal of Economic Behavior and Organization*, 15, pp. 159–69.

Dyer, Alan W. (1986), 'Veblen on scientific creativity', *Journal of Economic Issues*, 20(1), March, pp. 21–41.

Edgell, Stephen and Jules Townshend (1993), 'Marx and Veblen on human nature, history, and capitalism: vive la différence!', *Journal of Economic Issues*, 27(3), September, pp. 721–39.

Emery, Fred E. (ed.) (1981), *Systems Thinking*, 2 vols, Harmondsworth: Penguin.

Fox, Alan (1974), *Beyond Contract: Work, Power and Trust Relations*, London: Faber and Faber.

Friedman, Milton (1953), 'The methodology of positive economics', in M. Friedman, *Essays in Positive Economics*, Chicago: University of Chicago Press, pp. 3–43.

Fukuyama, Francis (1992), *The End of History and the Last Man*, New York: Free Press.

Giddens, Anthony (1984), *The Constitution of Society: Outline of the Theory of Structuration*, Cambridge: Polity Press.

Hahn, Frank H. (1988), 'On monetary theory', *Economic Journal*, 98(4), December, pp. 957–73.

Hampden-Turner, Charles and Alfons Trompenaars (1993), *The Seven Cultures of Capitalism: Value Systems for Creating Wealth in the United States, Japan, Germany, France, Britain, Sweden, and the Netherlands*, New York: Currency Doubleday.

Harris, Abram L. (1932), 'Types of institutionalism', *Journal of Political Economy*, 40(4), December, pp. 721–49.

Hayek, Friedrich A. (ed.) (1935), *Collectivist Economic Planning*, London: George Routledge. Reprinted 1975 by Augustus Kelley.

Hayek, Friedrich A. (1982), *Law, Legislation and Liberty*, 3–volume combined edition, London: Routledge and Kegan Paul.

Hill, Forest G. (1958), 'Veblen and Marx', in D.F. Dowd (ed.), *Thorstein Veblen: A Critical Appraisal*, Ithaca, NY: Cornell University Press, pp. 129–49.

Hirschman, Albert O. (1985), 'Against parsimony: three ways of complicating some categories of economic discourse', *Economics and Philosophy*, 1(1), March, pp. 7–21.

Hirshleifer, Jack (1977), 'Economics from a biological viewpoint', *Journal of Law and Economics*, 20(1), April, pp. 1–52.

Hodgson, Geoffrey M. (1984), *The Democratic Economy: A New Look at Planning, Markets and Power*, Harmondsworth: Penguin.

Hodgson, Geoffrey M. (1988), *Economics and Institutions: A Manifesto for a Modern Institutional Economics*, Cambridge and Philadelphia: Polity Press and University of Pennsylvania Press.

Hodgson, Geoffrey M. (1992a), 'The reconstruction of economics: is there still a place for neoclassical theory?', *Journal of Economic Issues*, 26(3), September, pp. 749–67.

Hodgson, Geoffrey M. (1992b), 'Thorstein Veblen and post-Darwinian economics', *Cambridge Journal of Economics*, 16(3), September, pp. 285–301.

Hodgson, Geoffrey M. (1993a), 'Institutional economics: surveying the "old" and the "new"', *Metroeconomica*, 44(1), pp. 1–28.

Hodgson, Geoffrey M. (1993b), *Economics and Evolution: Bringing Life Back into Economics*, Cambridge and Ann Arbor: Polity Press and University of Michigan Press.

Hodgson, Geoffrey M. (1994), 'Optimisation and evolution: Winter's critique of Friedman revisited', *Cambridge Journal of Economics*, 18(4), August, pp. 413–30. Reprinted in Geoffrey M. Hodgson (1999), *Evolution and Institutions: On Evolutionary Economics and the Evolution of Economics*, Cheltenham: Edward Elgar.

Hodgson, Geoffrey M. (1999), *Economics and Utopia: Why the Learning Economy is Not the End of History*, London and New York: Routledge.

Hodgson, Geoffrey M. (2001), *How Economics Forgot History: The Problem of Historical Specificity in Social Science*, London and New York: Routledge.

Johnson, Chalmers (1982), *MITI and the Japanese Miracle: The Growth of Industrial Policy, 1925–1975*, Stanford: Stanford University Press.

Kaldor, Nicholas (1985), *Economics without Equilibrium*, Cardiff: University College Cardiff Press.

Kapp, K. William (1976), 'The nature and significance of institutional economics', *Kyklos*, 29, Fasc. 2, pp. 209–32.

Khalil, Elias L. (1990), 'Rationality and social labor in Marx', *Critical Review*, 4(1–2), Winter–Spring, pp. 239–65.

Kornai, Janos (1971), *Anti-equilibrium: On Economic Systems Theory and the Tasks of Research*, Amsterdam: North-Holland. Reprinted 1991, New York: Augustus Kelley.

Kropotkin, Petr A. (1972), *Mutual Aid: A Factor of Evolution*, 1st edition published 1902, London: Allen Lane.

Laszlo, Ervin (1987), *Evolution: The Grand Synthesis*, Boston, MA: New Science Library/Shambhala.

Lippi, Marco (1979), *Value and Naturalism in Marx*, London: NLB.

Loasby, Brian J. (1976), *Choice, Complexity and Ignorance: An Enquiry into Economic Theory and the Practice of Decision Making*, Cambridge: Cambridge University Press.

Luhmann, Niklas (1984), *Soziale System: Grundriss einer allgemeinen Theorie*, Frankfurt am Main: Suhrkamp.

Machlup, Fritz (1967), 'Theories of the firm: marginalist, behavioral, managerial', *American Economic Review*, 57(1), March, pp. 1–33.

Marx, Karl (1973), *The Revolutions of 1848: Political Writings – Volume 1*, edited and introduced by David Fernbach, Harmondsworth: Penguin.

Marx, Karl (1976), *Capital*, Vol. 1, translated by B. Fowkes from the fourth German edition of 1890, Harmondsworth: Pelican.

Marx, Karl (1981), *Capital*, Vol. 3, translated by David Fernbach from the German edition of 1894, Harmondsworth: Pelican.

Marx, Karl and Frederick Engels (1982), *Karl Marx and Frederick Engels, Collected Works, Vol. 38, Letters 1844–51*, London: Lawrence and Wishart.

McKelvey, Maureen (1993), 'Japanese institutions supporting innovation', in Sven-Erik Sjöstrand (ed.), *Institutional Change: Theory and Empirical Findings*, Armonk, NY: Sharpe, pp. 199–225.

Mead, Margaret (1937), *Cooperation and Competition among Primitive Peoples*, New York: McGraw-Hill.

Miller, James G. (1978), *Living Systems*, New York: McGraw-Hill.

Mirowski, Philip (1987), 'The philosophical bases of institutional economics', *Journal of Economic Issues*, 21(3), September, pp. 1001–38.

Mirowski, Philip (1989), *More Heat than Light: Economics as Social Physics, Physics as Nature's Economics*, Cambridge: Cambridge University Press.

Mises, Ludwig von (1949), *Human Action: A Treatise on Economics*, London: William Hodge.

Morishima, Michio (1982), *Why Has Japan 'Succeeded'? Western Technology and the Japanese Ethos*, Cambridge: Cambridge University Press.

Myrdal, Gunnar (1957), *Economic Theory and Underdeveloped Regions*, London: Duckworth.

Nelson, Richard R. (1991), 'Why do firms differ, and how does it matter?', *Strategic Management Journal*, 12, Special Issue (Winter), pp. 61–74.

Nicolaides, Phedon (1988), 'Limits to the expansion of neoclassical economics', *Cambridge Journal of Economics*, 12(3), September, pp. 313–28.

Orrù, Marco (1993), 'Institutional cooperation in Japanese and German capitalism', in Sven-Erik Sjöstrand (ed.), *Institutional Change: Theory and Empirical Findings*, Armonk, NY: Sharpe, pp. 171–98.

Polanyi, Karl (1944), *The Great Transformation*, New York: Rinehart.

Reinheimer, Herman (1913), *Evolution by Co-operation: A Study in Bioeconomics*, London: Kegan, Paul, Trench, Trubner.

Robbins, Lionel (1932), *An Essay on the Nature and Significance of Economic Science*, 1st edition, London: Macmillan.

Sahlins, Marshall D. (1972), *Stone Age Economics*, London: Tavistock.

Schumpeter, Joseph A. (1976), *Capitalism, Socialism and Democracy*, 5th edition (1st edition 1942), London: George Allen & Unwin.

Sheridan, Kyoko (1993), *Governing the Japanese Economy*, Cambridge: Polity Press.

Simon, Herbert A. (1991), 'Organizations and markets', *Journal of Economic Perspectives*, 5(2), Spring, pp. 25–44.

Sjöstrand, Sven-Erik (ed.) (1993), *Institutional Change: Theory and Empirical Findings*, Armonk, NY: Sharpe.

Tomlinson, James (1982), *The Unequal Struggle? British Socialism and the Capitalist Enterprise*, London: Methuen.

Tomlinson, James (1990), *Hayek and the Market*, London: Pluto Press.

Udéhn, Lars (1992), 'The limits of economic imperialism', in Ulf Himmelstrand (ed.), *Interfaces in Economic and Social Analysis*, London: Routledge, pp. 239–80.

Vanberg, Viktor J. (1986), 'Spontaneous market order and social rules: a critique of F.A. Hayek's theory of cultural evolution', *Economics and Philosophy*, 2, June, pp. 75–100.

Veblen, Thorstein B. (1899), *The Theory of the Leisure Class: An Economic Study of Institutions*, New York: Macmillan.

Veblen, Thorstein B. (1919), *The Place of Science in Modern Civilisation and Other Essays*, New York: Huebsch.

Weber, Max (1968), *Economy and Society*, 2 vols, Berkeley: University of California Press.

Whitley, Richard (1994), 'Dominant forms of economic organization in market economies', *Organization Studies*, 15(2), pp. 153–82.

Whitley, Richard (1999) *Divergent Capitalisms: The Social Structuring and Change of Business Systems*, Oxford and New York: Oxford University Press.

Whittington, Richard C. (1989), *Corporate Strategies in Recession and Recovery: Social Structure and Strategic Choice*, London: Unwin Hyman.

Williams, David (1994), *Japan: Beyond the End of History*, London: Routledge.

Williamson, Oliver E. (1975), *Markets and Hierarchies: Analysis and Anti-trust Implications: A Study in the Economics of Internal Organization*, New York: Free Press.

Winter Jr, Sidney G. (1964), 'Economic "natural selection" and the theory of the firm', *Yale Economic Essays*, 4(1), pp. 225–72.

Young, Allyn A. (1928), 'Increasing returns and economic progress', *Economic Journal*, 38(4), December, pp. 527–42.

Index

Abramowitz, M. 32, 33
absolute pluralism 129–30
Adams, Walter 13
administered (discretionary) pricing 3,
    10–21
Aglietta, Michel xv, 101, 102, 105, 106
agriculture, price system in 7
Albert, Michel 212
Alchian, A. A. 76
Amable, B. 109
Amariglio, J. L. 138
Amendola, G. 106
American Economic Review xiii
André, C. 103
Aoki, Masahiko xviii
Appelbaum, E. 151, 157
Archer, Margaret S. xxii
Arrow, Kenneth 26, 28, 40, 204
Arthur, W. Brian 97, 191, 217
Asanuma, B. 79
assets, specificity 76–7, 78, 85, 87, 89–90
Association for Evolutionary Economics
    xvi
Association for Institutional Thought
    xvi
Australia, wage bargaining in 156
Austria, wage differentials in 158
Austrian economics xiv, xv–xvi, 62
    market process 62–74
        discovery versus creation 69–74
        Hayekian view 66–7, 205–8
        Kirznerian view 63–6
        Lachmannian view 67–8
    power in 49, 54–7, 59–60
Ayres, Clarence E. xvi, 4

Bacdayan, P. 116
Barber, B. 80, 81
bargaining systems 149–50, 151–8
    aggregate wage flexibility 157
    measurement 154–6

theoretical considerations 151–4
    unemployment and employment
        trends and 158–62
    wage differentials 157–8
Basalla, G. 81
Baumol, W. 160
Becker, Gary xiv, 203
Beksiak, J. 193
Berger, P. L. 80
Berle, Adolf 8, 13
Bertalanffy, Ludwig von 218
Blair, John M. 14, 21
Blanchflower, D. G. 154, 157
Blau, P. M. 40
Blaug, Mark xvi
Blois, K. J. 77
Böhm-Bawerk, E. 54–5
Boland, L. A. 139, 140, 141, 142
Boulding, Kenneth E. xv
Bowles, S. 58
Boyer, R. 101, 102, 103, 109, 111, 168
Brada, J. 193
Brown, V. 139
Bruno, Michael 153, 157, 163
Burawoy, Michael 214
Bush, Paul Dale 5
business (trade) cycle 70, 71

Caldwell, Bruce J. xvi, 140, 142–3
Calmfors, L. 152, 157, 158, 160
Campbell, Donald T. xxi
Canada 32
capital
    capital theory xiv, xv
    human capital 31–2
capitalism
    institutions and employment perform-
        ance in different growth regimes
        149–63
        unemployment and employment
            trends 150–1, 158–62